MW01006801

LOOKING FOR HEMINGWAY

Books by Tony Castro

Chicano Power: The Emergence of Mexican America

Mickey Mantle: America's Prodigal Son

The Prince of South Waco: American Dreams and Great Expectations

DiMag & Mick: Sibling Rivals, Yankee Blood Brothers

Mantle: The Best There Ever Was

LOOKING FOR HEMINGWAY

The Lost Generation and the Final Rite of Passage

TONY CASTRO

LYONS
PRESS

Guilford, Connecticut

An imprint of The Rowman & Littlefield Publishing Group, Inc.
4501 Forbes Blvd., Ste. 200
Lanham, MD 20706
www.rowman.com

Distributed by NATIONAL BOOK NETWORK

Copyright © 2016 by Tony Castro
Paperback edition 2019

All rights reserved. No part of this book may be reproduced in any form or by any electronic or mechanical means, including information storage and retrieval systems, without written permission from the publisher, except by a reviewer who may quote passages in a review.

British Library Cataloguing in Publication Information Available

Library of Congress Cataloging-in-Publication Data available

ISBN 978-1-4930-4195-4 (paperback)
ISBN 978-1-4930-1822-2 (e-book)

∞™ The paper used in this publication meets the minimum requirements of American National Standard for Information Sciences—Permanence of Paper for Printed Library Materials, ANSI/NISO Z39.48-1992.

Printed in the United States of America

For Renee

The wine was as good as when you were twenty-one, and the food as marvelous as always. There were the same songs and good new ones. . . . The faces that were young once were old as mine but everyone remembered how we were.

—ERNEST HEMINGWAY, SPAIN, 1959

Contents

Contents

PROLOGUE

When you go to war as a boy, you have a great illusion of immortality.
Other people get killed, not you.

—ERNEST HEMINGWAY

ON DECEMBER 9, 1979, THE SECOND SUNDAY OF THE FINAL MONTH OF the alchemically dreamy age that American author Tom Wolfe, the stylish sage of the New Journalism literary movement, had christened the "Me Decade," the *New York Times* published what any reader on a lazy Manhattan weekend might have taken to be just another of the innocuous engagement announcements that were traditionally the serene province of people with moneyed pedigrees recognized by the country's newspaper of record. There was nothing unusually extraordinary in the details. In fact, there was almost a genteel reservation compared to how the spawn of diplomats and Wall Street titans usually dropped in a casual mention of the elite schools attended by the couple.

> *The engagement of Diana Radway, daughter of the Marchioness of Linlithgow of London and the late John S. Radway of New York, to Timothy Logan Bakewell Davis, son of Mr. and Mrs. William Nathan Davis of Madrid and London, has been announced. A wedding is planned in February in London.*
>
> *Miss Radway expects to graduate from Columbia University next month. Her fiancé, an alumnus of Eton College, in Windsor, England, is a partner of the Business, a film production company in Beverly Hills, Calif.*

The two-paragraph announcement was enough to justify Wolfe's belief that the revolutionary 1960s had produced a class change ushered in by the economic boom of postwar America that afforded Americans a new sense of self-determination. You could be what or whomever you chose to be: wealthy, entitled, privileged, and of a rarified, socially elite class a stratosphere above which you were born. And so, though the *New York Times* identified Timothy Logan Bakewell Davis as being from Madrid and London, both his parents were Americans—American expatriates living abroad, but Americans nevertheless—as was their son, the model of a new American archetype.

Timothy Logan Bakewell Davis. One middle name didn't suffice. Years later, there would be some confusion over his first name among California hospital administrators, court clerks, and government officials whose records listed his legal name as Thomas. Perhaps it was only fitting, as for decades there would be similar confusion over what the exact name of his father might actually have been. Who was William Nathan Davis? No one knew for certain, not even his loved ones, though there was considerably less mystery surrounding his only son. Timothy Logan Bakewell Davis, known affectionately as Teo by his family and friends, was twenty-eight years of age at the time of his engagement and about to tear the pants off the literary creative world in the opinion of several who had met him. Wherever he went, people were overwhelmed with his European smarts and charm, most recently in Houston, Texas, where he left a vapor trail of jet-set impressions, just as he did in New York and Los Angeles, where he had relocated for a screenwriting fellowship at the American Film Institute.

"When Teo spoke, so softly and yet so knowingly in that aristocratic Eton accent of his, it was like getting an intoxicating whiff of Oxbridge," recalled Maxine Mesinger, the longtime celebrity gossip columnist of the *Houston Chronicle* who had met Davis on her rounds of the city's social circuit. "You wanted to immediately fall in love with him. You couldn't help but be impressed."

Not the least of those who had become Teophiles was Hollywood screenwriter-director Walter Hill, the filmmaker who would come to be known for reinventing the American action movie, with classics spanning from *The Getaway* to *The Warriors*. No Hollywood figure could have been a more perfect match for Teo at the time. Their connection, though they didn't realize it when they met, was Ernest Hemingway. As a student at Michigan State University, Hill had become obsessed with Hemingway's writing, even taking on the novelist's belief that "the hardest thing to do is write clearly and simply, and make your point in an elegant way." And Teo? Well, Teo could talk extensively and knowingly about Ernest Hemingway, as he could about many other subjects, including film—and even about Hill's early screenplays that had been produced, films such as *The Getaway* and *The Drowning Pool*, not to mention his directorial debut, *Hard Times*. Hill had recently met Davis at a Hollywood Hills party hosted by Tracy Tynan, the costume-designer daughter of English theater critic Kenneth Tynan, and Hill had done with Davis what he ordinarily hated doing with anyone, especially someone he barely knew: He had engaged in a discussion about his films.

"I was very surprised how well he knew my films," Hill recalled. "Usually I don't like to talk about a detailed analysis of my films, but he actually had a rather fresh approach. And if you know Teo, he's a very engaging fellow, and so we got to be friendly, and I encouraged him to become a screenwriter."

In an afternoon's conversation with a reluctant Walter Hill, Teo had verbally seduced a seasoned Hollywood filmmaker into an artistic autopsy of his work. But then Teo could have that kind of impact on people. When he was twenty-two, he had landed a newspaper reporting job at the *Houston Chronicle*, where he impressed an editor who hired him on the spot despite not having any professional journalistic experience or even knowing how to type. In New York, after leaving Houston to join his fiancée in Manhattan, a magazine editor was so charmed by Teo that he had given him a freelance assignment without seeing any of his work. It was an enormous leap of faith, especially since Teo actually had little writing to show. As with Walter Hill, each time it had been someone established in their respective field who in just conversing with Teo had been so overwhelmed with his knowledge and understanding of literature, journalism, and cinema—often accompanied by well-formed, strong opinions—that he left little doubt of succeeding in whatever he put his mind to. No one so young and articulate, they figured, could talk with the depth, passion, and intellect found in Teo and not rise quickly to the top. There was inevitability, it seemed, in Teo Davis rarely found in even the most ambitious young men his age.

"Ah, to be the fabled and famously debonair Teo Davis, a Connecticut Yankee in King Arthur's Court if ever one," the Texas author Larry L. King said in mock jest after meeting Davis at a mid-1970s Willie Nelson concert in Houston, where the consummate Texas cowboy professor had lost the attention of two beauties who were enthralled with whatever Davis was telling them in that ever-so-charming English accent.

Destiny, though, can sometimes be swept up in a whirlwind, and Davis's life had been unpredictably tumultuous since his carefree days growing up in the south of Spain amid fabulous wealth and the social climbing of his American expatriate parents. At their historic villa in Málaga called La Consula, Bill and Anne Davis had shown off a magnificent art collection that included several Jackson Pollock paintings while entertaining in extravagant fashion the literati and celebrities of the Western world, among them Noel Coward; Laurence Olivier and Vivien Leigh; and Kenneth Tynan and his wife, the writer Elaine Dundy—though their ultimate showpiece, everyone said, had been Ernest Hemingway, the most famous writer of the twentieth century. In her memoir, *Life Itself!*, Dundy had labeled Bill and Anne "the Gerald Murphys of the fifties, transferred to the new high bohemian playground of the Gold Coast of Spain," an allusion to the wealthy American expatriate couple known for their own lavish soirees on the French Riviera, where they entertained writers and artists of the Lost Generation in the 1920s. "Or had we died and awakened in the Murphys's villa on the Riviera in the twenties," wondered Dundy, "with Scotty and Zelda about to come rolling in any minute?" Bill Davis was "a New Yorker by origin, a snob, and a social climber," according to Jeremy Lewis's biography of Teo's uncle, Cyril Connolly, who was the leading British literary critic of the time. "He sent his son to Eton and fought a long and successful campaign to become a member of White's. . . . Something of a bully and drinking companion of Ernest Hemingway's, Bill Davis had the battered, coarse-grained, narrow-eyed features of a professional pugilist." The ever-so-famous White's was one of those elite watering holes Americans would have no knowledge about unless they were social climbers like the Davises. It was the exclusive London gentlemen's club that dated back to the seventeenth century and a membership that Davis came to cherish. However, it was admission to

Eton for his son that became Bill Davis's crowning glory—Eton, which had produced nineteen British prime ministers, thirty-seven holders of the Victoria Cross, not to mention that famous quote often attributed to the Duke of Wellington that "the Battle of Waterloo was won on the playing fields of Eton," no matter that the duke evidently never said that.

In the final years of his life and forever more, Ernest Hemingway would become inexorably linked to the Davis family and to Teo, too. For more than half a century after the Davises had hosted the quintessential American writer in an extended months-long stay in 1959 and again in 1960, all those who became acquainted with Teo could ever really recall of him was that in his childhood he had known Hemingway and was said to have actually been bounced on his lap, momentarily softening the irritable, aging genius of letters in his final years. That was what one of the Hemingway biographies maintained, anyway. And, of course, it made for great small talk, especially among social climbers in Houston's ambitious society world. Had Teo Davis really known Ernest Hemingway? Could those stories of Hemingway spending a better portion of his final days with the Davises at their palatial European estate possibly be true? Was Teo Davis the beneficiary of some kind of special literary acumen that had been magically passed on to him by Papa Hemingway? Hire the young man, pay him what he wants, and typing be damned!

And beyond that, as the exclusive world of the Hamptons in Long Island had wondered with the mythical Jay Gatsby, where did all that family money come from?

No one, especially in Texas, where great wealth and accompanying braggadocio is rarely a mystery for long, seemed to know.

"Teo was an exotic who always seemed drugged or drunk," recalled Chase Untermeyer, a reporter at the *Houston Chronicle* in the 1970s while Teo was on the staff who later became ambassador to Qatar under President George W. Bush. "He also showed how easy it was to break into Houston society in the 1970s with just a tuxedo and an Eton accent."

And, of course, Hemingway.

For social climbing may have been the consummate American non-contact sport of the twentieth century and beyond. Forget about the stage mothers and the Little League fathers and all their own frustrations at their lives' failures that they pump into the dreams they attempt to live out through their children, and think more of Jay Gatsby, F. Scott Fitzgerald's title character in *The Great Gatsby*, whose rags-to-riches rise became a cultural touchstone in twentieth-century America. For with the wealthy, especially the newly rich, of which the Davises were possibly the poster-couple example of post–World War II Americans, there was no expense to spare on ramping up. Whatever the cost to make the right connections, the Davises appeared to have had the most important requisite. As social arbiter David Patrick Columbia, publisher of the *New York Social Diary*, known as a Standard & Poor's index for the exceptional and rich, put it: "It's all about money, because, if you don't have the money, you can't do it. Everything is an exchange . . . and it's taken for granted."

So the Davises had parlayed their beautiful hacienda in Málaga, their real-life counterpart to Gatsby's lavish mansion in the mythical village of West Egg, into a wonderful opportunity for their children, not the least of that investment being Hemingway. It made for the greatest of conversation openers you could have, and Teo grew up using it, though not obtrusively, never in the I-knew-Hemingway fashion that he could have. However, it seemed that was what everyone first said of Teo even before they introduced you to him, so how could there not be an anticipation and an expectation? Few who had known Teo could ever tell you much more about him than those stories of Hemingway living for months at the Davis estate in Spain.

"It wasn't that Teo bragged about it—he didn't—I don't think I ever really heard him talk about Hemingway staying at his home," said Peter Heyne, a fashion reporter for *Women's Wear Daily* in Houston who was Teo's roommate in the mid-1970s. "I don't know exactly how that all became common knowledge. It just did, and I think people's curiosity did the rest."

Hemingway's visits with the Davises in Spain in 1959 and more briefly in 1960 had come as he wrestled in his final years with the credo that defined his life—grace under pressure—and as he tried reaching back for one more whiff of youth: the bullfights, the adoring Spaniards, the lovely young girls, even the young matador son of the bullfighter from the 1920s after whom he modeled the romantic matador Romero in *The Sun Also Rises*. Hemingway was about to turn sixty in 1959 in what became a last hurrah for him in Spain and an attempt to relive the past. He had set out for Spain to write an epilogue for a reissue of his bullfighting nonfiction classic, *Death in the Afternoon*, but it would not be as simple as he had planned. When *Life* magazine editors heard of his trip, they quickly asked him to expand the piece into an article of a few thousand words, which they hoped to publish as successfully as they had his Pulitzer Prize–winning novella, *The Old Man and the Sea*. It would put in motion an unexpected twist to how Hemingway would spend his sunset year in his beloved Spain. In the coming months, with Teo's father manically driving him all around Spain, Hemingway lived his life following the *mano-a-mano* duel between the world's two leading matadors at the time, Antonio Ordoñez and his brother-in-law Luis Miguel Dominguín. It became a quixotic adventure that ultimately produced Hemingway's posthumously published book, *The Dangerous Summer*.

For William Nathan "Bill" Davis, it was a lifelong dream come true. Davis was reputed to be the son of a wealthy Californian, not a New Yorker, as some mistakenly thought, who had business interests in Spain. However, that may have been just another story told and possibly concocted by Davis himself. In a Christie's auction in December 2013, for a Hemingway-autographed letter to Davis dated March 31, 1942, Davis was identified as "a wealthy patron of the arts from Indianapolis and a graduate of Yale (1929). Booth Tarkington based his *Magnificent Ambersons* on the Davis family. He met Hemingway in 1931, but also counted among his friends Jackson Pollack [*sic*], Cyril Connelly [*sic*], Peggy Guggenheim, John Dos Passos and other creative artists. . . . As this (and the following letters) reveal, Hemingway considered him one of his closest and most trusted friends."

"Hemingway biographers," the auction catalog further stated, "have neglected the importance of this friendship with Nathan William Davis (ca. 1906–ca. 1985)."

Signing the letter "Hemingstein," Hemingway addressed the airmail envelope to "Mr. and Mrs. William Davis" at "Uraguay 69, Mejico DF" and made the salutation on his Finca Vigía stationery in Cuba to "Dear Bill and Emily." Emily presumably was another wife, possibly Bill's first or his second, because there had been at least one other spouse before Anne. "We had a wonderful time with you guys," Hemingway wrote. "Marty [Martha Gellhorn] says she wrote you all the news. . . . We have never had any more fun than with you both nor ever liked anybody more. Will try to get some pictures of the pictures to send you to make sure to have something to lure you down here. We look forward to you coming as big thing of this summer." Then in a jocular postscript, he added, "You might let our friends know from time to time that I am proceeding leisurely through the various Mexican states working on that book *The Farewell to Arms Boys Take Telespalteper.*"

The letter, sold by a private collector, was purchased for $15,000 and may have revealed yet another dark side of the Hemingway personality. According to biographer Kenneth S. Lynn, Hemingway occasionally signed letters "Hemingstein" since "he was enough of an anti-Semite to find Jewish names funny just because they were Jewish." It was not unusual for Hemingway to use derogatory terms for Jews, blacks, Italians, and Frenchmen, though American scholar James Nagel, author of *Ernest Hemingway: The Writer in Context*, maintained that while "it is awkward for those of us sympathetic to Hemingway to read a not-very-veiled anti-Semitism that arises from time to time . . . you're not quite sure those feelings really ran in Hemingway." As for the Davises, the auction catalog including the "Hemingstein" letter maintained that "the recipient of this letter (Davis) was himself Jewish," although Teo Davis denied this years later.

Bill Davis, however, was a friend and admirer of the author, who would have forgiven virtually anything in Hemingway. "Having Hemingway as his houseguest," Lynn wrote in his biography *Hemingway*, "represented the fulfillment of Davis' social dream, and he considered it a privilege to wait on him personally." Hemingway, in turn, loved everything about La Consula, from the sixty-foot swimming pool where he could exercise every day to the wide veranda where he worked in the mornings. La Consula was whitewashed inside and out, with white marble floors and white-linen-covered furniture leading up to white walls covered in those Jackson Pollock paintings, some Goya prints, and large maps. In letters written from the estate, an admiring Hemingway went out of his way to mention the Esparto grass reed-plated mats in the corridors and rooms and how the house was full of books.

Hemingway, of course, was only the most recent visitor to be overwhelmed by the beauty and presence of La Consula. The villa had long had its historic importance, but the Davises renewed its life and turned it into a salon and retreat for intellectuals, artists, and the wealthy, especially those who were English. Foremost among them was the Davises' in-law Cyril Connolly, who came to be known as La Consula's "presiding genius, even in his absence." Throughout Europe, the Davises had gained the reputation of entertaining on a grand, lavish scale, with Bill delighting as a host, a role that gave him grateful guests and power. In her book *Tears Before Bedtime*, Connolly's second wife, Barbara Skelton, wrote that Bill loved "getting his guests drunk, to watch their reactions. And wait for their indiscretions. He liked manipulating people. . . . He was a perfectionist, a flatterer of the famous who dragooned servants, chose delicious food, brought the best flamenco and went to the best bullfights."

No one would question that Bill and Anne Davis were an enigma among the locals of the neighboring village of Churriana, who knew little of them beyond their wealth and extravagance. Certainly, few of those they entertained knew anything more about them either. They were neither writers nor celebrities, although they hosted some of the most famous people in the world. Talk among the locals was that Bill Davis had moved to Spain with the Jackson Pollocks after his divorce from a previous wife and couldn't return to the United States for fear that his ex would claim her share of the property. Before Anne, he apparently had been married to socialite Beatrice Diaz Davis, the daughter of immigrant Colombian parents. Bill, though, never talked to his guests at La Consula of how or why that marriage ended. Someone who knew Bea, as she was known, said she carried a torch for Bill the rest of her life and had tracked him down as living in the south of Spain.

The English writer Jonathan Gaythorne-Hardy remembered Davis as a "big, balding, shambling man with a deep hoarse, mechanically indistinct voice who walked with a slight slouch or list, as if holed below the water line." The young journalist Valerie Danby-Smith, who later married Hemingway's son Gregory, met the Davises that summer of 1959 and remembered in an interview years later that "when Bill wrote to Ernest and said he heard he was coming to Spain, could he be his host, maybe it's because he didn't know him very well that Ernest accepted. Mary always said she was very surprised, because normally they didn't stay at other people's houses. They either rented one or they stayed in hotels, for that independence."

Bill Davis, though, was one who seemed to relish being an enigma. He was pleasant, for the most part, and unselfish in the way he entertained. The one disturbing thing most of his guests remembered about Davis was that he called his wife Anne "squaw" for reasons no one knew or could understand. Anne did not appear to have any Native American features about her. If she was Native American, she could have been the richest among all of the American tribes, for she may have been as wealthy as Bill, if not more so. Anne Bakewell could actually trace her family back to John James Audubon, the French-born ornithologist, naturalist, and painter. Anne's great aunt Lucy Bakewell had married Audubon in 1808, six months after he had arrived in Kentucky. For a while in the early 1800s, Audubon was even a partner in a riverfront business there with Anne's great-grandfather Thomas W. Bakewell, whose fortune apparently had come from yet another uncle, Benjamin Bakewell, who owned a commission house in New York. Later, it was the Bakewell's money that allowed Audubon to pursue his dream to create an American ornithology after he had been jailed for debt and shattered by bankruptcy. It was also Lucy Bakewell who promoted Audubon's watercolors to the New York Historical Society, explaining the paintings and the hardships in painting them while showing a winning sense of humor. "If I were jealous," she told a committee at the Historical Society, "I would have a bitter time of it, for every bird is my rival."

The story of how Anne's mother came into her own wealth was a convoluted tale that had left her enormously comfortable. According to numerous accounts, her mother regularly came to the financial aid of Anne's older sister, Jean, while she was married to Cyril Connolly. References in several books call Anne the older sister; however, according to birth and U.S. Census documents, Anne was the younger sister by two years, having been born in 1913 in Pittsburgh, Pennsylvania. Anne and

Jean were the children of William Mullins and Gertrude Paxton Logan Bakewell of 5529 Fifth Avenue in Pittsburgh, with a summer home in Hyannis Port, Massachusetts, and a winter home in Daytona, Florida, replete with yachts named *Waheva* and *Sirene*. And get the name Gertrude Paxton *Logan* Bakewell. Anne's mother was a distant relative of James Logan, a historic figure in Pennsylvania, where he was chief justice of the state supreme court in the 1800s. It also explains the full breadth of Teo's name in his *New York Times* betrothal announcement: Timothy Logan Bakewell Davis. It was no surprise then that the Bakewells, who married in 1909, were listed in the Pittsburgh *Social Register* and the *Pittsburgh and Allegheny Blue Book* of that period. By the 1920 census, though, Gertrude Bakewell had resettled with her two daughters and their younger brother, Thomas, in South Pasadena, California, with no mention of their father. By 1930, Gertrude Bakewell had remarried to a well-to-do Princeton-educated lawyer who went by the curious and possibly preppy name D. Lish Warner, and the new Warner-Bakewell family was living in Baltimore, Maryland.

Meanwhile, the Bakewell wealth underwrote an upward lifestyle in Europe. According to immigration and travel records, both sisters made numerous trips abroad to France and England during the 1920s. Frances Jean Bakewell married Cyril Connolly in New York on April 5, 1930, beginning a whirlwind lifestyle in the fast lane of London intellectual circles that included a brief friendship with Edith Wharton and Aldous Huxley. Jean soon developed a series of health issues that left her with a chronic weight problem and unable to bear children. In 1939, she left Connolly, returning to New York and later becoming the wife of Laurence Vail, the former husband of Peggy Guggenheim. Jean's health problems continued, though, and on July 16, 1950, she died of a stroke at the age of thirty-nine while on a trip to Paris. Vail took charge of Jean's body, interring it in the Vail family vault at Père Lachaise Cemetery in Paris. The only person notified at all of her death was Jean's brother, Thomas Bakewell of New York City. That same year Connolly married the writer Barbara Skelton, whom he later divorced, and in 1959 married Deirdre Craven, a granddaughter of James Craig, first Viscount Craigavon.

Anne Bakewell had been as active socially and personally as her older sister. She had married and in 1934 had a son, of whom little was ever said in later years. She also followed her sister in returning to the United States in the 1940s, where she carried on a chaotic love affair with Clement Greenberg, recognized by many as the greatest art critic of the twentieth century. It was Greenberg who charted and celebrated the rise of abstract expressionism in the 1940s and 1950s and who was among the first to acclaim the work of Jackson Pollock. In their tempestuous relationship, the two were often quarrelling and breaking up, as Greenberg wrote in one of his letters to Harold Lazarus, a friend and former classmate at Syracuse University.

Annie left for Baltimore on her way to Mexico the beginning of this week. We're through forever, even as friends. As usual, you're right: you warned me once, "Remember, she's Jeanie's sister." It would have been even correcter [sic] to say: she's her mother's daughter. The only thing I can explain her behavior by is lesbianism, and I suppose that is the explanation.

In another letter, Greenberg boasted of being involved with "the ideal sex object, which is Annie, and as always the ideal sex object is what I don't want to marry & in some ways have contempt for, but it remains the ideal, perfect, irreplaceable sex object." Then in a fit of jealous rage, he lamented that though he still desired Annie, "in the characteristic way of the Bakewells, she has brought another man into this situation, the longest of Peggy G[uggenheim]'s latest lovers," who apparently happened to have been Bill Davis, for whom she eventually left Greenberg.

In their own way, it could be said then, Bill Davis and Annie Bakewell were a match made in abstract art heaven. With their fortunes and Jackson Pollock paintings, they married and made their way to Spain, where Annie's former brother-in-law Cyril Connolly connected them to La Consula. Even after their divorce and Jean's death, Connolly remained close to Annie and her new husband. His letters to them were filled with terms of endearment such as "Darling Annie Dearest Bill" or "Dear Anniebill," often with thoughts of their children. They were equally effusive in their concern for his well-being, and his role as the home's top intellectual remained intact. Connolly was La Consula's "house writer and master of ceremonies," said Kenneth Tynan, who believed that La Consula gave the Davises' in-law "a momentary glimpse of Eden from the wastelands of middle age." Jean, called "Jeanie" by her loved ones, had been the love of Connolly's life, and he was devoted to her memory, as were the Davises. They named their daughter after her, though she would go by her childhood nickname Nena for the rest of her life. Bill and Anne were also loyally devoted to each other. In her memoir about life with her father-in-law, Valerie Hemingway remembered Bill as a Dickensian-faced man who had been a taxi driver in San Francisco, as he had been in Mexico City, where Hemingway met him again later and began calling him "Negro." Later, at least one biographer, A. E. Hotchner, maintained that the name was given to Davis by bullfighter Antonio Ordoñez. The matador joked that Hemingway's handwriting was so bad that Davis, who "had beautiful handwriting was EH's 'negro' or ghostwriter and the nickname stuck." *Negro*, however, is hardly Spanish for *ghostwriter*, and Hemingway's own correspondence shows that he called Bill Davis by that name long before Ordoñez ever met him. But while there may have been a history of Hemingway's nickname for Davis, no one could adequately explain his wealth.

"El Negro was quiet and acquiescent with Ernest, his demeanor more that of a chauffeur or paid servant than lord of the manor," Valerie Hemingway wrote, "but I detected a cynicism or cruel streak as I observed his behavior with lesser beings in the entourage." By one account, perhaps the one most accepted by many friends and relatives, Davis had been born in California in either 1906 or 1907 and had first visited Spain in 1926 with his father. There his interest in Hemingway had intensified, and Davis had wrangled a brief introduction. It was Hemingway's second wife, Pauline Pfeiffer, who years later arranged Davis's reunion with Ernest. In 1941, a year after she had divorced Hemingway, Pfeiffer met Davis in San Francisco, where she maintained an apartment in addition to her home in Key West, Florida. Later that year, Bill reconnected with Ernest in Sun Valley, Idaho. By then, Hemingway was already married to novelist and journalist Martha Gellhorn; and in the spring of 1942, the

Hemingways visited Davis in Mexico, where he was living with Emily, apparently his first wife. In Mexico, according to at least one account, Davis had also known Leon Trotsky, one of the fathers of the Russian Revolution, who had been granted asylum in the late 1930s and settled in Coyoacán on the outskirts of Mexico City. By then, though, Davis was already an effete literary connoisseur and, like Hemingway, a Hispanophile and bullfight aficionado.

"My father had an obsession in his life," said Teo, looking back years later on his family history, "and that was Hemingway."

In late April 1959, that obsession was seemingly fulfilled in Spain. There, as the Hemingways settled in at La Consula in the cool, marbled warmth of their adjoining rooms on the upper level, the Davises' two friendly hounds followed Ernest and positioned themselves like protective sentries at each side of his bed. Hemingway eyed the dogs and then the carved wooden crucifix on the wall above his bed and, evidently seeing that beast and God were looking over him, let out a laugh that could be heard throughout the villa.

It was an extraordinary start of what would be the house's most incredible summer. Mary Hemingway later wrote in her memoirs that the Davises had indeed been unusual people. Annie Davis, she said, was "an American who had lived abroad so long she seemed to us European." The Davises also did not permit a telephone or radios in their home, so their only means of communicating with the outside world was by mail or telegram. It made for an idyllic cocoon of privacy for Hemingway, who in his advancing years was increasingly becoming less of a people person.

Teo remembered that the first days of the Hemingways' stay at the Davis home brought with it an immediate *Upstairs Downstairs* class clash on how the hacienda was operated by the household staff and how Ernest behaved. Starting in the mornings, Ernest was usually writing by daybreak, the time when the cooks were beginning to prepare breakfast, the gardeners tending the lawns and plants, and the maids straightening the house from the night before. Their work was meticulously planned, as the Davises insisted on La Consula always looking immaculate and yet as if not a care in the world were given to the house appearing that way. "Semi-invisible servants were there to make your beds, to wash and iron and put away your clothes, to attend to your every need and desire, and to cook delicious meals," recalled regular guest Elaine Dundy. Hemingway, too, was his own creature of habit, writing from the time the sun rose, preferring to be disturbed only by the sound of the morning birds, and finishing around midday, when his creative juices had given out. The rhythm of the house, however, had long ago been established, quickly creating conflict. For Hemingway, annoyance would take over and override his manners. He didn't want the maids coming anywhere near his work, much less touching his papers, especially a large board titled "So as Not to Kid Myself," which tabulated the number of words he had written each day and which he insisted remain attached to a wall and in plain sight.

Not surprisingly, Hemingway got his way at La Consula. Nevertheless, the villa was constantly filled with commotion those months in 1959 when the Hemingways were guests. Teo recalled that life on the estate during that period centered around "Papa," as he also came to call Ernest. He loved Fats Waller, the American jazz pianist and entertainer who had become far more famous after his death in 1943 than he was in life; and the Davises always had Fats Waller songs like "Ain't Misbehavin'" and "Honeysuckle Rose" blaring from their loudspeakers by the pool. Hemingway's favorite was "Your Feet's Too Big." He did not really sing in tune but instead loved to encourage other people to perform. Often the turmoil at La Consula was simply the departure and return of Hemingway and his cadre of friends and bullfight aficionados, which sometimes even included matadors themselves. At Hemingway's festive sixtieth birthday party that summer at the Davis home, Teo recalled, the bullfighter Antonio Ordoñez himself led a local hook and ladder company in putting out a blaze that had been set off by a fireworks display.

That party, the most fabulous birthday celebration Teo would ever see in his life, left a permanent impression on him, and not all for the best. Teo had turned eight that April, a birthday celebrated with his sister and the servants, who baked him a cake, just days before the Hemingways' arrival. Later that summer, seeing the birthday feast for Ernest, Teo dreamed that one day his parents might throw a similar bash for him. They never did, not even close.

Yet Teo found Ernest to be the closest to a grandfather he would know. As a child, he never knew his grandparents on either side. Bill Davis never spoke about his family, and Cyril Connolly was the only one on Annie's side of the family whom Teo would come to know. But there was never the immediate connection he had known with Hemingway, whom he found to be almost like a human relic who ached and bellowed in the mornings, often angry and morose but at the same time nearly childlike in the way he approached life. Few were aware then that Hemingway had begun suffering from depression and paranoia, which would be with him until the end of his life.

"Timoteo," Hemingway said to him one morning. "You are the one person who never asks me that same damn question everyone else always asks: What are you working on?"

It was obvious, Teo would one day conclude, that Ernest was clearly struggling to work—to work because he had to, because he was expected to, because retirement was out of the question. As Hemingway would say later that summer to his longtime friend and editor, A. E. Hotchner, who had come to Málaga for the birthday party: "Retire? Unlike your baseball player and your prizefighter and your matador, how does a writer retire? No one accepts that his legs are shot or the whiplash gone from his reflexes. Everywhere he goes, he hears the same damn question: What are you working on?"

Often after he had finished writing for the morning, Ernest went out of his way to talk to Teo, who was usually outside playing on the wide verandas, and to ask the child about his life. He had seen a baseball, a glove, and a bat in the house and tried talking baseball to the youngster, only to learn that Teo had no real knowledge about the sport, having grown up in Europe and never even having seen a game. Hemingway, however, had been raised with baseball. In Cuba, at his Finca Vigía estate, Ernest had even laid out a baseball field for his two sons from his second marriage to Pauline Pfeiffer—Gregory, known then to family and friends as "Gigi," and Patrick. The two youngsters played on a youth team Hemingway organized called the Gigi All-Stars, along with children of members of the household staff and other boys in the neighborhood. Ernest personally equipped the team and dressed them in white flannel uniforms. Gigi and Patrick lived with their mother but would visit Ernest often when they were young. Hemingway himself would sometimes play in the games. Other times Hemingway would pile the kids into his Chrysler and transport them to games at the private Club de Cazadores (the Hunters' Club). This was also where Ernest would go skeet shooting, and it was open exclusively to whites. The six dark-skinned Cuban boys on the team raised some eyebrows, but no one was about to challenge Hemingway, who never had a problem having all his team's players admitted and served.

"Papa would bat, too," recalled Oscar Blas, who at seventy-eight years of age in 2008, was one of seven surviving players. "When he got a hit, he would make one of the little kids run for him. . . . When he played, he seemed like our big brother. He had as much fun as we did."

Another player, Rene Villarreal, eventually went to work for Hemingway at Finca Vigía and developed a friendship with the Hemingways that spanned three decades. "As the Gigi All-Stars' boys grew up, they got jobs and moved on," he said in an interview years later. "A couple became baseball players in local minor leagues. There was no more baseball played at the finca after the boys grew up. Those were indeed innocent and happy times."

So it was understandable how in Spain, Teo's baseball bat and glove would awaken in Ernest an old love and possibly another memory of his youth. J. Gerald Kennedy, a Hemingway scholar at Louisiana State University, later wrote how as a child Hemingway owned a huge collection of baseball cards and posters but lost track of them, much like most American boys did as they grew up. Teo recalled a sadness crossing Ernest's eyes when Teo told him that he didn't really keep up with baseball.

"Just as well," Hemingway lamented. "Without the great DiMaggio, the game's not what it was."

Finally, one day Ernest managed to make use of Teo's unused baseball equipment when he and A. E. Hotchner decided to show Antonio Ordoñez how to play the game. Hemingway believed the bullfighter to be an exceptional athlete who could have been a major league middle infielder had he grown up in America. According to Valerie Hemingway, Ordoñez acquitted himself well that afternoon, enjoying himself so much that he offered to teach Hotchner how to be a bullfighter just to show his gratitude. Teo took it all in, laughing as Ernest volunteered to be the editor's manager.

"How are your reflexes?" Ordoñez asked Hotchner.

To show Hotchner's agility, Hemingway surprised him by tossing wineglasses and cutlery at him, which he quickly caught.

"Hemingway was a different person in the morning than he was in the afternoon, and, I imagine, than he was in the evening," Teo recalled. "But that may have just been symptomatic of his age. He turned sixty that summer, but his mileage. Well, his mileage was much higher."

Teo remembered how on some mornings his childish squealing with Ernest chasing him down the long halls of the estate awakened the other guests, who delighted in seeing the aging writer's increasingly grumpy demeanor soften, even if only for a few fleeting moments. For Teo, too, these were much-needed displays of emotion that were sadly missing from his relationship with his parents. Neither Bill nor Anne Davis was affectionate with their children, and Teo would lament that "I cannot recall my parents ever telling me they loved me."

Perhaps, in their minds, they did express their love, just simply in another manner. Who can ever judge the intricate relationships of fathers and sons, parents and children? For certain, that summer would forever change the lives of Bill and Anne Davis and their children—though arguably not for the better—and it would eventually come to evoke mixed, embittered feelings, especially in Teo.

"Hemingway became my parents' overriding interest and obsession," Teo said, looking back more than half a century later. He continued,

I don't know if I had any formed impressions about Hemingway at the time. Except that the time was all-consuming with him. This was the pinnacle of my parents' lives, and I think that this is something that I would come to understand in the coming years. For most families, the kids occupy front and center. In our family, it was Hemingway. It wasn't me, nor my sister. Nothing we could ever do or dream to do mattered to them. My parents were narcissists. It was all about them, and this would only become increasingly apparent—that we didn't matter much. My parents were in their own separate world, and we weren't part of that world. This was true even more so after Hemingway died. They became the center of attention of everyone who was trying to write about Hemingway with any depth. They wanted to talk to Bill and Anne Davis. This became their life. We were not. After we returned from boarding school, they didn't want much of anything to do with us.

And why would they. We weren't Hemingway.

I

"Fiesta, Sí!"

*Every man's life ends the same way. It is only the details of how he
lived and how he died that distinguish one man from another.*
—ERNEST HEMINGWAY

ERNEST HEMINGWAY WAS IN THE MIDDLE OF HIS LATE MORNING SWIM
in La Consula's sixty-foot pool when he heard the happy commotion of his wife Mary, along with Bill and Annie Davis, welcoming
one of his many friends who had begun arriving for what promised
to be the biggest birthday celebration known throughout Málaga and
the surrounding Andalusia part of Spain. Mary Hemingway had flown
in champagne from Paris, Chinese food from London, codfish from
Madrid, and friends from all over the world, including the maharajah
of Cooch Behar, American diplomat David Bruce and wife Evangeline, Italian royalty, Spanish aristocrats, and actress Lauren Bacall. There
were also fireworks directed by an expert from Valencia, carnival booths,
and a live orchestra. Ernest Hemingway was turning sixty years old on
July 21, 1959, and Mary wanted it to be a party that would be fitting
for the most celebrated writer in America, if not the world. This had
not been why Hemingway had come to Spain, having sought one more
whiff of the country so closely linked to his early fame in the 1920s.
However, he was never one to turn down a celebration in his name. And
perhaps no friend was further up his own personal guest list than the
one whose voice he immediately recognized. He remembered the distinctive pitch of Charles Trueman Lanham's voice as clearly as the day

he had met him in Normandy, where Hemingway was reporting on the D-day invasion for *Collier's* magazine.

"I want you to know that if you ever yield one foot of ground without my direct order, I will court martial you!" Lanham's words to his troops as he assumed command of his regiment had stuck in Hemingway's steel-trap memory.

In World War II, there had been few soldiers more courageous than Buck Lanham, as he was known. A colonel at the time of the D-day invasion, Lanham had commanded the U.S. Twenty-Second Infantry Regiment in Normandy in July 1944 and was the first American officer to lead a break through the German defensive Siegfried line on September 14, 1944. Hemingway had accompanied American troops as they stormed to shore on Omaha Beach, but as a civilian correspondent he was not allowed to land himself. He then had attached himself with Lanham's regiment as it made its way to Paris. Later, Lanham led a breakout in the Battle of the Bulge after surviving a bloody ordeal in the Battle of Huertgen Forest. There in the Huertgen Forest, the regiment suffered massive losses: 80 percent casualties in eighteen days. But Lanham had still been awarded the Distinguished Service Cross, and only a few people had ever impressed Hemingway the way Lanham had. "Buck is the finest and bravest and most intelligent military commander I have known," Hemingway later said of Lanham. He held such standing in Hemingway's hall of heroes that when Hemingway learned he was getting the Nobel Prize for Literature in 1954, Buck Lanham had been the first friend he called, receiving his congratulations.

"I'm thinking of telling them to shove it," Hemingway told his friend.

"Don't be a jackass," Lanham said.

"Well, maybe not." Hemingway was still recovering from injuries in back-to-back airplane crashes in Africa in which he had nearly been killed and needed the prize money. "There's thirty-five thousand dollars."

Five years later, Lanham didn't have to think twice about flying from his home in Washington, DC, to the south of Spain to celebrate Hemingway's sixtieth birthday. In his swim trunks and dripping wet in the midsummer sun, Ernest rushed out of the pool, where he had been having a playful swim with Teddy Jo Paulson, an American tourist and one of the young women he had been chasing after since the Fiesta de San Fermín in Pamplona earlier in the month. He hurried to embrace Lanham, who had become one of Hemingway's closest friends and with whom he kept up a steady correspondence for seventeen years. That correspondence totaled more than six hundred pages, which Hemingway biographer Carlos Baker would call "the longest, fullest, and most informative sequence of Hemingway letters to come to light." While convalescing from injuries, Hemingway even took to considering Lanham as a father confessor. Now Lanham had an early birthday present for his friend and presented Hemingway with an affectionately inscribed history of the Twenty-Second Infantry Regiment.

"War seemed to bring out the best in him," Lanham would later say of his friend. "In war, old Hemingstein, as he called himself, was magnificent. And in peacetime he could really be insufferable."

Drying his hands with a towel, Ernest adjusted his wire-rimmed glasses, which Mary had handed him, and made a quick study of the book. He seemed surprised and became teary-eyed, with emotion reddening his broad face with pinky cheeks and tan brow, which was offset by his mussed white hair and white beard. The C-shaped scar, caused by an accident in which he brought a skylight down on his own head, was clearly visible high on the left side of his forehead.

"Buck." Ernest choked as he said the name. "Too much, Buck. Too much."

Ernest handed Mary the book and embraced Buck again. For Hemingway, there was no one who epitomized courage more than Buck Lanham, a career soldier who had been widely decorated for his repeated acts of courage and bravery. If Hemingway could have been anyone else, he would have wanted to be Buck Lanham. Years later, this also would be the impression of distinguished Washington, DC, lawyer Jacob A. Stein, who had befriended Lanham in the 1970s and talked to him about Lanham's own friendship with Hemingway and the writer's obsession with courage.

"That is all he wanted to talk about," said Lanham, who was a short-story author and published poet as well as a soldier. "Courage for me was something I happened to be born with. Luck and courage. Without luck, courage often means a short life expectancy. . . . I told him courage is not what a sober person discusses in public. I wanted to talk about my short stories. No interest. He wanted to talk about this grace-under-pressure crap."

In 1959, it may have been fitting that Hemingway's thoughts about courage were foremost on his mind, not just because he was about to celebrate reaching his sexagenarian stage but for the challenge he now faced in his life: having set out in the twilight of his life on a quixotic quest to recapture the sentimental Spain of his early success in the 1920s only to sadly confront, *mano a mano*, a final rite of passage that would test all the credos of bravery and grace under pressure he had lived by. It would be the fabled writer's last hurrah. For at that time of his life, Hemingway was at that age that we dread: old, losing our train of thought, unable to do what once came so easily, too quick to show our frustration at our slowness but still holding on to the hope of one last glimmer of youth. What would unfold, Pulitzer Prize–winning novelist William Kennedy would later write in the *New York Times*, was "a prismatic vision of the dying artist, a complex and profoundly dramatic story of a man's extraordinary effort to stay alive."

If ever a birthday party could break up the tension and pressure that had already built up that summer, it was the lavish celebration Mary Hemingway was planning. Nevertheless, the days leading up to this birthday had not been easy ones for Ernest's fourth wife, his harsh mistreatment of whom had worn away much of her love. She was a small, wiry woman with lively blue eyes and a tanned face with sharply creased features. She also knew how unfaithful Ernest could be. He had been married each time he had taken up with the next wife. When Mary met Ernest in London in 1944, she had been a correspondent for *Time* magazine, and Ernest was still married to his third wife, journalist and writer Martha Gellhorn, who had inspired him to write his most famous novel, *For Whom the Bell Tolls*. Mary was familiar with Ernest's mating rituals, but she also knew what no one else did, given Ernest's machismo bravado: The great Hemingway was no longer the virile man he pretended to be. However, that didn't keep him from treating her cruelly, flirting shamelessly with almost any young woman who gave him attention since arriving in Spain. Then in the days before the party, after the running of the bulls at the Fiesta de San Fermín, Mary had broken a toe slipping on a stone in a creek bed as Ernest sought to retrace for his entourage an exploration from the 1920s along the Irati River outside Pamplona. In incredible pain, she could barely walk but received no sympathy from Ernest, who continued his pursuit of one particular young woman he had added to his entourage of friends and fans. His behavior was clearly obvious and an embarrassment to those around him. "He was noticeably cold and distant and indifferent to [Mary] at times, as though he were a stranger living at her side," observed writer José Luis Castillo-Puche, the Spaniard who had befriended Hemingway in the 1950s. Mary, though, remained undaunted in following through with her elaborate plans for the birthday party.

And what a party it became that night.

From the upper veranda of La Consula, not far from Ernest's second-floor bedroom, the Spanish orchestra that Bill Davis had hired, which included members of the Pamplonesa band, played the celebratory music of the Fiesta de San Fermín, including *pasadobles* and *jotas* that were familiar from the streets of Pamplona. Whether by intention or not, the celebration, which began around noon on July 21 and continued for two days, took on the semblance of the recently completed Pamplona *feria*, which had lasted eight and a half days, replete with its Basque culture, traditions, music, song, dance, and fellowship.

"Fiesta, sí!" became the mantra for the night, a reference to one of the slogans often heard during the Fiesta de San Fermín and the running of the bulls in Pamplona. Hemingway had first shown up there in 1923 with his first wife, Hadley Richardson, and the experience had made an impression on the twenty-three-year-old American journalist. "Bullfighting is not a sport—it is a tragedy," had been the headline in the *Toronto Star* on his first dispatch from Pamplona.

However, *"Fiesta, sí!"* also carried a second, perhaps more significant meaning for Hemingway. Americans knew the novel that had catapulted him to fame as *The Sun Also Rises*, which had been published in the United States in 1926 by Scribner's. Through much of Europe, though, the novel was known as *Fiesta*, the title that the London publishing house Jonathan

Cape gave it and continued using for years. And on that partying night in the south of Spain, the novel was celebrating a birthday of its own, for it had been on July 21, 1925, that Hemingway began the book, finishing the first draft in two months. The novel was heavily autobiographical, based on Ernest and Hadley's third visit to Pamplona in 1925, when they brought a group of American and British expatriates with them from Paris. The disintegration of the fictitious group in *The Sun Also Rises* closely paralleled what happened in real life, while Hemingway also portrayed the post–World War I "Lost Generation"—thought by many to have been drunkenly decadent, wildly self-indulgent, and irretrievably ruined—as remarkably resilient and still holding promise.

These themes were not that dissimilar from what had emerged in the two and a half months of Hemingway's 1959 visit to Spain. In 1959, Ernest chased young women as unashamedly as he had pursued the beautiful and recently divorced British socialite Lady Duff Twysden in 1925, being as insensitive to Mary as he had been to Hadley, all the while soaking up another Lost Generation's ambivalence to convention. *The Sun Also Rises* had changed Hemingway, as it had Pamplona, whose quaint village festival exploded into an international event after the book's incredible popularity. Hemingway saw this firsthand when he returned to Pamplona for the last time in 1959. "Forty thousand tourists have been added," he observed with some surprise. "There were not twenty tourists when I first went there nearly four decades ago."

"*Fiesta, sí!*" Hemingway swigged more wine and threw his arm around Antonio Ordoñez, the bullfighter phenom whose father, Cayetano Ordoñez, had honored Ernest's wife Hadley a generation earlier by presenting her, from the bullring, the ear of a bull he killed. It had been Cayetano, no less, who had been the model for the romantic character Romero, the dashing bullfighter whom Lady Brett Ashley, the fictitious counterpart of Lady Duff Twysden, cavalierly ran off with in *The Sun Also Rises*.

Guitar players seemed to follow Hemingway everywhere he went at his party, serenading him with folk songs, including some he had taught them that dated back to the Spanish Civil War, among them "*Los Cuatro Generales*," a song about General Francisco Franco, who would go on to

6

become the long-entrenched dictator of Spain, and the fascist generals who led the coup against the democratic Spanish Republic in the 1930s.

> *Los cuatro generales*
> *Mamita mia*
> *Se han alzado, que se han alzado.*
> *Para la Nochebuena . . . Mamita mia*
> *Seran ahorcados . . .*
> (The four insurgent generals . . .
> *Mamita mia*
> They tried to betray us . . .
> At Christmas, holy evening . . .
> *Mamita mia*
> They'll all be hanging . . .)

Flamenco dancers performed among the Japanese lanterns in the gardens amid the sound of fireworks in the background. For a while, there were also the distinct cracking sounds of gunshots as Hemingway shot lit cigarettes dangling from the mouth of Antonio Ordoñez. Their friendship had not been one of chance. The fact that Antonio happened to be the son of Cayetano Ordoñez may have been a sign of just how much Ernest was trying to re-create his youth, choosing to befriend and align himself with the younger version of the bullfighter who had enchanted him in the 1920s. Antonio Ordoñez, as much as anyone or anything, was the reason Hemingway was now in Spain, having come there to write about his *mano a mano* bullfighting duel with his brother-in-law. It was an unusual opportunity; *mano a manos* are rare occurrences since it is not often that there are two matadors of such a high caliber fighting at the same time. It was this rarity that Hemingway hoped to capture. As for Ordoñez, the charismatic young Spaniard epitomized Hemingway's idealized vision of courage, much as Buck Lanham did, but perhaps never more so than as he stood his ground that night, holding a lit Camel between his lips as he somehow also whistled through the smoke the two-note melody from the "Colonel Bogey March," a near half-century-old tune popularized in World War II.

It was impossible not to marvel at Hemingway, with the marksmanship of a military sniper, shooting the cigarette from Ordoñez's lips. He did it repeatedly—a photograph would document the feat for posterity, showing Buck Lanham at Hemingway's side—with surgical skill and the steadiness of a big-game hunter on a safari. The buzz at La Consula mounted through the night as the story spread that the great Ordoñez was risking lips, life, and future by having the world-famous hunter Hemingway shoot cigarettes out of his mouth with a potentially deadly .22 rifle that he had a history of using for amusement in order to blast cigarettes out of the hands, and occasionally from the lips, of willing participants. It would be years before an archival librarian would study the photograph and argue that it was, in fact, a much safer weapon that Hemingway had fired at Ordoñez's mouth. "The way the breach works, it folds in half," concluded Megh Testerman of the John F. Kennedy Library in Boston, which houses the largest collection of Hemingway's papers and documents. "Some may have mistook it for a .22 but it's an air rifle."

That night, though, no one would steal the thunder from Hemingway.

Among the guests that Hemingway most sought to impress with his shooting prowess that night was a nineteen-year-old aspiring Irish journalist, Valerie Danby-Smith, on whom he had set his romantic sights. He had met her in Pamplona and insisted that she join his entourage, or *cuadrilla*. When Danby-Smith balked, saying she needed to continue working to support herself, Hemingway created a job for her. She would become his traveling secretary. And that night, impress her he did. "Mary rented a shooting gallery from a traveling carnival, and it became the main attraction when Ernest, to the horror and fascination of onlookers, blasted the ash from Antonio's cigarette with a .22 rifle as he held the butt between his lips," Danby-Smith, who later married Ernest's youngest son, Gregory, said of the event in her memoir, *Running with the Bulls*.

Ordoñez had first witnessed Hemingway shooting cigarettes out of someone's grasp in 1956 when Ernest had been in Spain and shot the ashes off Gauloises that their Italian chauffeur Mario held up as a target in his hand. It had been unusually windy that late afternoon after the bullfighting *feria* in Zaragoza, and Hemingway had used a .22 rifle and impressed his *cuadrilla* of friends. However, at the La Consula party, it turned out that Antonio and Ernest had indeed led onlookers to believe Ernest was using a .22 rifle when in fact it had been an air gun from the carnival gallery armory. "Hemingway shot cigarettes out of my mouth with pellets from the kind of air gun you use at a fair stand," Ordoñez would later say. "They were not real bullets, but they could damage your face. Later on, at El Escorial outside of Madrid, he shot cigarettes out of my mouth using real bullets."

Real bullets from a .22 or pellets from an air gun, it was quite a show. Seven times Hemingway clipped the end of the cigarette that Ordoñez gripped with his lips, while he puffed on them to see how short he could get them.

"Ernesto," Antonio finally said. "We've gone as far as we can go. The last one just brushed my lips."

The crowd of spectators, applauding each time Hemingway shot off the cigarette, burst into laughter at Ordoñez's remark and cheered the two men. Then Bhaiya, the maharajah of Cooch Behar, an independent Indian principality, whom Hemingway had met in Zaragoza in 1956, insisted that Ernest shoot a cigarette from his lips as well. Hemingway obliged, with the maharajah starting out using an ebony holder for his cigarette before finally abandoning it to match Ordoñez.

How courageous of the ever-brave matador, someone said to Ordoñez in Spanish after Hemingway had shot the last Camel out of his lips.

"Courageous? Only in my dreams," Ordoñez shot back. "All matadors are afraid." Later he expanded on that thought: "From the moment the bull enters the ring, I become afraid—and I remain afraid until I have killed him and the mules have dragged the bull out. No man is without fear. It's a fear that can never be conquered, but only controlled. That's why at the start of every [bullfighting] season I know that I will be gored, and it's foolish to pray that you won't be gored. So I pray only that if I am hurt, that I am not mortally wounded."

Already that season, Ordoñez—who was twenty-seven years of age, though his slender face and frame made him look even younger—had been gored seriously enough that the injury effectively had paid for Hemingway's extravagant birthday party. Throughout Mary's long weeks of planning, Ernest had complained bitterly that she was foolishly spending his money to host this party. One day she finally confessed that she was paying for the party with her own money, which she had earned by selling *Sports Illustrated* a lengthy story about Ordóñez's recuperation, much of it done at La Consula.

Ordóñez and his wife, Carmen, were among the original forty invited guests, though at least that many crashed the party, which celebrated both Ernest's and Carmen's birthdays. Of course, many more would later maintain they were in attendance or their relatives would claim someone in their family had been there and offer first- and secondhand accounts. When Hemingway learned that he shared a birthday with Carmen, he had insisted that her birthday be commemorated along with his. Ultimately, the three-layered cake that Mary ordered for the party had ninety candles on it: sixty for Ernest and thirty for Carmen. Nothing was left to chance. The Chinese food from London included fifty pounds of sweet and sour turkey that shared the cuisinery limelight with casseroles of codfish and shrimp and several baked hams. Bill Davis himself took care of ordering the booze: six cases of rose wine, four cases of champagne, and an assortment of whiskey, gin, and cognac.

Although the drinking started earlier, the party didn't officially begin until 10 p.m., and for some resembled a Spanish version of a feast Jay Gatsby might have hosted. The Davises were wealthy, after all, and knew how to throw lavish and extravagant parties. From time to time, Bill Davis had even been known to use that line from *The Great Gatsby*: "And I like large parties. They're so intimate. At small parties there isn't any privacy." And this party for Hemingway might have been even bigger if Davis had been able to snatch the guest everyone in the West had sought for years—Russian prima ballerina Maya Plisetskaya, who spent much of her career as a captive under fierce scrutiny and at the murderous whim of Joseph Stalin's regime but still shimmered as one of the greatest dancers of the twentieth century. Fearing she might defect to the West, Russian authorities had never allowed Plisetskaya to travel afar with the Bolshoi Ballet, shameful considering that many regarded her as the greatest ballerina in the world. Finally, in 1959 Premier Nikita Khrushchev lifted her travel restrictions, and the Davises, along with Hemingway, joined in seeking her company. She could not fit in a visit to Spain, Davis was finally told by friends in London. The party guest list was impressive, nonetheless. From Hemingway's vantage point, Antonio and Carmen Ordoñez led the list of guests, followed closely by Buck Lanham, Gianfranco and Cristina Ivancich, and, of course, Lauren Bacall, who kept such a low profile that she wondered many years later whether she had actually been there. Gianfranco's sister Adriana had been Ernest's great love a decade earlier, having then been nineteen, the same age Valerie Danby-Smith was in 1959. Mary saw a number of parallels between Ernest's obsessive infatuation with both young women, and she was trying to ride out his puppy love with Valerie the way she had his relationship with the gorgeous Venetian beauty Adriana. However, Mary couldn't cover all of Ernest's flirtations. Another guest who had Hemingway's attention was Beverly Bentley, a sexy, blond actress with a number of film and Broadway credits who had also joined Hemingway's *cuadrilla* that summer. Four years later, she became Norman Mailer's fourth wife.

"You remind me of Marlene Dietrich," Hemingway had said to Bentley when they met, and what a line it proved to be. Ernest had met the German singer-actress aboard a French ocean liner in 1934, when Hemingway was returning to Key West via Paris after a safari in East Africa and Dietrich was headed back to Hollywood after visiting relatives in Nazi Germany on one of her last trips home. Theirs became a great platonic romance, much of it carried on over moving love letters. In a correspondence dated June 19, 1950, at 4 a.m., Hemingway wrote: "You are getting so beautiful they will have to make passport pictures of you 9 feet tall. . . . What do you really want to do for a life work? Break everybody's heart for a dime? You could always break mine for a nickel and I'd bring the nickel."

The love letters exemplified Hemingway the hunter, chasing prey, be it women who caught his attention or animals with whom he wanted to prove his manhood in a different way. That night at La Consula, he celebrated sixty years of life and conquests and the hopes that there was still more ahead, for his sixtieth birthday party had turned into a crucible of intense experience both for the writer and for his guests, some emerging forever changed—at least in their perception of the man they came to celebrate. Had any novelist ever stood astride the culture as did Hemingway at his height, almost narcissistically so?

"He was bigger than life, like some kind of Greek god, Zeus or Apollo, and what he said to you weren't just words—they were like thunderbolts of wisdom from Olympus. You had to be there to appreciate the sheer magnitude of Hemingway," Teddy Jo Paulson, the young woman with whom Ernest had been swimming the afternoon that Buck Lanham arrived, recalled in an interview a quarter of a century later. Paulson, a beautiful college sorority girl from Williston, North Dakota, had just graduated from Northwestern University and would be going on to graduate school at the University of Chicago. She and her girlfriend Mary Schoonmaker had been on a tour of Europe that would take them to ninety-two cities in sixty-two days when they met Hemingway in Pamplona. They had been roommates and Kappa Kappa Gamma sorority sisters at Northwestern, and Teddy Jo would later be Mary's maid of honor at her wedding. They were guests of the Hemingways at the *corrida* in Pamplona, with Ernest insisting Teddy Jo sit next to him in the front row, from which he never hesitated in talking to the bullfighters and carried on a running dialogue with Antonio Ordoñez about his bulls. Ordoñez dedicated one of his bulls to Hemingway and his *cuadrilla*, giving Paulson an ear from his second bull of the day. For Mary Schoonmaker, watching that day's death of the bulls had painfully touched a nerve, as it did for a lot of Americans unaccustomed to bullfighting. A native of Evanston, Indiana, and a member of the Southern aristocracy from that area, Mary had grown up an equestrian and was passionate about animals. However, her differences with Ernest on the treatment of animals aside, Mary acquiesced to changing a third of their travel itinerary in order to join Ernest's *cuadrilla* at La Consula so that they could be at his birthday party, which became the height of their summer vacation and the source of stories for years to come.

Perhaps the twentieth century's most influential writer, Hemingway would have loved nothing more than to have gone down as a cultural symbol, certainly of masculinity, as well as of bravery and courage. He had become just that, especially in the postwar America of the mid-twentieth century, which like all societies had the need for heroic, bigger-than-life figures not because they created them but because icons like Hemingway expressed a deep psychological aspect of human existence. Hemingway the creative genius knew this all too well and, consciously or not, had provided it in the construction he presented in his life and in his fiction. For like most heroes, if Ernest Hemingway had not existed, he would have been invented, as was a good portion of what the public knew of him. "Hemingway combined a scrupulous honesty in his fiction with a tendency to distort and rewrite the story of his life," his biographer Jeffrey Meyers wrote in a memoir about Ernest. "He had a literary reputation among expatriate writers before he had published a word of fiction. *The Sun Also Rises* created the most powerful literary image of Spain and of the Lost Generation and quickly influenced American youth. They 'drank like his heroes and heroines, cultivated a hard-boiled melancholy and talked in page after page of Hemingway dialogue,' Malcolm Cowley recalled." In many ways, then, Hemingway was all that America wanted itself to be in his time, and he was also all that America feared it could never be. He was the hero of America's romance with boldness, its celebration of courage, a nation's Arthurian self-confidence in machismo strength during a time when it last thought might did make right. Hemingway typified the very fabric of a national culture of which Americans could whimsically reassure themselves every time they looked at a Norman Rockwell painting on the cover of the *Saturday Evening Post*, even as the world was changing. For as the poet Rolf Humphries noted, in the profession of anxiousness, there is an element of fashion. What better face to put on that than Ernest Hemingway's?

No one could have agreed more than Hemingway's host, Bill Davis, who spent much of the evening near the writer, making sure his famous guest didn't want for anything. Hemingway had hardly been out of Davis's sight since his arrival in April. Ernest appreciated that, as well as how Bill had been an all-knowing friend. "He loved food and knew good food and knew where to get it in any country better than anyone I had ever known," Hemingway would later write about Davis in his bullfighting stories for *Life*.

He is a strange man and has made a life of finding out things about people, country, food, wine, sports, books, architecture, music, painting, and all of learning and living. When he came to Spain first he had based on Madrid and then had driven with Annie through every province in Spain. There was no town in Spain he did not know, literally, and he knew the wines, the local cooking, the special things to eat and the good places to eat in all towns large and small. He was a wonderful traveling companion for me, and he was an iron man driving.

Davis would have been at Hemingway's side simply because of their friendship, though there were some who saw him as Ernest's "jealous watchdog," out to dissuade anyone from thinking they could replace him. However, at the party there was a less selfish reason for the American expatriate to stick so close to Hemingway. In their time together since the Hemingways' arrival from the United States, Bill had noticed Ernest growing increasingly more short-tempered than usual. Hemingway, he knew, could be verbally combative and sometimes mean-spirited, but it was rarely a wrath directed at any of his close friends. The night before the party, however, had produced an ugly scene that had left Hemingway unnerved and Davis concerned over this further sign of Hemingway's mental deterioration. José Luis Castillo-Puche would later describe Hemingway at this time as "a pathetically lonely and a pathologically devious man."

On the night before the birthday party, at a dinner-dance at the Hotel Miramar in Málaga, Davis and other guests had witnessed a nasty, petty side of Hemingway and how he could now inexplicably and irrationally turn on his loved ones. Ernest had been seated when Buck Lanham, who had just danced with David Bruce's wife, Evangeline, passed behind Ernest's chair as he was returning to their table. Lanham had glanced at his wristwatch and seen that midnight was only twenty minutes away. He put his arm around Hemingway as he announced that they could start celebrating his sixtieth birthday in a matter of minutes. Then as his hand swept away from his friend's shoulder, Lanham momentarily grazed the back of Hemingway's head. It was innocent enough, but Hemingway erupted as if ready to fight. Yelling as if his head had been burned, Ernest let loose a string of vile profanity.

No one, not even Lanham, was allowed to touch his head, Hemingway screamed at his friend.

The outburst dramatically silenced their table, with everyone staring at Hemingway in disbelief. Lanham momentarily froze, stunned by Hemingway's unexpected behavior. Then just as quickly, Lanham's surprise turned to anger. The proud military man, who had interceded with superiors on Hemingway's behalf on more than one occasion during World War II, stormed off through the garden adjoining the hotel dance hall and stood seething outside the facade under its open towers facing the sea.

"Jackass," a waiter heard Lanham mumble as he approached him with a tray of champagne flutes. Lanham waved the waiter away and again muttered angrily under his breath, "Fucking jackass."

Moments later, Hemingway caught up with Lanham, who looked at him coldly. Hemingway knew he had seriously damaged an important friendship, perhaps irreparably. Weeping, he asked Lanham for his forgiveness and may have been surprised to find that his friend was not so easily placated. Ernest blamed his behavior on his vanity. The top of his head was bald, he explained, and he tried hiding the baldness by combing what was left of his gray hair forward.

"If Lanham would forgive him, he said he would go to the barber the next day and have his goddamn hair cut short like Lanham's," biographer Carlos Baker wrote of the incident.

"Stop talking like a jackass," Lanham told Hemingway. Clearly, for Lanham the word was a favorite term of playful derision, but at this moment he seemed to say it without any playfulness.

Hemingway's friendship with Lanham would survive the incident, but it left Lanham convinced that Hemingway was now suffering from some mental disorder. The five concussions Ernest had sustained during his life—could they have led to his mental deterioration? There was also what biographer Michael Reynolds called "too many late nights, too much wine for too many days, too much adulation and not enough solitude—whatever the cause, Ernest was going down into his depressed persona." For Lanham, though, it wasn't just Hemingway's erratic lashing out that made him wonder about his emotional well-being. He was also put off by Ernest's embarrassing attempts to seduce young women—to which others seemed to turn a blind eye—his heartless mistreatment of his wife Mary, and the increasing vulgar obscenity that now peppered his language.

Mary feared that the incident with Buck had spoiled the birthday party she had lovingly planned, but Bill Davis and A. E. Hotchner interceded, according to Buck's account. Hemingway had had a bad night, they insisted. Although Buck suspected there was more to Ernest's volatile behavior, he was not going to spoil the celebration. By noon, the incident appeared to be behind them as guests began arriving at La Consula. By all accounts, Hemingway was the life of the party and back to his familiar old form.

Part of the reason for this may also have been the watchful eye of Antonio Ordoñez, who had assumed the role of a protective son, though there was more to it. He knew that Ernest held in his hands Antonio's own legacy and that of bullfighting during his lifetime. Whatever Ernest wrote for *Life* magazine, correctly or not, would establish how the Western world saw Antonio in the history of Spain's sport of life and death. And Antonio, who had already secured from Ernest the assurance that he was a greater matador than his heroic father, wanted to be known as the greatest bullfighter of all. He had arrived in Málaga using a cane to walk as he recovered from the goring, and La Consula had quickly proven to be the ideal elixir for the injury. On his first morning, Antonio had walked from the first-floor bedroom he and Carmen were using up to the second floor, where Ernest had put aside the day's writing to visit with the bullfighter.

"Let's go," he said to Ernest, urging him to join him in a walk around the villa's grounds. Then he had put the cane down on Ernest's bed. "The cane's finished," he said. "You keep the cane."

Ordoñez began mending under Hemingway's care as the writer took charge of changing the bandages and dressing on the wound. They continued taking long walks, talking about bullfighting, planning Antonio's return to the bullring, and then swimming in the afternoon once the summer sun had heated the water. They spent time joking about developing a writing partnership together, possibly including Bill Davis because Ordoñez facetiously maintained that it was "Negro," as they called Davis, who was the real writing brains behind Hemingway's success.

"Maybe we better keep on selling the stuff under your name alone until mine is better known as a writer," Ordoñez told Hemingway at one point, according to the *Life* article. "How are we doing under your name?"

"We're getting by," Hemingway said.

"Is it true we can only win that Swedish prize once?" Ordoñez was referring to the Nobel Prize.

"Yes," Hemingway said.

"What injustice," said Ordoñez.

Antonio was nearby on the night of the party as Ernest and Carmen opened their gifts and then blew out the candles on their cake. As the cake was being served, the Andalusian sky lit up with a final fireworks display that seemed to go on forever. Ernest's mood had been uplifted by all the attention from his guests, especially having Ordoñez nearby, the symbol of his father, who, after all, Hemingway had portrayed as the heroic, manly matador Pedro Romero who could so openly seduce Lady Brett Ashley in *The Sun Also Rises*. Perhaps the only thing better in Ernest's mind might have been to have had Lady Duff Twysden herself present. However, the real life model for his Lady Brett had died more than two decades earlier, on June 27, 1938, of tuberculosis at the age of forty-six in Santa Fe, New Mexico.

It was almost half an hour later that panic broke out among the party's guests underneath one of the palm trees as stray fireworks ignited it. The fire triggered Bill Davis's worst fear—that his prized showcase villa could go up in smoke. Davis quickly rounded up some of his guests and waiters to help contain the flames by hosing down the surrounding trees, shrubbery, and the adjoining parts of the villa. The ever-fearless Ordoñez was at the forefront, using a garden hose to fight the fire and directing others in using buckets of water to douse the areas of potential danger. For a moment, however, the panic seemed to grow as guests realized that no one could call for emergency help because there were no telephones at La Consula, a point on which Bill and Annie Davis had taken great pride. Now as that decision seemed increasingly foolish, Davis hastily dispatched someone to a neighboring house outside the estate to use the phone there to call the fire department.

About the same time that fire engine sirens could be heard in the distance, the orchestra began playing music again, soon drowning out the siren's wails, when it appeared that Ordoñez and the others had successfully contained the blaze to one palm tree, which continued to burn. Minutes later, a fire brigade from Málaga arrived and with professional firefighting equipment, quickly extinguished the fire and made sure there were no simmering embers. The excitement and brush with danger briefly seemed as if it might have been part of the planned celebration, which immediately took on a new life. Hemingway gave celebratory *abrazos* to the firefighters and led his guests in cheering them and insisting that they join the party. As midnight turned into the early hours of the morning, the fire engine became another party favor as the firefighters gave guests rides down the long villa drive and around La Consula, the siren sounding the triumph of the night.

"Fiesta, sí!" Hemingway cried as he danced into the next day with his guests. *"Fiesta, sí!"*

2

La Consula

To me heaven would be a big bullring with me holding two barrera seats.

—ERNEST HEMINGWAY, 1925 LETTER
TO F. SCOTT FITZGERALD

THE OVERWHELMING SUCCESS OF ERNEST HEMINGWAY'S SIXTIETH birthday party, which would become one of the most celebrated events in his life, hardly came as a surprise to his devoted wife Mary, nor to Bill and Annie Davis, who could take pride that it had occurred at their majestic villa. From the moment she had first seen La Consula, Mary Hemingway felt the breathtaking estate on the Costa del Sol of the Mediterranean was the perfect location for Ernest's sixtieth birthday that summer. When they arrived at La Consula that spring afternoon, the Hemingways were pleasantly surprised by what they saw. The nineteenth-century mansion that belonged to Ernest's friends rose gracefully behind twin iron gates. The doors alone were over fifteen feet high and were made of heavy carved oak. Outside, the rich vegetation, which included palm and acacia trees, pines, lilies, and vines, all reminded the Hemingways of their finca in Cuba.

The summer of 1959 in Spain hadn't yet begun for Ernest Hemingway, but he was already calling it the greatest summer of his life. Ernest and Mary had crossed the Atlantic Ocean on board the SS *Constitution*, bound for Algeciras in the south of Spain, and Ernest soon began sending cables to his longtime friend A. E. Hotchner, urging him to join his *cuadrilla* that summer as he intended to travel around Spain catching a series of bullfights involving Antonio Ordoñez, the *torero* Ernest was convinced was greater than even the legendary Manolete. "Hotch, there never was such a summer in prospect," Hemingway wrote in his cable. The campaign trail Ernest had begun to outline was dizzying and exhausting, as it would take many almost all-night drives over the rugged Spanish geography to make the daily *corridas* that packed the schedule. The Hemingways had been on the *Constitution* since April 26, when they boarded it in New York after a hurried trip to their Finca Vigía in Cuba, and Ernest was ripe with enthusiasm. His publisher, Charles Scribner's Sons, had decided to reissue his 1932 nonfictional bullfighting account, *Death in the Afternoon*, and Hemingway saw the opportunity to update it with the upcoming summer's *mano a mano* duels between Ordoñez and his brother-in-law Luis Miguel Dominguín, who had come out of retirement. It would be, to the non-bullfighting aficionado, the bullfighters' equivalent of baseball's World Series. Bullfights traditionally consisted of three matadors, each fighting two bulls. However, in a dangerously demanding *mano a mano*, there would be only two matadors dividing the afternoon's roster of six bulls.

Ernest's temperament on the transatlantic voyage swung wildly from optimism to despair, with Mary unable to squelch her husband's notorious dark moods. For some time, Ernest had been having difficulty writing, a task made even more troublesome by the distractions brought on by his increasing fame. He was struggling with the memoir that would become *A Moveable Feast*, and he was juggling the writing on that with trying to wrap up *The Garden of Eden*. Making the work that much more difficult had been shifting gears while writing at his Finca Vigía, especially under the increasing uncertainty of the Cuban Revolution, which had culminated on New Year's Day when Fidel Castro's rebels had ousted the country's dictator, Fulgencio Batista. At the time, Ernest and Mary had been at the old mining town of Ketchum, Idaho, looking for a house they would eventually buy from New York Yankees owner Bob Topping. For weeks after the overthrow, Hemingway had been mentally kicking himself for having commented at all about Castro and the revolution when the *New York Times* and the wire services had tracked him down.

He had told the *Times* that he was "delighted." Only after Mary reminded him that it was still uncertain what the Castro government had in store did Ernest reconsider, especially given that his home and personal property was still in Cuba. He finally called the *Times*' newsroom and changed the word to *hopeful*.

In 1958, Hemingway had received an invitation from his friend Bill Davis to visit him and his family at their home in Málaga. Ernest had given it serious consideration and then accepted the invitation. The offer, though, appealed to him for reasons that had little to do with friendship and much more because he thought a luxurious, out-of-the-way retreat would help seclude him, when he needed to be, for the writing he hoped to finish. Hemingway also loved to be catered to, and he knew that his wealthy friend's expansive hacienda home with servants at the ready would be like having a five-star hotel of his own at his disposal. Then the *mano a mano* between Ordoñez and Dominguín developed, and the idea of staying with the Davises seemed heaven-made for the fateful summer of 1959.

The trip across the Atlantic took more than a week, at times exasperating Hemingway, who was in no mood for extended life at sea, over which he had no control. The novelty of the *Constitution*'s recent history also wore off quickly. On April 4, 1956, Grace Kelly and fifty of her family and bridal members, as well as her poodle, had boarded the ship for an eight-day trip to Monaco, where she married Prince Rainier. On his trip, Ernest spent days roaming the ship, enjoying the recognition that came often, as there was no mistaking the image that had become synonymous with literature in the 1950s. Hemingway loved children, and he spent one afternoon watching a sister and brother playing table tennis on deck, an event captured by their father on a black-and-white eight-millimeter home movie.

When the ship arrived at Algeciras in the south of Spain in late April, Ernest's friend Bill Davis was waiting at the dock to meet the Hemingways with a pink Ford he had rented for the occasion. Hemingway insisted the color was salmon pink, and Davis and his guest made a big fuss over the color. It was actually called "Pembrook Coral," and it was an English Ford, according to the lease papers Davis signed in Gibraltar.

Mary had never met Bill, but he quickly made a positive impression with an extensive late afternoon picnic lunch that his wife Annie had prepared in a basket accompanied by wine. The Hemingways, in turn, made an equally positive impression on Davis, who had hoped to be their exclusive host during their stay. His new guests had twenty-one pieces of luggage—most of them extra-large Valpaks designed by Ernest and bearing his geometric-shaped coat of arms, which he had also designed—which Davis somehow managed to get into the car as well as tie to the roof and the top of the trunk.

Hemingway looked as if he had just stepped out of a men's fashion magazine. He wore one of his favorite red-plaid wool shirts, a wool necktie, a tan wool sweater-vest, a tight-fitting brown tweed jacket with sleeves too short for his arms, gray flannel slacks, Argyle socks, and loafers. He breathed hard, seeming hot in the warm humidity, and looking distinguished with his distinctive white mustache and ragged, half-inch full white beard. His gray hair was thinning on top, where the increasing baldness was partially hidden by a comb-over from the back. His face was tanned and ruddy, setting off the steel-rimmed spectacles that created a studied, professorial look. All the while, Hemingway had one arm around a scuffed, dilapidated briefcase pasted up with travel stickers—a briefcase containing his valuable unfinished manuscripts in progress. He reminded Davis that they also had several shotguns that had to be cleared through customs with a police permit. As Hemingway recalled it in the *Life* magazine report on that summer:

> *Once the guns were stowed with the other baggage we were off, now in the twilight to climb up through the handsome white town and out through the old Arab-like part of it onto the tree-bordered narrow black-surfaced road that runs around the bay and then, out of the marshy country, climbs up to cross the jutting finger of contoured land that spatulates out into a narrow plain with Gibraltar rising at the end as though the finger touched a giant dinosaur of stone. There was a customs control at the base of the finger as a first check on smuggling from the Rock or as a nuisance value unit in the cold war to make the British give it up. The civil guards waved us through as we*

went from Algeciras and we started, in the dark now, climbing and descending the roller coaster contours of the road that parallels the sea from Gibraltar to Málaga.

It was an eighty-six-mile trip back to his home in the village of Churriana, Davis told his new guests, and with traffic the drive could take up to two hours. Hemingway was immediately put off. Small things could distract him, such as not approving of the chauffeur driving them to the Davis estate. "I thought the driver that Bill Davis . . . had hired in Málaga drove very badly especially through the packed main streets of the small fishing towns we passed through where the people were out for the evening paseo," he later wrote. "But I thought, since we had come from driving American roads, perhaps I was only nervous. He made me nervous all right; but it was from cause as we found out later." However, Hemingway felt relieved to be back on terra firma, as he put it, especially in Spain and even more so as he learned that Davis had already gone to the trouble of finding a stand-up desk that he favored for writing longhand. He had developed the habit of writing standing up because of back problems stemming from an injury he had suffered in World War I and sometimes boasted that Thomas Jefferson had, after all, written the *Declaration of Independence* standing up as well. "Writing and travel broaden your ass if not your mind," he would write in a letter a year later, "and I like to write standing up."

Upon finally driving past the lamp-lit arch at the entrance and onto the long, graveled driveway lined by cypress trees leading to the Davis home, both Ernest and Mary were struck by the resplendent beauty of the estate. For the Hemingways, it recalled the grandeur of their Key West house and the privacy of the Finca Vigía. Hemingway later told friends it was a forested garden as lovely as the Botanico in Madrid, which he had always loved, and that he could not have picked out a more fitting name, La Consula, given to the estate because it had been built in 1856 for the consul of Prussia, Don Juan Roz. It had been neglected during and after the Spanish Civil War and was virtually ruined, allowing Davis to buy La Consula in the summer of 1953 for $50,000. The Davises had been looking for a house in the south of Spain, and they were able to completely restore it. They had been led to this hacienda by Anne's brother-in-law

Cyril Connolly, a literary critic regarded by many as Britain's leading intellectual.

Connolly had introduced Bill and Anne to English writers Gerald Brenan and his wife, Gamel Woolsey, who had lived in the nearby village of Churriana before the Spanish Civil War. Brenan and his wife had returned to the area in 1949 but had not been able to move into their own house until after the New Year in 1953. Their sprawling home, a villa that dated to the eighteenth century, was known for its big tower and a romantic cobbled courtyard where doves splashed and cooed around a fountain. Although Brenan had been a Republican supporter during the civil war, he and his wife nevertheless had fled Spain after sheltering the estate's former owner, Don Carlos Crooke Lario, a member of Málaga's wealthy merchant class. Lario was a well-known Falangist Franco supporter, and the Brenans feared they had incurred the wrath of the working-class syndicates that held Churriana. "Don Carlos was in great danger and we were obliged, every time armed lorries entered the village, to conceal him in a secret cavity in the roof of the bathroom," Brenan explained in his book *The Face of Spain*. "Eventually after considerable risk and anxiety to all of us, I obtained a pass for him and put him on a British destroyer." When the Brenans returned, it was to a Spain still under reconstruction and now firmly ruled by a dictator. Their village, though, was as beautiful and scenic as they remembered it. "All around us lay the broad, flat, richly cultivated fields, spreading like a lake of green water to the edges of the mountains," Brenan wrote. "A team of oxen was ploughing and from far away a boy's voice, carried in gusts of wind." They wished they could instead own La Consula, but they did the next best thing. Later, they tipped their friend Connolly to La Consula, who made the connection to the Davises. "Cyril brought an American couple called the Davies," Brenan wrote of them in one of his letters to his literary friend Ralph Partridge, misspelling the Davises' surname. "I like them as they worship everything Spanish. Annie is good looking and Bill is slow and his voice is like a force of Nature, soothing to the ear but difficult to understand."

Bill and Annie were also loyally devoted to each other, and they saw the Hemingway visit as the pinnacle of their lives at La Consula. It was commonly believed that Ernest had not been in Spain in twenty years, not since the Spanish Civil War; but Bill Davis knew that to be wrong. Hemingway had been in Spain twice in the 1950s: in 1953 on his way to Africa and again in 1956, just before the massive renovations to La Consula were completed. Those visits, though, had been low-key trips, even though Ernest was still being celebrated for *The Old Man and the Sea* and the Nobel Prize he was awarded in 1954. Since then, their showcase villa finally done, the Davises had made several overtures to Ernest, with their invitation to visit in the summer of 1959 being only the latest of their attempts to host Ernest and Mary. "Bill had been pestering Hemingway to come for a year," Jonathan Gathorne-Hardy wrote in his biography of Davis's neighbor Gerald Brenan, "and after checking with Kenneth Tynan that the house was comfortable and exacting a promise of complete privacy, [Hemingway] arrived for five months of bullfighting. . . . Bill in an ecstasy of snobbish and sycophantic excitement turned La Consula into a fortress, but Gerald and Gamel were asked to lunch."

Brenan later told biographer Jeffrey Meyers that Hemingway's "presence" had intimidated him. "It was as if, when he was in a room, there wasn't enough air for the rest of us," he said.

No one could deny that Hemingway's long-awaited visit in full worldwide triumph was now a coup not only for Bill and Annie Davis but also for Spain and the Costa del Sol. For in Spain, Ernest Hemingway was no ordinary writer—he was a Christ. It had been the ideal time, as it turned out, for the Davises to have moved to the south of Spain, which in the 1950s still retained its quaint, Spanish-countryside appeal. Spain was the most insular of European countries, even more so than England, and in the mid-1950s it was inundated with tourists, American bases, and soldiers, sailors, airmen, and money, all having an impact on the Spanish character. The relative strength of the dollar or pound sterling, and the grinding poverty of Spanish society, made places like Churriana relatively inexpensive for foreigners. The village was also close to both Málaga and the beaches of Torremolinos, and not far from the airport—what there was of one. It was more of a landing strip with a bar and a restaurant from where one could watch the planes landing and taking off. At the time, Churriana had a reputation of being a quiet backwater of a village with only one car in an impoverished Spain whose children too often were hungry and dressed in rags. The conditions made it possible for a few like the Davises, especially, to have large household staffs—maids, cooks, nannies, gardeners—as well as for others in the tourist invasion to enjoy a lifestyle they might not have had elsewhere. In one of her letters, Gamel Woolsey told a friend: "One of the things I love so much in Spanish life and which you will like is that the servants are not servants, so much as attendants. If Gerald and I begin working in the garden in the afternoon gradually all the servants gather around us. If we are watering, they help us. If we are pruning bushes, they gather up the twigs and begin clearing leaves." However, there was a price to pay in the envy of other neighbors. "Envy and admiration of us take the form of moral disapproval," Brenan later told John Crosby of the *New York Herald Tribune* in the 1960s. "I suppose all countries with a low standard of living suffer from envy. They disapprove of the high standard of living. There's an immense amount of prosperity among the serving classes. One of the things that has made Málaga women very bitter is that the price of servants has gone way up. The cost of food has doubled."

With the arrival of foreigners came a great loosening of the rigid, almost medieval structure of social life in the Spanish countryside, something Brenan came to personally observe. "Women used to have love affairs within the family," he said in an interview. "There was no social life at all, nothing we'd call social life. In Málaga society, people who made money one hundred fifty years ago mixed only with the family. Men expected absolute purity and chastity of their girls, but they were always trying to get off with the foreign girls." The symbol of that foreign influence in the south of Spain, said Brenan, was none other than the bikini. "The bikini presented an insoluble police problem," he said. "The police [officer] would go up to a woman wearing a bikini and say: 'It's forbidden to wear a two-piece suit.' Then he'd scratch his head and say: 'But I don't know which piece to tell you to take off.'"

The village of Churriana was small, with its charm making it a refuge for people who were growing tired of the coast and the increasing invasion of tourists. Among other American expatriates who were neighbors of the Davises were American sculptor Bayard Osborn, a series of his wives, and his daughter Io, who was Annie Davis's godchild. Io Osborn often made use of the huge swimming pool at La Consula, including the time she surprised Ernest Hemingway. "Hemingway was a taciturn old man in my eyes and yes, he was revered as a bullfighting expert," she recalled. "I jumped on him in the Consula swimming pool. His reaction was dramatic and very scary, but I was later offered the opportunity to apologize and he repaid my humility by teaching me to play backgammon. That is my contribution to this strange and wonderful slice of history." It all made their village, as her stepmother Pilar remembered, one of the prime areas of their country. "There were only two places to be back then—either in Cadaques in Catalonia, where the Guiness family had their home, or in Churriana," Io said. "They were the two poles, and generally speaking artists gravitated to Cadaques, which of course had Salvador Dalí, while literary people came to Churriana." As Brenan put it in his own correspondence at the time: "I get sick of the Spanish. I didn't come here because I loved Spain. I like it here because of the climate and because it's cheap. . . . I have a few Spanish friends in Málaga, but I hardly ever see them. In Churriana, I just know shopkeepers and servants. We don't know any Spaniards here at all."

It was an aristocratic view of life in the south of Spain that was common not only with Brenan but also among many of the American expatriates, according to Pilar Osborn. "Gerald, however, was a charming old fogey, as long as you had something he found attractive," she said in an interview. "I used to go over to his house and read him my poetry. I made him laugh with all my old stories of Cuba. He had this typical aristocratic habit of the time of always flicking the remains of his sherry glass at the wall before topping up. My husband picked up the habit from him. It meant you constantly had to keep whitewashing the walls and meant putting down white carpets was impossible."

It was customary among those grand villa owners to drop in on one another's houses in the evenings for informal, long dinner parties that often went into the early morning. As for La Consula, its soirees were by far the biggest and most talked about, which was exactly what Bill and Annie Davis had sought to have when they bought the villa.

Until the Hemingway visits, the second occurring in 1960, the Davises' premier social event had been New Year's Eve 1956, when the guests included Laurence Olivier and Vivian Leigh. The year had been a difficult one for the two actors. Leigh became pregnant in 1956 and withdrew from the production of Noel Coward's comedy *South Sea Bubble*. However, the day after her final performance in the play, she miscarried and entered a period of depression that lasted for months. Meanwhile, Olivier had his hands full directing and producing a film version of *The Sleeping Prince*, retitled *The Prince and the Showgirl*. Because of Leigh's condition, he had cast Marilyn Monroe as the showgirl, eventually forced to endure Monroe's eccentric prima donna behavior. By this time, Gerald Brenan and Gamel Woolsey had become the Davises' dearest friends and were sat next to Olivier and Leigh. Brenan, though, found himself in the embarrassing position of being unable to remember a single film in which Leigh had appeared, not even the two for which she had won Academy Awards for Best Actress—for roles as Scarlett O'Hara in *Gone with the Wind* in 1939 and Blanche DuBois in *A Streetcar Named Desire* in 1951.

Leigh dazzled everyone with her beauty. As Davis's friend Elaine Dundy said in her memoir: "Her face had the kind of delicacy of carving so fine-grained you could not fully appreciate it at a regular distance: the kind that was forever caught in her close-ups. In contrast, Olivier appeared solid, almost stolid. I searched his face for traces of the features of Heathcliff that turned a whole generation of schoolgirls my age into frenzied idolators. I found them in his eyes, still set in tunnels so deep that I got lost looking into them."

It was a sign of Bill Davis's social-climbing juggernaut having switched into high gear as he worked to make a statement of his home as the salon of its day. It had been a heady rise for someone who collected celebrated people as he did expensive art—and who, to many, didn't look the part.

"Bill Davis had the battered, coarse-grained, narrow-eyed features of a professional pugilist," author Jeremy Lewis wrote in his biography of Cyril Connolly. "He liked to correspond with Connolly about his collection of first editions but was probably more at home talking about 'a good-looking natural cock-sucker [female]' and once admitted to [Connolly's second wife] Barbara that what he really enjoyed in life was farting in company, peeing on lavatory seats (preferably when women were about to use them) and blowing his nose into his fingers."

That April, from the moment Davis picked up the Hemingways at the ship dock, it was obvious that their friendship was a perfect pairing for the summer. Davis didn't intrude. He was deferential, almost servant-like. He also struck people as having "a strange personality," according to Valerie Danby-Smith. "It wasn't one of these effusive things," she recalled.

"He was very much a laid-back, quiet, almost self-effacing type. Ernest called him 'Negro' the whole time, because he had very thick lips and he felt he had this sort of Negroid . . . you know? So that was almost like using him as a servant, in a way. He drove the car. He was like the chauffeur, he was not so much like the host. He let the Hemingways use the house as if it were their own house. He didn't do the big thing of 'I'm the host, I'm hosting the Hemingways.' He really took a back seat, and his wife Annie was just the most delightful person, just a wonderful, warm person. There were two children who were about eight and ten or eleven at the time, so it was a family house. But the family was very much in the background."

For the Davises, the social economy of Churriana was perfect for what they wanted to accomplish. It was no coincidence that so many allusions were made to Gerald and Sara Murphy's Villa America at Cap d'Antibes on the Riviera during the 1920s. "The Murphys were among the first Americans I ever met," Russian composer Igor Stravinsky once said, "and they gave me the most agreeable impression of the United States." They were well known for their generous hospitality and flair for parties, and they created a vibrant social circle that included a great number of artists and writers of the Lost Generation. Gerald, born in Boston to the family that owned the Mark Cross Company, had befriended Cole Porter at Yale and later had a brief but significant career as a painter. His wife, Sara Sherman Wiborg, had been born into wealth in Cincinnati, Ohio, and was the great-niece of Civil War general William Tecumseh Sherman. When they later set up their salon on the French Riviera, in addition to their friend Cole Porter, their circle of artists and writers included especially Zelda and F. Scott Fitzgerald, John Dos Passos, Jean Cocteau,

Pablo Picasso, Archibald MacLeish, John O'Hara, Dorothy Parker, Robert Benchley, and, of course, Ernest Hemingway.

"Once upon a time there was a prince and a princess," said Donald Ogden Stewart. "That's exactly how a description of the Murphys should begin. They were both rich; he was handsome; she was beautiful; they had three golden children. They loved each other, they enjoyed their own company, and they had the gift of making life enchantingly pleasurable for those who were fortunate enough to be their friends."

The Murphys, living their lives abroad after World War I, helped form the perfect context for Bill and Annie Davis and their role in Europe after World War II. For if Gerald and Sara Murphy had been the beautiful couple of the Lost Generation of the 1920s, as many called them, the Davises apparently had become the beautiful couple of the Lost Generation of the 1950s.

3

The Dying Artist

*That is what we are supposed to do when we are at our best—make
it all up—but make it up so truly that later it will happen that way.*
—ERNEST HEMINGWAY, 1934 LETTER
TO F. SCOTT FITZGERALD

ERNEST HEMINGWAY'S ARRIVAL IN SPAIN THAT SPRING WAS THE BIG-
gest news on the Continent, bringing with it heightened expectations
of the upcoming bullfighting season. It would be months, and not until
early 1960, before the world would be able to read Ernest's new epilogue
of *Death in the Afternoon*, which was the reason for his trip. However, the
buzz in the New York offices of Time Life had created a demand for a
jump on any new Hemingway book publication. The editors of *Life* and
Sports Illustrated wasted no time in waging quiet campaigns to make a
deal in which Hemingway's coverage would be serialized to each magazine's respective audience.

Sports Illustrated was in the fifth year since its founding, and its editors argued that it would be the perfect placement for what was obviously
a world sporting event covered by the consummate sportsman. However,
Sports Illustrated would be no match against *Life* and its publishing relationship with Hemingway. In 1952, the magazine had published *The Old
Man and the Sea* to unprecedented success. With Hemingway's photograph on the cover, *Life* sold 5.3 million copies of the magazine in the first
two days alone. The magazine also was part of the book's and Hemingway's literary triumph. The novel won the Pulitzer Prize in 1953, and

Hemingway was awarded the Nobel Prize for Literature in 1954. When the magazine's editors heard of Hemingway's plan to write an epilogue for his 1932 book, *Death in the Afternoon*, they asked him to expand the piece into a *Life* article, which they hoped would be as successful as the publication of *The Old Man and the Sea*.

As they settled into what he thought would be a relaxing summer of bullfight watching in Spain, Ernest now was suddenly thrust back into the world of journalism. This was the writing career that had given him his start, though he came to disdain it. "Journalism, after a point has been reached," he once wrote, "can be a daily self-destruction for a serious creative writer." However, journalism and nonfiction had been the essence of *Death in the Afternoon*, as it would be for the book that eventually came out of his time in Spain in 1959, *The Dangerous Summer*, as well as for his posthumous tour de force, *A Moveable Feast*. "He lived all his life with his own *mano a mano* between nonfiction and fiction, primarily believing that fiction was supreme," the *New York Times* wrote of Hemingway's tightrope walk between being a journalist and a novelist. In defending his preference to be known for his fiction, Hemingway told George Plimpton that "you make something through your invention that is not a representation but a whole new thing truer than anything true and alive, and you make it alive, and if you make it well enough, you give it immortality."

Life went into a full-court press in its campaign to have Hemingway write a series of articles on the *mano a mano* between Antonio Ordóñez and Luis Miguel Dominguín. The deal, though, was really about Hemingway. He was the star, and journalism was secondary; for Hemingway, though a bullfighting aficionado and the writer most closely identified with the sport, hardly had the objectivity and the position of being an unbiased observer to write or report on such a bullfighting spectacle. He had completely missed the career of Manolete, regarded by most as the greatest bullfighter in history. Because of the civil war, Hemingway had self-exiled himself from Spain for fourteen years during the time that Manolete ruled the sport. When Hemingway finally broke down and caught Manolete in the bullring, it was in Mexico in the winter of 1947, six months before the great matador died from a goring. Hemingway not only denied Manolete's greatness, he also disparaged him by claiming he was a fraud and that he fought ineffective bulls whose horns had been ground down in order to lessen the danger. This, sadly, was an indication not only of how wrong Hemingway may have been but also of how removed he was from Spain and from bullfighting. Later, even James Michener concluded in his introduction to *The Dangerous Summer*, "For an American outsider like Hemingway, no matter his long service to the art, to barge into Spain and denigrate Manolete was like a Spaniard sticking his nose into Augusta and claiming that Bobby Jones did not know how to play golf." Unfortunately, by the time Hemingway had finally seen Manolete in the bullring, he was where all great athletes ultimately find themselves: over the hill and a shell of what they had once been. The irony was that, approaching sixty and having difficulty doing what he once did so brilliantly, Hemingway now found himself in the same place.

But this, after all, was the same Hemingway who had disparaged the father of the very bullfighter he had come to Spain to watch, Antonio Ordoñez. It was a sad note that he resorted to tearing down one matador in order to elevate another instead of explaining objectively and in detail what made one better than the other and why. It was one man's opinion anyway, one which most Spaniards didn't share, at least in regard to Manolete. Nevertheless, Hemingway's criticism of Cayetano Ordoñez in *Death in the Afternoon* had not stopped Antonio's father, who fought as Niño de la Palma, from going on to a solid career, topped off after his retirement when he became director of the Lisbon School of Bullfighting. Several generations of his heirs also became bullfighters, with his son Antonio developing into one of the country's greatest. Ordoñez would eventually become Hemingway's friend and business partner and would be among the first to defend him against his harsh criticism of Manolete. The aged Hemingway, who was so scurrilous in his attack of Spain's national saint of the bullring, was a man perhaps more sympathetically seen by someone like Ordoñez, who was not wedded to his reputation and belonging to a newer generation of Spaniards.

Hemingway's fame, though, was such that few dared to publicly challenge his bullfighting expertise. One of his rare critics was the Spanish writer José Luis Castillo-Puche, a man almost two decades Hemingway's junior, who became close to him in his final trips to Spain and wondered if Hemingway hadn't been suckered by the promoters of the 1959 *mano a mano* series, all to help advance Antonio Ordoñez's career. The *mano a mano*, Castillo-Puche felt, had been a publicity stunt, and it succeeded in wrestling in a prized but unexpected catch in Hemingway. "Everything we know about Hemingway in Spain began with [José Luis] Castillo-Puche," said Susan Beegel, editor of the *Hemingway Review*, in an interview. "To understand Hemingway's books on Spain, you must understand Spain. Castillo-Puche provided that bridge." Allen Josephs, a former president of the Hemingway Society, said Castillo-Puche was "unquestionably the Spanish writer who felt closest to Hemingway. He was a young man when they met. He was willing to put up with Hemingway's idiosyncrasies, and he clearly understood the importance of Hemingway's writing for Spain, and Spain for Hemingway." However, there was a more serious relationship, or lack of one, between Hemingway and Spain that had developed by his 1959 trip. "Ernesto was no longer a fascinating figure to people in Spain," wrote Castillo-Puche. "He had become a sort of joke, in fact."

Ernest Hemingway, however, was a rarity as a novelist who never wrote a novel about America but instead celebrated all that was Spain, its culture and its lifestyle, as few non-Spaniards ever had—and who was able to understand its nuances and complexities in a way that captivated the world, even at a time when the country's politics were buried in the past. Hemingway, as former *New York Times* Madrid bureau chief James M. Markham would later put it, was someone "who had done so much to fix Spain in the contemporary imagination." Hemingway's Spain, Markham once remarked, was "a tragic Spain of impassioned living and violent dying, a nation of Goyas and Garcia Lorcas that seemed cast to his own virile, existentialist morality."

For Hemingway, his relationship with Spain had long been a literary love affair, a match that had been made by Gertrude Stein, who suggested he travel there in 1923 to experience bullfighting. It was also Stein, the expatriate American writer who befriended Hemingway in Paris in the 1920s, who had coined the name "the Lost Generation." Hemingway had gone to the Feria de San Fermín in Pamplona at Stein's urging and experienced "the running of the bulls," which led to writing *The Sun Also*

Rises, published in 1926. In 1932, he returned to Spain to research *Death in the Afternoon*, his manifesto on bullfighting, which was first published in *Esquire* and later as a book.

It would be Pamplona, through its immortalization in *The Sun Also Rises*, that would become most closely associated with Hemingway. Some would argue, in fact, that it was Hemingway who made San Fermín the internationally renowned festival that it became. In 1968, the town fathers of Pamplona put up a bust of Hemingway next to the Plaza de Toros on a small pedestrian way that also bears his name. In Spanish, the writing on the pedestal reads, "Ernest Hemingway, Nobel Literature Prize laureate, friend of this town and admirer of its fiestas, which he was able to describe and spread."

Hemingway himself would come to question what he had done for Spain, lamenting about the impact of his work in *The Dangerous Summer*: "I've written Pamplona once and for keeps. It is all there as it always was except forty thousand tourists have been added. . . . Now on some days they say there are close to a hundred thousand in the town." Many natives came to share that opinion. "There is a debate over whether or not Hemingway was positive for the identity of the *sanfermines*," said Julian Balduz, a former mayor of Pamplona. "What happened is that Hemingway put the *sanfermines* at the disposition of the whole world, and the whole world doesn't fit into Pamplona."

It would be a debate still argued well after Hemingway's death, and in a sense Ernest would become an ideal metaphor for the twentieth-century history of Spain, whose defining period may well have been the 1930s and the country's civil war. When Hemingway had spent time in Spain in the 1920s, the country had been ruled by a military dictatorship with a monarchy that stood as a symbol of that nation's glorious past. He stayed at the Pension Aguillar because that was where the bullfighters lived; and although he never ran with the bulls in Pamplona, he tried his hand in amateur bullfighting competitions. All the while, Spain was in the grip of political upheaval that eroded support for the military government as well as the monarchy, leading King Alfonso XIII to give in to popular sentiment for establishing a republic. In the elections of 1931, Socialists and liberal Republicans captured control of Spain, forcing King Alfonso XIII to flee the country while forming the Second Spanish Republic. Over the next five years, Spain went through three democratic elections, and the uncertainty fueled the unrest and chaos in a country that had not yet shed its feudal and clerical past. It proved to be the perfect conditions for two of the Spanish institutions that had long exercised repressive power under the old monarchy—the military and the Roman Catholic Church—to lead the overthrow of the republic.

The civil war began on July 17, 1936, when General Francisco Franco launched a rebellion from Spanish Morocco, leading the Nationalists, supported by Nazi Germany and Fascist Italy, against the Republicans, who were loyal to the democratically elected Spanish Republic. There in Spain in April of 1937, the Lost Generation of 1920s Paris reunited briefly in Madrid when Hemingway returned as a correspondent to cover the civil war. It would be those experiences that he drew upon for numerous short stories as well as for the novel *For Whom the Bell Tolls*, published in 1940.

However, Hemingway was hardly objective in his reporting of that war, being a staunch supporter of the Republican troops and often putting himself in danger while supporting that side. In her book *Hotel Florida*, named after the hotel where Ernest, Martha Gellhorn, and many other reporters covering the Spanish Civil War stayed, author Amanda Vaill portrayed how Hemingway and others struggled with how to portray the conflict to the outside world. "Hemingway is a man who wanted to write one true sentence, who told people to write the truest sentence that you know," Vaill said in an interview. "That was his mantra. But I feel that of all of them, he was the one who practiced the most deception of himself and others. The Spanish government was less prepared to win than he wanted them to be, but he didn't want to report that. He didn't want to see it, and maybe he didn't see it. He wrote things that had true things in them and led readers to believe something, but the truth was something else. And the truth was often something he did know but he just didn't want to say."

In a 1951 letter to Carlos Baker, Hemingway sought to explain his reporting role in Spain. "There were at least five parties in the Spanish Civil War on the Republic side," he wrote. "I tried to understand and evaluate all five (very difficult) and belonged to none. . . . I had no party but a deep interest in and love for the Republic. . . . In Spain I had, and have, many friends on the other side. I tried to write truly about them, too. Politically, I was always on the side of the Republic from the day it was declared and for a long time before."

Half a million Spaniards died in their civil war, which was finally won in 1939 by Franco, who established a fascist autocratic dictatorship and eventually restored the monarchy, making King Juan Carlos I his successor. However, Franco's repressive rule, lasting more than three decades—until he died in 1975—was notoriously known for its concentration camps, forced labor, and executions of political and ideological enemies, as well as for causing the deaths of hundreds of thousands of Spaniards.

"Hemingway is an ambiguous character in Spanish history because he was more or less well liked by both the Republicans and the Fascists," Spanish historian Paco Pereda said of Hemingway's place in the country's civil war. "It was his political beliefs that did it for the Republicans and the fact that he liked bullfighting, drinking, hunting, and powerful emotions [that pleased] the Fascists."

Hemingway reportedly "spent some of his energies trying to lobby the Republican side to protect bullfighting even though it was heavily implicated with the pro-Franco rebels." After the war, according to author Douglas Edward Laprade, Spanish censors struggled from 1953 into the 1970s trying to strike a "balance between celebrating certain Hemingway prose (basking in the glow of international recognition he gave bullfighting) while censoring other things Hemingway wrote. The popularity of the film *For Whom the Bell Tolls* (in 1943), however, proved too much to ban outright, and so apparently it was also screened, though with more politically delicate segments edited out."

Meanwhile, on this trip especially, Hemingway was having to delicately balance his own role in Spain. He knew that he was too popular in that country to have his work banned, as censors did with some writers, and yet he was aware that his visits to Franco's Spain in the 1950s were made well before the country made its momentous transition to democracy. It was in this climate that Hemingway was making what he knew would be a highly publicized visit in 1959, replete with the glory and fanfare of a returning prodigal son.

In 1959, then, the bullfighting *mano a mano* had, for the moment, married Hemingway to Spain, as well as to La Consula. In the first ten days at La Consula, Hemingway mapped out a preface to a new school edition of his short stories. It was a seemingly useless exercise, explaining that the wife of the main character on *The Short Happy Life of Frances Macomber* was someone "I invented . . . complete with handles from first bitch I knew," as if this were going to get into a book aimed at teenage students. It was as if the author's mind was elsewhere, which perhaps it was. Ernest was preoccupied with planning the itinerary for the first few *corridas* of the season, which would take them in a zigzag geographical travel pattern that made sense only in Spain's bullfighting circuit. There was Zaragosa in the northeast part of Spain one day, Alicante in the southeast on the next, Barcelona back in the extreme northeast the following day, Burgos in the central part of the north on another day, and Málaga on the south coast capping that week. The hired driver, along with Bill Davis, would be at the wheel of the pink Ford, driving Hemingway and company up and down the countryside to make each bullfight, sometimes driving all night, as required by the eight-hour, 478-mile jaunt from Burgos to Málaga.

By then, though, the season already had more than its share of unexpected drama. On May 13 in Aranjuez, the Hemingway party had barely arrived on time, with Ernest cursing the driver Bill had hired to drive the Ford. That day's *corrida* was not one of the *mano a manos*, for Dominguín was not scheduled, so Ordoñez fought only two bulls that afternoon, with the second one charging out of the *toril* in full stride. Ordoñez immediately gave him a dozen tremendous *veronicas*. These were passes in which the matador holds the cape up in front of his body with both hands as the bull rushes past. After one round of the *picadors* weakening the bull, Ordoñez asked for *banderillas*, the long, wooden stem decorated with colored paper strips and a metal tipped dart at one end. In an art all its own, these are placed by the bullfighter or a *banderillero* on each side of the bull's lower neck. Ordoñez placed his own *banderillas* and then moved to using the *muleta*, the smaller red cape, stiffened with a rod on top, which the matador uses in the series of passes leading up to the kill. With the *muleta*, Ordoñez made four magnificent *estatuarios*, standing perfectly erect as the bull passed him with the *banderillas* dangling from his sides. Ordoñez had built a frenzy among the aficionados who were watching the world's leading matador as he moved in for the kill. Then, at that moment of truth, Ordoñez miscalculated. In what seemed like a blur, the bull charged too close to the matador, hooked upward toward Ordoñez's body, and caught him.

Ordoñez had been gored.

A look of terror crossed Hemingway's face as he saw Ordoñez bleeding but refusing to leave the ring. Acting as if nothing had happened, Ordoñez performed series after series of *derechazos*, passes with the right hand, every one slower and more beautifully elegant than the last, each punctuated with a graceful *pase de pecho* in which the bull's horns passed by his chest. All the while, blood covered his groin and upper leg. With his energy giving out, Ordoñez finally went in for a perfect kill, with the plaza erupting in a triumphant ovation. Blood dripping down his leg and his face drawn and pale, Ordoñez was awarded the bull's ears, its tail, and a hoof.

"I told you he's the greatest!" an ecstatic Hemingway shouted to Davis and the entourage. "He's probably the greatest bullfighter the world has ever seen! He's the greatest I've ever seen!"

4

The Politics of the *Corrida*

And how much better to die in all the happy period of undisillusioned
youth, to go out in a blaze of light, than to have your body worn out
and old and illusions shattered.

—ERNEST HEMINGWAY, 1918

NIÑO DE LA PALMA WAS THE NAME UNDER WHICH ERNEST HEMING-
way's favorite bullfighter of the 1920s, Cayetano Ordoñez, fought in his
early days in Spain when the young writer attended the San Fermín fiestas in the city of Pamplona. So brave and heroic was his handling of the
bulls that de la Palma was sometimes carried in triumph through the
streets outside the bullrings that he had just conquered. Hemingway was
no less equally moved, holding him in such high esteem that he used him
as his model for the bullfighter Pedro Romero in *The Sun Also Rises*. However, there had been more. Cayetano had been Hemingway's alter ego.

The short story from which *The Sun Also Rises* eventually developed
had originally been titled "Cayetano Ordoñez." It was the story about
the corruption of a young bullfighter by a group of bullfighting aficionado expatriates who eventually all become the characters in *The Sun
Also Rises*. It included the seductive British socialite Lady Duff Twysden with whom Cayetano had an affair, identical to the novel's romantic
tryst between Pedro Romero and Lady Brett Ashley. It was a fling that
had been set up by Hemingway, who was then married to his first wife,
Hadley. For in Cayetano, Hemingway saw the romantic, heroic character
he imagined himself to be but as a death-defying professional, wrapped

up in rural masculinity and courage. Ernest had been mesmerized by Cayetano on first sight in 1925, Cayetano's debut season in the bullring, when he saw him in a *corrida* in Madrid headlined by the veteran Juan Belmonte. "He did everything Belmonte did and did it better—kidding him—all the *adornos* and *desplantes* and all," an enthusiastic Hemingway wrote his friend Gertrude Stein in Paris. "Then he stepped out all by himself without any tricks, suave, *templando* with the cape and smooth and slow—splendid *banderilleros* and started with 5 *Naturales* with the *muleta*—beautiful, complete *faena* all linked up and then killed perfectly."

Hemingway, however, had a change of heart about de la Palma after the bullfighter committed what to Hemingway was a man's most unforgivable sin: In his eyes, de la Palma had cowered in the bullring after being gored and almost killed by a bull. He would never be the same again. In Hemingway's mind, in a series of *corridas* after his near-fatal goring, the bullfighter had failed to show grace under pressure, the author's ultimate credo. Crestfallen by Niño's lapse, Ernest wasn't hesitant about castigating him in *Death in the Afternoon*. De la Palma, he wrote, "started to be great but after his first severe goring developed a cowardice which was only equaled by his ability to avoid taking chances in the ring. . . . If you see Niño de la Palma, the chances are you will see cowardice in its least attractive form; its fat rumped, prematurely bald from using hair fixatives, prematurely senile form."

It was a cruel, mean-spirited indictment that perhaps only Hemingway, so beloved by the Spaniards that they would stand and applaud when he entered the *plaza de toros*, could get away with even though his sentiments about de la Palma were not universally shared. In fact, there had always been an undercurrent of resentment against Hemingway among Spaniards that was rarely touched upon by traditional North American literature, which historically idealized his relationship to Spain. He had self-exiled himself for two decades because of the Spanish Civil War, seeing not a single bullfight in Spain from 1933 until 1953. Instead, his perception of Spain and his expertise on bullfighting would be built on having spent roughly forty days in Spain during 1923, 1924, and 1925, as well as one trip in 1933. By the time he did return to Spain in 1953, Hemingway was at the top of the world—*The Old Man and the Sea* having just won the Pulitzer Prize—but he seemed exhausted by the country and bullfighting.

The perception of Hemingway and Spain as one, though, was already intractably emblazoned in literary annals. Perhaps it was indicative of Hemingway's stature in the traditional Spanish mind-set that the son of de la Palma would graciously open himself up and befriend the writer. Cayetano Ordoñez was already comfortably retired and enjoying his place in Spain's storied past as a promising matador who had never fulfilled his expectations but who had inspired the most famous bullfighter in literature. His offspring became one of the most famous bullfighting families in the history of Spain, with Antonio Ordoñez fulfilling the early promise his father had shown. By the late 1950s, Antonio was the country's pride of the ring, something he had taken up at the age of fourteen when he dropped out of school. "All I need to do," he would say about his limited formal education, "is to be able to sign my name on a check."

As for what Hemingway had said of Ordoñez's father, the young matador was almost philosophical, his reading of the situation belying that lack of formal schooling. "I have read Hemingway's criticism in *Death in the Afternoon*," he said. "But I believe that a bullfighter, a public figure who is judged by a mass audience, must learn to accept and to ignore destructive criticism. If a critic is negative about you, that means he has no understanding of what you are doing. I don't know about my father's friendship with Hemingway or his response to *The Sun Also Rises*." Clearly, Ordoñez the son was not claiming any sins of the father. Perhaps it was the fact that Hemingway elevated the son over the father in both achievement and courage that had mollified Ordoñez, for he had asked of Hemingway upon meeting him after a bullfight, his right hand bleeding from a sword cut in killing his second bull that afternoon: "Sit down on the bed. Tell me. Am I as good as my father?"

In Hemingway's eyes, the son had far exceeded the father. He also saw in Ordoñez what he wanted to think of himself insofar as his troubled relationship with his own father. He had excelled far beyond the provincial dreams of his father, and like Ordoñez, he ruled his world. Hemingway had begun following Antonio Ordoñez upon his return to Spain in 1953, and the friendship had bonded him once again with his adopted homeland. "It was strange going back to Spain again, the country I loved more than any other except my own," Hemingway would write about his first return to Spain since the country's Civil War. "It seemed too good to be true. . . . They say if you can stay away from bullfighting for a year, you can stay away from it forever. That is not true, but it has some truth in it . . . and I had been away for fourteen years." Hemingway was immediately taken with the young bullfighter. "I could see he had the three great requisites for a matador," he wrote after his first meeting with Ordoñez. "Courage, skill in his profession, and grace in the presence of death." Hemingway would eventually consider Ordoñez the world's greatest living bullfighter, and he would return to Spain several times during the 1950s to follow Ordoñez's career and admire his artistry.

However, there was more at play in the relationship between aging literary king and the young prince of the bullring. As 1959 approached, so did a landmark birthday for Hemingway. He would be turning sixty years old that summer, and despite the grandiose plans that wife Mary had in mind for a monumental birthday celebration, it was still turning sixty. He would be a sexagenarian, and he was feeling it. For the first time in his life, Hemingway confronted his mortality with every daily muscle pain, with every movement he could no longer make as easily as he once had, with the knowledge that he was now his mythical old man from *The Old Man and the Sea*, Santiago. Hemingway, in the words of James A. Michener, "was a lusty sixty-year-old man who had reason to fear that his own death was imminent." The friendship with Ordoñez, who had come to see himself as a protégé of Hemingway's model of the consummate courageous hero, now provided him with an imaginary alternative, if not of beating back aging, at least of denying it. Ordoñez allowed Hemingway to recapture the spirit of his own youth in Spain. Michener saw it as Hemingway's "return to those heroic days when he was young and learning about life in the bull rings in Spain."

Now, with the bullfighting season of 1959 looming ahead, Hemingway would get one more chance to live out his bullfighting passion through Ordoñez. However, if Ordoñez symbolized the youth that was behind Hemingway, there would be another bullfighter in the drama who would represent the old dreams of the aging Hemingway seeking one more moment of glory. He was Luis Miguel González Lucas Dominguín, the son of a famous matador of the Belmonte era, Domingo González Mateos, who fought under the name Domingo Dominguín. Of his three bullfighter sons, Luis Miguel Dominguín was a child prodigy, appearing at ten years of age in professional arenas with small bulls and adopting his father's name. A stylish showman who worshipped publicity, he eventually became the challenger to the great Manolete. He was adored in the flesh by a host of beautiful and famous women and dressed in costumes designed by his good friend Pablo Picasso, who created the brilliantly fabulous "suit of lights." Having killed his first bull at the age of fourteen, his huge following made him a millionaire by the mid-1950s when he decided to retire, declaring, "I have lost the feeling and when one loses the feeling one cannot play with one's life." It was said that Dominguín's rising star was what had pressured Manolete into the daring style that led to his tragic death in the bullring.

"Luis Miguel was a charmer," Hemingway would say of Dominguín, "dark, tall, no hips, just a touch too long in the neck for a bullfighter, with a grave mocking face that went from professional disdain to easy laughter."

Luis Miguel's charm had caused a stir in 1949 when he courted Angelita, the eighteen-year-old daughter of the Duke of Pino Hermoso, the nephew of King Alfonso as well as an amateur bullfighter. The duke did not want a commoner paying court to his daughter and had called on the country's dictator, Generalissimo Francisco Franco, who warned Spain's matador hero to stay away from the girl. A new, financially lucrative tour, keeping him out of Spain for months fighting bulls in Latin America, was quickly arranged for Dominguín. However, a week before Christmas, longing for Angelita, Spain's great bullfighter jumped on a flight to Madrid from Caracas, Venezuela, leaving his tour in such a rush that he left all his luggage behind. Back in Spain, Luis Miguel began seeing Angelita secretly until they were discovered and the angry duke locked up his daughter in her room. Undeterred, one night Angelita managed to slide down a rope made from bed sheets to a waiting Luis Miguel, who bundled her up and fled in a waiting car. The two young lovers vowed never to be separated again. Unfortunately, a watchman on the estate had seen the entire incident and alerted the duke, who again used his vast influence immediately. Spanish police launched an unprecedented national dragnet trying to capture the couple and thwart the elopement. All of Spain was agog over the romantic escape that tickled the imagination in an adventure befitting a Cervantes novel. Unfortunately for the heartbroken young couple, they were soon apprehended. Angelita was returned to her parents, and Luis Miguel was eventually released from custody.

The bullfighter's arrogance, though, did not sit well with many fans, Hemingway among them. His distaste for Dominguín came to a head in that summer of 1959 when Hemingway was in a restless state of mind, torn between the writing with which he had been struggling and the demands of following the bullfights. "The visit had the makings of a triumphal return tour," wrote biographer James R. Mellow, "and it was true that whenever he attended a bullfight, he was a favored visitor with the most difficult bulls dedicated to him." By then, however, Hemingway seemed most dismayed that Dominguín's personal lifestyle outside the bullring had exceeded that of the famous author, who had once given the matador his blessing. Dominguín had friendships with both General Franco and Picasso. He also had romantic liaisons with actresses from Lauren Bacall to Brigitte Bardot, from Zsa Zsa Gabor to Ava Gardner. Hemingway claimed to have introduced Dominguín to Gardner in 1953 while she was filming *The Barefoot Contessa*, though this was not how Gardner remembered their meeting. Gardner recalled meeting Dominguín in the lobby of the Hotel Alfonso VIII during *feria* in Seville while he was with his then girl-friend, a Portuguese-Thai beauty named Noelle, of whom Gardner would say, "Oh, what a charming creature." They all went out together that night, and Noelle would quickly see that the movie star was interested in her boyfriend. "I noticed the way she lifted her glass to him, danced with him, let her fingers glide over her back," Noelle recalled. "Later in the car, she pretended that there wasn't enough room and sat down smack on Miguelo's lap. I knew that this cat was bent on destroying my happiness."

At the time, Ava's husband Frank Sinatra was back in the United States, making *From Here to Eternity*, the film that would put his career back on track. It was also the period of Gardner's life when she began turning her back on Hollywood and became, like Hemingway, an expatriate seeking to redefine herself. "If I hadn't cared for Hollywood in its heyday," she later said, "it certainly had less attractions for me now that things seemed to be falling apart." When she befriended Hemingway, Gardner had already appeared in two film adaptations of his works, *The Killers* with Burt Lancaster in 1946, based on a short story, and *The Snows of Kilimanjaro* in 1952. "Of all the parts I've played, Cynthia was probably the first one I understood and felt comfortable with, the first role I truly wanted to play," Ava later said of her character in *The Snows of Kilimanjaro*. "This girl wasn't a tramp or a bitch or a real smart cookie. She was a good average girl with normal impulses." And Gardner seemingly was also on the same wave length with Hemingway, being, as the *New Yorker* once put it, "a Hemingway type of woman—she often drank with the writer."

Ava was also, as she told English writer Peter Evans, "so fucking tired of being Ava Gardner." She and Hemingway could talk endlessly about how their public personas too often got in the way of enjoying life. However, Hemingway had a need for his, he once famously told her. "Even though I am not a believer in analysis," he said to Ava, "I spend a helluva lot of time killing animals and fish so I won't kill myself." While staying with Hemingway at his Finca Vigía villa in Cuba, Gardner sometimes swam alone naked in his pool. "The water," Ernest once ordered his staff after Ava left the pool, "is not to be emptied." He also boasted to his friends who would visit: "Gentlemen, please remove your shoes and dip your feet reverently in the water of this pool, where Ava Gardner swam naked this morning." In Spain, Hemingway taught her the subtleties of the bullfighting tradition, and she became an aficionada along with being Dominguín's lover, whom she followed from *corrida* to *corrida*. "About all I can tell you about bullfighting," Ava later said, "I learned from Hemingway, you know?" Her life at that time was not unlike the role she played as Hemingway's greatest heroine, Lady Brett Ashley, in the film adaptation of his greatest novel, *The Sun Also Rises*. Dominguín considered her the most beautiful woman he had ever seen, with those dazzlingly high cheekbones and haughty green eyes. It was the kind of beauty, some said, that came along once in a hundred years and transfixed men and women alike. But Dominguín insisted that he liked her more for her humor and understanding. "Men," he said, "fall in love with a woman's faults rather than her qualities." For her part, Gardner later said, "It was a sort of madness, honey."

According to author and bullfighting historian Alexander Fiske-Harrison, after having seduced Gardner into bed, Dominguín got up, dressed, and headed toward the door. Gardner, who had just been nominated for an Academy Award for her role in the John Ford film *Mogambo*, asked her matador lover where he was going.

"Where am I going?" asked the excited Dominguín. "To tell everyone!"

The affair, heavily publicized throughout the world with photographs of the Hollywood movie star and heroic matador romantically close, led to the ever-temperamental Sinatra storming to Spain to get Gardner back. On a Sunday, Sinatra tracked Dominguín to a bar where the matador was celebrating a bullring triumph on top of his seduction of Gardner, and Sinatra didn't hesitate in confronting the matador.

"Do you know who I am?" Sinatra demanded.

Dominguín looked at Sinatra, accompanied by what appeared to be two gangster toughs, and refused to back down. He stood up from his seat, surprisingly much taller than the singer, a fact not lost on Sinatra. Nearby, half a dozen of Dominguín's bullring friends and associates also stood up, knives showing from their waists and looking more menacing than the American gangsters.

"Yes, Mr. Sinatra," Dominguín said. "I know exactly who you are. In this place, you are no one."

Late in his career, Dominguín would explain that the lure of being with a married woman was a lot like that of being a bullfighter.

"It is like being with the woman who pleases you most in the world when her husband comes in with a pistol," he said. "The bull is the woman, the husband and the pistol, all in one. No other life I know can give you all that."

Eventually, Dominguín and Gardner split up, torn apart by their equally fiery temperaments. In 1955, he married the Italian actress Lucia Bose, a former Miss Italy and a less challenging relationship. As Dominguín described it in one interview: "She speaks Italian. I speak Spanish.

We do not know what the other one says, and we get mad. It is perfect. But what is speaking? If you say nothing, you are always right."

The marriage broke the hearts of a string of young lovers Dominguín had already left behind. Years later, Dominguín told celebrity columnist Liz Smith that Gardner herself had been among those pining for him.

"When Ava got divorced she called me and told me I could marry her, but it was too late," Dominguín said. "The truth is I couldn't have gone on with her. She didn't leave me any time for my bulls!"

5

Hollywood in Spain

The most complicated subject that I know, since I am a man, is a man's life.

—Ernest Hemingway, *The Christmas Gift*

Although he had come to Spain for the bullfights, Ernest Hemingway had no hesitancy about stealing the thunder from the summer's *mano a mano* or from the matadors themselves. The *corridas*, the afternoons of bullfighting, were as much about the great author Hemingway watching them, in his mind, as they were about anyone in the bullring. Luis Miguel Dominguín may have been the only one to fully appreciate that, having quickly sensed that Ernest's interest had less to do with the bullfighting than with the search for something in his past, as well as the financial incentive. Dominguín understood this because he himself had agreed to the *mano a mano* with his brother-in-law primarily for the money that his own lifestyle necessitated. Deep down, though, there was another incentive behind Dominguín coming out of his comfortable retirement, an incentive not so dissimilar from Hemingway's own reason for this trip to Spain—the *gusano*, the worm that got inside every great matador and brought him back again and again to the bulls. "As a matter of fact," he said, "I never really lost sight of the bull's face. On my ranch I've fought them. I never really retired. You'll see."

For his part, Dominguín didn't care whether Hemingway was documenting the *mano a mano* for America or not. In his experience, few Americans understood bullfighting or cared for it. He also believed that

Hemingway overstated the mutual antipathy between himself and Antonio Ordoñez and only pretended to know bullfighting, when in fact he knew little about bulls and killing them in the bullring. "It is one thing to kill an animal when you are armed with a powerful weapon," Dominguín said once, a not-too-veiled reference to Hemingway's penchant for hunting. "It's another thing to kill a charging dangerous animal when the only thing you're armed with is your own *cojones.*" And there was no denying that the summer of 1959 would be not only a dangerous one but possibly a deadly one. In the first bullfight at Valencia, Dominguín swiftly dispatched two bulls. Then, when a gust of wind tore his *muleta* to one side as he went in for the kill, he was gored in the abdomen by the third animal.

In three weeks' time, though, Dominguín was back in the bullring, fighting in Bilbao, with his beautiful admirer Lauren Bacall looking on. Bacall was among those who felt strongly that Hemingway failed to understand Dominguín's greatness, having already overheard the famous author publicly bad-mouthing the matador. Years later, Bacall recalled that summer and how Dominguín granted her the unique privilege of being with him as he prepared for one of the bullfights. She watched as Dominguín wound up a lock of his hair at the back of his head, where he attached the bullfighter's false pigtail called the *añadido.* He then knelt before a makeshift altar on a dresser on which were arranged, row on row, dozens of religious trinkets and medals; pictures of saints; crucifixes; rosary beads; an image of the Virgin of Macarena, the patroness of bullfighters; and of Jesus of the Great Power, patron of the city of Seville and of bullfighters. And yet despite the religious appeal to the *corrida* gods, Dominguín was gored again, the eleventh goring of his career, but he refused to quit and finished the *corrida* in heroic fashion.

Afterward, bleeding as he hugged Bacall, Dominguín belittled the criticism about his bulls that some in his *cuadrilla* had heard coming from Hemingway.

'"Nobody knows about the bulls except the cows," he said, "and not all of them do."

It didn't stop Bacall from trying to change Hemingway's mind about Dominguín's own greatness as a matador, which she sought to do away from the *corridas,* over lunches and dinners throughout Spain as well as at La Consula. In Hollywood, Bacall had heard stories about Hemingway having been in Tinseltown years before her own arrival there, not trying to sell one of his novels but instead promoting *The Spanish Earth*, a 1937 film about the Spanish Civil War and a rare record of the famous writer's voice. Hemingway and a group of other writers covering that war—including Archibald MacLeish, John Dos Passos, and Lillian Hellman—had banded together to write and produce a film to raise money and awareness for the Spanish Republican cause. Hemingway himself contributed almost a third of the $18,000 they initially raised and hired the Dutch documentary filmmaker Joris Ivens, a passionate leftist, to make the movie. In mid-1937, Hemingway returned to America to deliver a stirring anti-Fascist speech to a crowd of thirty-five hundred at a writers' congress in New York. Then it was off to show the film to President Franklin D. Roosevelt in a meeting that Hemingway's future third wife, journalist Martha Gellhorn, arranged at the White House through her personal friend First Lady Eleanor Roosevelt. From Washington, DC, Hemingway, Gellhorn, and Ivens traveled cross-country to Los Angeles in order to raise money from Hollywood studio moguls and movie stars. Hemingway's old friend F. Scott Fitzgerald, who was in Hollywood trying to resurrect his sagging career, attended the film's screening at the house of Academy Award–winner Fredric March, where guests contributed $17,000 to buy ambulances for Spain.

At La Consula, Bacall played to Hemingway's ego by telling him the story she had heard from Hollywood friends years later. Their account was that Fitzgerald, in dreadful physical shape from trying to dry out from his alcoholism, had intentionally avoided Hemingway at the Hollywood screening because at that point their careers were polar opposites. Hemingway was now the toast of the literary world as he campaigned for the Loyalist side in the Spanish Civil War, while Fitzgerald was down and out in Hollywood, collaborating on mediocre films. "Ernest came like a whirlwind," Fitzgerald later described Hemingway's entrance at the screening to Max Perkins, who was his editor as well as Hemingway's. "I felt he was in a state of nervous tensity, that there was something almost religious about it." The Hollywood screening was the last time Hemingway and Fitzgerald saw each other. After Hemingway left Los Angeles,

Fitzgerald sent him a telegram: "THE PICTURE WAS BEYOND PRAISE AND SO WAS YOUR ATTITUDE."

The name Fitzgerald invoked great interest at La Consula, especially with Bill Davis, who had occasionally made inquiries about whether Scott might be traveling in London or Paris, where the Davises also had homes. English critic Cyril Connolly, Davis's brother-in-law, had often suggested Fitzgerald as a guest at La Consula and later would say that "Fitzgerald is now firmly established as a myth, an American version of the Dying God, an Adonis of letters"—although at another point he wrote that "Fitzgerald is overrated as a writer, that his importance, apart from *Gatsby* and a few stories, lies in his personality as the epitome of a historical moment."

"I lived in Scott's apartment for a while," the sultry looking Bacall told Hemingway and other guests at La Consula during one of her visits in 1959.

Her remark caused some raised eyebrows, as she expected.

"Not at the same time," she said, the moment she had captured the salon's attention. "He had lived at the Gardens of Allah, an old hotel on the [Sunset] Strip some years before I did."

In a 1985 interview, Bacall could not recall what Hemingway's response had been at that time. "His eyes got glassy," she said. "I remember that. I wondered if he wasn't just momentarily thinking back on what they had been like years earlier."

"His talent," Hemingway once said in recalling Fitzgerald, "was as natural as the pattern that was made by the dust on a butterfly's wings."

What had been most embedded in Bacall's memory about La Consula had been Bill Davis's graciousness and how he had helped guard her privacy in a couple of instances when other guests had asked personal questions. That was one of the drawbacks to the soirees Davis hosted at La Consula. There were the famous and glamorous literati, celebrities, and movie stars—but often there were also the star-struck guests of guests who sometimes didn't share the manners of their hosts. The Davises' neighbor Gerald Brenan, for instance, was known for his tireless philandering, particularly with young girls, even bringing them into his villa and throwing them in the face of his wife, Gamel Woolsey. On several occasions, when Gamel was away for summers in England, Brenan took one of those lovers—a young American named Hetty MacGee—to a party at La Consula, causing his wife to fret not over the betrayal but over the likelihood of Brenan's girl committing a social faux pas. Davis, who had dined at Brenan's house and had met MacGee, knew she had "an enthusiasm for bullfighters, gitanos, and flamenco" and made sure to have the men in Ordoñez's *cuadrilla* keep the girl occupied.

"He made being at his home comfortable, that I remember," Bacall recalled of Bill Davis, "and he did it even at his own expense. I couldn't believe how he answered to the name 'Negro,' which took me a while until I understood that Ernest used it as a term of endearment. They had a curious relationship, beyond friendship actually, and it was good to see that Ernest had a friend who was so unselfish in helping him and making him at home."

The Hemingways had quickly settled in for what would be a long summer that would test their endurance. There was a long, eleven-day stay in Madrid at the fiesta of San Isidro, where the drinking and partying wore out some of their friends. Then came *corridas* in Cordoba and Seville, which exhausted Annie Davis and Mary Hemingway, who both chose to catch up with their sleep and rest at La Consula. Hemingway and Bill Davis went on to Aranjuez, forty-two kilometers south of Madrid, and were glad they did. There, on May 13, Antonio Ordoñez was badly gored but heroically remained in the ring, killing his bull in a magnificent performance for which he was rewarded with both of the bull's ears, its tail, and a hoof before staggering to the hospital. Hemingway later hurried to Ordoñez's bedside, arriving with his own *cuadrilla*, whose presence rubber-stamped Hemingway's own celebrity. For in Ernest's mind, it was as if he weren't just living vicariously through the young Ordoñez, but instead it had been he who had faced death in the bullring that afternoon. In a sense, he had, for this was very much his own last *olé*, a glimpse into what novelist William Kennedy later called "a prismatic vision of the dying artist, a complex and profoundly dramatic story of a man's extraordinary effort to stay alive. . . . The *mano a mano* is also a story made to order for the dying man's need not to die. He creates Ordoñez as an immortal, for isn't that the status of all the very best dead people?"

Hemingway would even use Ordoñez's goring and the pain he suffered while recovering to start the second part of *The Dangerous Summer* series for *Life* magazine, which he called "The Pride of the Devil."

"Bill Davis and I stayed in Madrid until Antonio was out of danger," Hemingway wrote. "After the first night the pain really started and it increased up to and past the limit of tolerance. The clockwork suction pump kept the wound drawing. I hated to watch Antonio suffer and I did not want to be a witness to the agony he went through and how he fought nor to let the pain humiliate him as it rose in force like a wind ascending in the Beaufort scale. . . . In Spain pain is quite simply regarded as something a man has to take."

Of course, where else would Ordoñez recover after his release from the hospital but at the Davis estate, where soon Hemingway and the wounded bullfighter were off trapshooting. By this time, Hemingway's ever-growing *cuadrilla* was bigger than Ordoñez's, but Bill Davis insisted that Ordoñez recuperate at La Consula and that the partying continue, where each night now looked like the Paris salons of the 1920s.

"Darling, you're so thin and beautiful," the gorgeously long-limbed Slim Hayward said to Ernest at one of the parties, looking even lovelier than her guest, Lauren Bacall, who followed her friend's cue. "You're even bigger than I imagined," she said in her distinctively throaty voice, as if delivering a line from a film. According to one biography, "Hemingway puffed up his chest like a pouter pigeon." Two years after husband Humphrey Bogart's death, Bacall had just returned to the top of her stardom in the adventure film *North West Frontier*, which was a box office hit.

However, it was Hayward, who, though forty-one, was the scene stealer at La Consula, perhaps having had more practice than Bacall in real life, for some said she was one of those "women so incandescently, overwhelmingly charming that they need be nothing else in life." A New York socialite and fashion icon, she seemed to exemplify the American jet set of her time, and her share of lovers included William Randolph Hearst, William Holden, and Jimmy Stewart. She was also the ex-wife of director Howard Hawks, who had left his wife for her and modeled Lauren Bacall's character in *To Have and Have Not*—what some considered a travesty of Hemingway's novel of the same name—after her, down to renaming her Slim and even stealing one of his wife's lines that the film made famous: "You know how to whistle, don't you?"

Hawks had turned Hemingway's *To Have and Have Not* into a film, and they had hit it off as friends since both loved to hunt, fish, and drink. Hawks once told Ernest he could "make a movie out of the worst thing you ever wrote." When Hemingway asked, "What's the worst thing I've ever written?" Hawks answered, "That piece of shit called *To Have and Have Not*." "Ah, hell," Ernest shot back. "I needed the money!"

When her marriage to Howard Hawks hit the skids, Slim moved to Cuba to stay with Ernest and Mary, then his wife of six weeks, who was hardly thrilled by the visit—and whose resentment began building after Ernest's flirtatious greeting when he met the socialite at the airport.

"Miss Slimsky!" Hemingway blared. "Why don't we ever find each other *between* marriages?"

"There was an immediate and instant attraction between us, unstated but very, very strong," Hayward later said.

Hemingway adored her—he called her "Slimsky"—and the story that came out of their fling was that when he had once dropped his pants "in front of her, [standing] there in all his macho glory, she just kept reading her newspaper."

At the time, Slim was on top of the world. Everyone knew that she, not Hawks, had found Bacall to play opposite Bogart in *To Have and Have Not*, having discovered the screen Slim in a February 1943 issue of *Harper's Bazaar*. In 1946, Slim had just been named the Best Dressed Woman in the World by the designers and fashion editors of the New York Dress Institute, beating out the Duchess of Windsor, a four-time winner who was the runner-up. And she had Hemingway singing her praises, along with his constant attention. While in Cuba, Slim also met her second husband, theatrical producer Leland Hayward, who, along with David O. Selznick and Jennifer Jones, had imposed himself during a cruise layover, though an alleged one-night stand with Frank Sinatra reportedly led to Slim's breakup with Hawks after ten years of marriage.

Did it all sound like a Lady Brett Ashley, more so even than Ava Gardner? And the chutzpah? Slim had charmed her first husband, Howard Hawks, by announcing to the Hollywood director that she had no wish to be an actress. She caught the eye and interest of her second husband, Leland Hayward, by defining the word *spoonerism*—a humorous mistake in which a speaker switches the first sounds of two or more words, as in "red door" as opposed to "dead roar." In 1947, Slim went to see another former lover, Clark Gable, off as he departed for Europe in 1947 and later received a postcard from him telling her, "You were wonderful." Just what exactly had she done so wonderfully, Hayward demanded to know. Slim batted her eyelashes and said, "I was just wonderful being wonderful."

Was it any wonder that Truman Capote used Slim as the unflattering model for the fictional Lady Coolbirth of his infamous *Answered Prayers*—and paid dearly for it? After the article was published in *Esquire*, she never spoke to Capote again. And soon the fictional Lady Brett Ashley had nothing on Slim. She married British financial whiz Sir Kenneth Keith and became known as Lady Keith. But during her time at La Consula, she was still plain Slim Hayward, a lifelong pal of Hemingway, whom she once almost blew away with a shotgun.

"I had never known anyone so intelligent," Slim later said of Ernest. "His mind was like a light . . . illuminating corners in your own head that you didn't even know were there. He had a tremendous influence on my thinking, my literary taste, my enjoyment of things simple and open, my recognition and distaste of pomposity."

Who knows what might have happened between them if Slim hadn't been put off by Hemingway's personal appearance and hygiene. A fashion plate, she couldn't deal with Ernest wearing the same clothes for days at a time, which reinforced her impression that he wasn't as clean as she wanted her men to be.

They carried on a correspondence through the years. At one point in 1953, as Ernest basked in the praise over *The Old Man and the Sea*—which Slim had read in its early drafts—he wrote her that he was "burned black by the sun" in Cuba, asking how she would feel about him piercing his ears and getting tribal marks.

At La Consula, Ernest recounted the story of how he had barely escaped death by Slim's hand while entertaining her on a partridge hunting trip in Ketchum. What made the incident especially frightening, Ernest told his audience in the villa's huge living room, was that Slim was no beginning hunter. He said that William Faulkner had asked Howard Hawks, "Am I a better bird-shot than Hemingway?" "No, you're not," said Hawks, "but my wife Slim's better than either of you!" The day of near tragedy, Ernest, Mary, and Slim were returning home with a bag of birds when Ernest saw yet another partridge and stopped the Lincoln. Piling out of the car, they loaded their shotguns and had the weapons cocked, awaiting the sight of partridges. Slim sat on the fender of the car, where, finally giving up hope of getting more birds, she pumped out two shells from her sixteen-gauge automatic, believing she had emptied the chamber. She didn't realize that there were still more cartridges in the shotgun, having forgotten that she had removed the plug to allow the insertion of more shells. Slim didn't want to leave the weapon cocked and pulled the trigger, not realizing that Ernest had bent over in front of her to retie his boot shoelaces. A split second sooner or later and the exploding gunshot would have killed Hemingway. Fortunately, all Ernest got was the singeing of the hairs on the back of his neck.

Ah, shucks, Slim said, charming the *cuadrilla* the way she had seduced Ernest. Hadn't she run the bulls in Spain, something he never did, visited him in Cuba and Key West, and hunted with him in Idaho? Her one regret, she said, was that she never hunted with him in Africa and that she never got Ernest on a golf course.

"A Hemingway sentence," she said, after all, "is like a well hit golf ball."

6

The Rich Are Different

The rich were dull and they drank too much, or they played too much backgammon.
—ERNEST HEMINGWAY, *THE SNOWS OF KILIMANJARO*

ALTHOUGH HE WAS ARGUABLY THE WEALTHIEST WRITER IN AMERICA, the last thing anyone thought would be weighing most on Ernest Hemingway that summer of 1959 was the same headache that troubles the least successful of artists—money. With the socialist revolution having swept Cuba, Ernest had come to grips with the likelihood that he would lose his estate on the island, his boat *Pilar*, and anything of value still at La Finca Vigía. He was also worried that he would never return to Cuba to retrieve the manuscripts he had left there in a bank vault. He knew the heartbreak of losing his manuscripts through carelessness on his own part, but the possibility of having his work confiscated through a new government's nationalization of the country was unthinkable. All that was one more reason why the *Life* magazine assignment was now so important to him, as were the books he was hoping to finally finish that summer. The last thing Hemingway expected was another major financial setback.

However, a sense of foreboding seemed to come over Ernest when he returned to La Consula after a *corrida* and found a letter from his tax lawyer, Alfred Rice, waiting for him. "I have shockingly bad news waiting for you," the letter began. Hemingway seethed with growing anger as he took in the gist of a monumental error by his lawyer on his 1957 tax return—a mistake that was going to cost him $28,000 in back taxes. He didn't know it then, but the error had actually been substantially more, a $45,000 mistake on which a total of $48,000, including interest, would soon be due. "Because it is entirely my neglect," Rice wrote, "I will pay the interest instead of you on the additional tax." Hemingway was furious, and this wasn't the first time his tax lawyer's mistakes had cost him. In a December 7, 1957, letter to A. E. Hotchner, Hemingway had complained bitterly about a previous, unexpected tax liability from years past that he blamed on Rice and "what at best could be overall ignorance." Nevertheless, Hemingway continued to employ Rice and, even after his death, Rice still represented Mary Hemingway.

Exhausted from a full day of travel, Hemingway felt physically sick and drank even more that night, with Bill Davis indulging him by having him sample different wines from the cellar. For a man who enjoyed the finer things in life—excellent wine and great food among them—Ernest never looked forward to paying for them. In his younger years, while married to Hadley, who had grown up in relative splendor, he chose to live over a sawmill because he preferred to spend his wife's money on wine and travel. He had even sentimentalized that time in *A Moveable Feast*, as "the early days when we were very poor and very happy." Even in Paris, according to the Hemingway Resource Center, "they could have afforded much better; with Hemingway's job and Hadley's trust fund, their annual income was $3,000, a decent sum in the inflated economies of Europe at the time."

The fact that Hemingway would now, in 1959, live almost exclusively off the hospitality of Bill and Annie Davis, who also always picked up Ernest's drinking and food tabs throughout Spain, was not unusual in the least bit. For Ernest had lived almost his entire life, even while on top of the literary world, on the kindness of family and friends, if not of strangers. A wealthy uncle, Gus, of his second wife, Pauline, helped the couple buy their Key West home and later provided Ernest with a $25,000 loan that allowed him to spend three months hunting in Africa while gathering material for his future writing. "He had no problem with paying for their Paris apartment, their cars, their Key West home, their African safari, and all sorts of other financial support," Ruth Hawkins, author of

Unbelievable Happiness and Final Sorrow: The Hemingway-Pfeiffer Marriage, said in an interview with Allie Baker of the Hemingway Project. "Gus also loved being a part of Hemingway's research—such as when he learned that Hemingway wanted to do a book on bullfighting. Gus sent a message to his plant manager in Spain, telling him to round up everything that was ever written on bullfighting, send it to Ernest, and send him the bill. Gus even agreed to finance efforts by Hemingway and [bullfighter] Sidney Franklin to build a bullfight ring in Cuba, which went awry when Cuban legislators demanded payoffs."

Hemingway justified the paradox of taking from the wealthy while at the same time damning their intrusion into the arts by, as biographer Jeffrey Meyers put it, defining "himself in opposition to the very rich who lived on unearned income because he wrote for a living and made enough money to support himself." At the same time, on a personal level Hemingway had more in common with the rich than he did with the common man. When he died in 1961, he left a gross estate of over $1.4 million, with wife Mary as the sole beneficiary. His estate stock portfolio included holdings in thirty-six companies, mostly blue-chip securities—including AT&T, Eastman Kodak, General Motors, and Bethlehem Steel—which apparently provided him with more income in the five years preceding his death than did his published works. His debts totaling $58,529 were mainly for federal and state income taxes. Hemingway's tax problems had haunted him half his life, frightening him into often believing the Internal Revenue Service (IRS) and Federal Bureau of Investigation (FBI) had agents trailing him, which fed his paranoia in his later years. A. E. Hotchner, his friend and author of *Papa Hemingway* and *Hemingway and His World*, joined up with Ernest at La Consula in the summer of 1959 and helped him edit the *Life* magazine story, which eventually turned into a series of articles. The next year Hotchner joined Hemingway again, in Ketchum, Idaho, and found his friend believing federal agents were there in that town chasing him.

"It's the worst hell. The goddamnedest hell," Hotchner remembered Hemingway telling him as they rode from the train station. "They've bugged everything. That's why we're using [friend] Duke [MacMullen]'s car. Mine's bugged. Everything's bugged. Can't use the phone. Mail intercepted."

"We rode for miles in silence," Hotchner wrote, reminiscing about Hemingway in the *New York Times* fifty years after his death. "As we turned into Ketchum, Ernest said quietly: 'Duke, pull over. Cut your lights.' He peered across the street at a bank. Two men were working inside. 'What is it?' I asked.

"'Auditors. The FBI's got them going over my account.'

"'But how do you know?'

"'Why would two auditors be working in the middle of the night? Of course it's my account.'"

It seemed to his friend that Hemingway, whose physical and mental well-being were already in doubt while in Spain in 1959, had finally lost all touch with reality and was in need of psychiatric help, which he soon got in late 1960 when he was admitted to St. Mary's Hospital in Rochester, Minnesota, where he underwent electric shock treatments. As Hotchner lamented Hemingway's decline, he also could later console himself that there had been some basis for what seemed to be Hemingway's irrational fears:

> *This man, who had stood his ground against charging water buffaloes, who had flown missions over Germany, who had refused to accept the prevailing style of writing but, enduring rejection and poverty, had insisted on writing in his own unique way, this man, my deepest friend, was afraid—afraid that the F.B.I. was after him, that his body was disintegrating, that his friends had turned on him, that living was no longer an option.*
>
> *Decades later, in response to a Freedom of Information petition, the FBI released its Hemingway file. It revealed that beginning in the 1940s J. Edgar Hoover had placed Ernest under surveillance because he was suspicious of Ernest's activities in Cuba. Over the following years, agents filed reports on him and tapped his phones. The surveillance continued all through his confinement at St. Mary's Hospital. It is likely that the phone outside his room was tapped after all.*

In Spain in 1959, Hemingway thought he could relieve his mind of those worries, especially with his expenses being covered by his friend

Bill Davis, until he received Alfred Rice's letter about his 1957 tax return problems. Rice had further irritated Hemingway by also informing him that he expected to be paid 10 percent of all film and television earnings as his cost for reading all of the contracts on Ernest's behalf. Davis tried to assuage Hemingway's distress by suggesting that possibly his own tax attorneys in London should go over his taxes or refer him to their associates in the United States. Hemingway was too distressed emotionally to give it serious consideration at that moment. He confided to Davis about his long-standing problems with the IRS dating back to the 1930s. Then Davis did something that he didn't often do for friends, except for Cyril Connolly, his brother-in-law: Davis offered to lend Hemingway whatever sum he needed to pay his back taxes, as well as to settle with the Cuban authorities to secure the return of his property, especially the manuscripts in a bank vault. He wondered whether together he and Hemingway might not make a trip to Cuba in order to make a personal appeal. This was the story that circulated around Churriana, where villagers passed on the account by word of mouth as part of a trail of gossip about the Davises, whose fabulous wealth made them the talk of the town.

"My father would have done anything for Hemingway, anything at all, with no expense spared," Davis's son, Teo, said half a century later. "I don't know if Hemingway completely understood just how devoted my father was to him."

Bill and his wife Annie viewed the support of writers like Cyril Connolly and Ernest Hemingway as part of their own contribution to the arts, as if their loans or gifts were endowments to artists, allowing them to devote their time to their creativity instead of being worried about their finances. Their family fortune in the 1950s was estimated at $45 million, modest compared with the billions of J. Paul Getty, believed to have been the richest American at the time. The Davis wealth is based on estimates from their London banking and financial records examined by European sources, in addition to the likely value at the time of La Consula and the art on the estate. Davis himself left no record of the total cost incurred in hosting the Hemingways for almost half a year in 1959. However, it is likely that the final price tag was in the tens of thousands of dollars, upward of $75,000, for food and liquor at La Consula. The bigger expenditures were for meals and accommodations, sometimes for the entire *cuadrilla*, while on the road all over Spain for the *corridas*. The *cuadrilla* was never fewer than seven friends and hangers-on and sometimes included more than twenty. Davis apparently even paid the salary of Hemingway's young personal assistant in the early months; they had met in May, and Ernest insisted she be part of his retinue and be employed at $250 a month plus virtually all living costs.

Her name was Valerie Danby-Smith, a nineteen-year-old Irishwoman who had been a freelance journalist when she met Hemingway and was disarmed completely when she asked him how it felt to be back in Spain for the first time since the civil war, unaware of Ernest's earlier trips in the 1950s. In his biography, Carlos Baker wrote that "evidently believing . . . that a miraculous renewal of youth could be achieved by association with a nineteen-year-old girl, [Hemingway] adopted Valerie Danby-Smith as his secretary, insisting on having her at his elbow during meals, at the bullfights, and in the car."

"He said, 'You'll learn far more from me about writing and journalism if you work for me for the summer.' And he was absolutely right," recalled Valerie, who later was married for a while to Ernest's youngest son, Gregory, and wrote a book about her time in Spain that summer under the name Valerie Hemingway. When the two met, Valerie was working for a Belgian news service, which had assigned her to interview Hemingway while he was at the *fiesta de San Fermín* in Pamplona. "I knew very little about him," said Valerie, who was raised largely in a Dublin convent. "His books were banned in Ireland because of the country's very strict Catholic code. We didn't read him. His books had cursing in them, we were told. He was divorced and had affairs. . . . We talked about Ireland and its literary scene, how I had smuggled a James Joyce book into Ireland, and then he started asking me questions. . . . Of course, I knew of Hemingway, but I only read one book. It was quite by accident. It was *The Sun Also Rises*, which was called *Fiesta* in Ireland. . . . I didn't understand why it was banned. At the convent, I had no idea, really, why a book would be banned. It was a little paperback with a watercolor of a bullring on the cover. I'd never heard of [a] bullring at that point. I slipped that book in my pocket. I never did return it."

Valerie told Ernest that she stole the book from the home of a girl-friend's uncle, who was on the censorship board, and Hemingway roared. He was immediately smitten by her youth and her looks. "Her creamy complexion, pink cheeks and tangled dark hair," Bernice Kert wrote in *The Hemingway Women*, "reminded some people of Goya's Duchess of Alba." It would be a curious relationship. According to several accounts, Ernest fell in love with Valerie, whose presence was one of the causes of increasing friction in his marriage that summer. Mary Hemingway had had to endure this scene before, as Valerie was hardly Ernest's first ingé-nue, though she would be his last. He took her under his wing that sum-mer, and they became inseparable as he entertained her with his stories and taught her about life, war, guns, and, of course, bulls. Hemingway, according to some versions of their friendship, would eventually discuss marriage with Valerie, who politely passed on the idea.

In Spain during the summer of 1959, Valerie soon became ensconced at La Consula, which in Spanish tradition awakened late except for the household staff; the Davises two children, Teo and Nena; and, of course, Hemingway. Ernest's attention was divided on several writing projects, including that summer's bullfighting *mano a mano*, his unfinished novels, and his memoir about his early years in Paris, which was posthumously published as *A Moveable Feast*. Hemingway had begun work on the book in 1957 but put it aside while reworking *The Garden of Eden*. Ernest didn't return to work on the memoir until he had moved into the house of New York Yankees owner Dan Topping in Ketchum, Idaho. The manuscript was among the works that Hemingway took with him to Spain in 1959, where he hoped to get back to it. One day that summer, Hemingway came downstairs with several chapters from the memoir. "I remember reading them and thinking how wonderful it must have been to have been poor and a writer and living in Paris in the Twenties," Valerie wrote in a 1964 article in *Saturday Review* magazine.

Some of the manuscript was still in longhand, but the more recent pages were typewritten, knocked out on a Halda, a Swedish-made type-writer Bill Davis bought for Ernest that spring when Hemingway had sent him a list of items he needed at La Consula for his work and com-fort. Davis also bought, at Ernest's request, a standup writing desk, which was actually a podium similar to those used in churches. Ernest preferred to write standing up so as to relieve the strain on his lower back. Hemingway took the typewriter on some of his travels around Spain that summer as well as on a trip to Paris. The Halda was considerably lighter than most typewriters of that day, and Ernest could pack it in its original leatherette case, which eventually bore tattered transportation stickers from the American Export Line and the French Line. Ernest later left the typewriter at La Consula, and Bill ultimately willed it to Teo and Nena. Four decades later, they sold the typewriter at auction. "I was a young girl living with my parents at our house, La Consula, which was in Churriana, Málaga, Spain, when Ernest Hemingway lived with my family at La Consula during 1959 while he wrote *The Dangerous Summer*, and I saw him use this typewriter on several occasions while writing that manuscript," Nena Davis wrote in a letter of authenticity for the auction in late 2001. "It was thereafter kept by my father at La Consula and always referred to as 'Ernest's typewriter.' In 1975, La Consula was sold to the King, Juan Carlos, and my parents moved all of the art, books and memorabilia to their apartment in Madrid, Spain, including this typewriter. When my parents died in 1985, my brother Thomas and I were the inheritors of my parents' estate and thus we came into possession of Ernest's typewriter." The typewriter sold for $65,000.

In 1959, Bill Davis went to such great extremes to accommodate the Hemingways that Ernest's actual expenses that summer were few, though he imagined that the costs for the extravagant birthday party Mary was planning were coming out of his pocket. In fact, Mary paid for much of the party, with Bill and Annie Davis footing part of it themselves. It was yet part of how Hemingway could never accept the notion that he was, if not rich, then certainly financially comfortable and would be for the rest of his life. In American pop culture, this might have seemed fitting. Several generations in the twentieth century grew up having heard of a legendary exchange about "rich people" that supposedly took place between F. Scott Fitzgerald and Ernest Hemingway. Fitzgerald was to have said either "The rich are different from you and me" or "The rich are different from us"—to which Hemingway was to have responded, "Yes, they have more money." In fact, however, this repartee never actually occurred, but instead is based on what Fitzgerald and Hemingway each wrote, and it eventually became woven into legend.

Fitzgerald's short story titled "The Rich Boy," written in 1925 and included in a 1926 *Redbook* magazine collection, included this paragraph:

> *Let me tell you about the very rich. They are different from you and me. They possess and enjoy early, and it does something to them, makes them soft where we are hard, and cynical where we are trustful, in a way that, unless you were born rich, it is very difficult to understand. They think, deep in their hearts, that they are better than we are because we had to discover the compensations and refuges of life for ourselves. Even when they enter deep into our world or sink below us, they still think that they are better than we are. They are different.*

Some years later, Hemingway mocked those famous opening lines of Fitzgerald's "The Rich Boy" in his short story "The Snows of Kilimanjaro," published in 1936 by *Esquire* magazine, writing:

> *The rich were dull and they drank too much, or they played too much backgammon. They were dull and they were repetitious. He remembered poor Scott Fitzgerald and his romantic awe of them and how he had started a story once that began, 'The very rich are different from you and me.' And how someone had said to Scott, Yes, they have more money. But that was not humorous to Scott. He thought they were a special glamorous race and when he found they weren't it wrecked him as much as any other thing that wrecked him.*

Furious, Fitzgerald complained to both Hemingway and their mutual editor, Maxwell Perkins, who oversaw both writers' work at the Charles Scribner's Sons book company. Hemingway's response appeared to only anger Fitzgerald even more in that the other man gave neither an apology nor an adequate explanation for using Fitzgerald's name as a foil in the story. Caught in the middle of his two star writers, Perkins tried to heal their differences, as editors often do. Two years later, when Scribner's reprinted *The Snows of Kilimanjaro* in an anthology of Hemingway stories, as well as in most subsequent reprintings, Hemingway changed the name "Scott Fitzgerald" to "Julian." However, the Hemingway-Fitzgerald feud over this didn't end there. Fitzgerald himself may have further locked the mythical version of the exchange with Hemingway into literary history by jotting into a personal notebook the entry: "They have more money. (Ernest's wisecrack.)" Then the critic Edmund Wilson apparently sealed the exchange into an anecdote he created when he used entries from Fitzgerald's notebooks—including the one about "Ernest's wisecrack"— in a collection of his essays and unpublished writings in a book titled *The Crack-Up*, published in 1945, five years after Fitzgerald's death. In an explanatory footnote, Wilson wrote: "Fitzgerald had said, 'The rich are different from us.' Hemingway had replied, 'Yes, they have more money.'"

Finally, calling it a "famous exchange" that "everyone knows," literary critic Lionel Trilling repeated the story—as if it had actually happened in a conversation between Fitzgerald and Hemingway—into popular posterity in a review and essay about *The Crack-Up* in the *Nation*.

There was also another version of the story. Ben Sonnenberg, the American publisher of the literary magazine *Grand Street*, lived at La Consula for a while in 1960 and in his memoir wrote that "Bill (Davis) told me what Ernest Hemingway had told him about his famous exchange with Scott Fitzgerald (about the rich). 'Ernest didn't say, "Yes, they have more money." What he said was, "Yes, they don't give a fuck," and a hoor who was sitting at the bar with them said, "Neither do I."'"

Yet despite all his condescension about the rich, in his personal life Hemingway would eventually backtrack about his criticism that Fitzgerald's downfall had been his romantic awe and infatuation with the rich. For as the summer of 1959 at La Consula would show, Ernest preferred to spend the money of the rich rather than his own. Hemingway's own life, it would seem, had come full circle from that moment when fame from *The Sun Also Rises* had assured him of a different life. As Alfred Kazin was later to observe in the *Atlantic*'s 1964 publication of *A Moveable Feast* about the collapse of Hemingway's marriage to Hadley Richardson:

The rich come in and spoil everything. Once there was a writer, with a wife and a young baby. He was perfectly innocent, the virtuous apprentice, a devoted husband—until he published his first novel, whereupon the "rich" saw that he was a comer and took him up. The winter that he and Hadley went skiing in Austria "was like a happy and innocent winter in childhood" compared to the next winter, a nightmare winter disguised as the greatest fun of all, and the murderous summer that was to follow. It was that year that the rich showed up.

Hemingway was never shy, when drinking with friends like Davis, of excoriating himself for the demise of what he thought had been an idyllic first marriage, blaming it on the predatory rich who had followed him, Hadley, and their child Bumby to their favorite ski resort in Austria. But then, this was what further made Hemingway so fascinating to Davis, who told Cyril Connolly and other friends that the confidences shared in friendship offered more about a famous person like Hemingway than all the biographies combined. Those firsthand anecdotes added to what Davis already knew from his reading of *The Snows of Kilimanjaro*, in which Hemingway blamed the writer-narrator Harry for drinking and cavorting with the rich and wasting away his talent. "It was strange, too, wasn't it," Harry admits in his thoughts, "that when he fell in love with another woman, that woman should always have more money than the last one." The allusion in real life was to Pauline. In her book about *The Sun Also Rises*, author Linda Wagner-Martin suspects that Hemingway similarly despaired of his first-rate literary falloff in the years after *A Farewell to Arms*, blaming Pauline, although it was "her money that gave him the chance to spend what he had not earned and was not paying for" in the years before his comeback.

After that, as the most celebrated writer in the world and without a realistic worry beyond those in his imagination, Hemingway could no longer flaunt his youthful poverty like a badge of honor, his need to wear old clothes or to skip meals to save money. For he was now, whether he wanted to admit it or live that life, a member of that group who was different than most other people.

Hemingway himself would later admit in a letter to Charles Scribner, his publisher, that he had a special fondness for those among the wealthy who could rise above their money to display the courage that set certain people apart. "The gentry has always been those who didn't give a god-damn," he wrote. "It has nothing to do with where you went to school (the poor bastards suffer and sweat that thing out). . . . The real gentry are almost as tough as the really good gangsters."

7

Who Was Hemingway?

God knows I had not wanted to fall in love with her. I had not wanted
to fall in love with any one. But God knows I had.
                    —ERNEST HEMINGWAY, *A FAREWELL TO ARMS*

FROM THE EARLY DAYS OF THE HEMINGWAYS' STAY AT LA CONSULA,
Annie and Bill Davis couldn't help but notice the growing antagonism
between Ernest and Mary, often played out as a soap opera with their
home as the stage. They felt for Mary and, like others unexpectedly caught
seeing the devastation in another couple's marriage, found it difficult to
pretend they had not just witnessed the hell that tired love can wreak. It
was a pretense that Mary appeared all too happy to join, though she later
wrote that she sensed something changing in Ernest or perhaps in her or
maybe in both of them at the time.

In her own way, though, Mary Hemingway had shown herself to be
the strongest of all four of Ernest's wives, confidently able to enjoy the
highs and to tolerate the lows of their marriage. They met in Paris in
the summer of 1944, and Ernest had declared his love almost immediately, telling her, "You're beautiful, like a May fly." Hemingway, however,
had also described her as "a smirking, useless female war correspondent."
Worse, he was not hesitant about mistreating her in public, once throwing wine in her face in front of friends and another time smashing her
typewriter. However, nothing, not even Ernest's open womanizing, could
deter her love as she dedicated herself to protecting his image and reputation, even long after his death. She also put her own journalism career

73

aside in order to devote part of their married life to typing Hemingway's letters, reading his manuscripts, and managing the household while trying to maintain her independence in her husband's shadow.

In 1959, Hemingway began a new round of public humiliation of Mary soon after he met Valerie Danby-Smith. As they drove around Spain, he insisted that Valerie ride between him and Bill Davis in the front seat of the pink Ford, while relegating Mary to the back seat or to another car she shared with Annie Davis. By then, the Hemingway *cuadrilla* included the writer Peter Buckley and Dr. George Saviers of Sun Valley, Idaho, and their wives, along with two young American schoolteachers who had been invited along, Mary Schoonmaker and Teddy Jo Paulson. Biographer Kenneth Schuyler Lynn compared Ernest's behavior to how he had treated his first wife in the 1920s, which lead to their breakup. "Hemingway," he wrote, "played up to Valerie and froze out Mary with the same blatancy with which he had cozied up to Duff Twysden right in front of Hadley in the self-same cafes." Hemingway's mistreatment reached a low on a picnic trip out of Pamplona to the Irati River, where Mary fell as she climbed over two rocks and broke the third toe of her right foot in two places. The pain was incredible as she tried walking back to safety without much help or concern from her husband, who finally barked out without feeling, "I'm sorry you broke your toe."

Mary was understandably miserable for the remainder of the Pamplona festival, where she had difficulty limping around and watched Ernest flirting with the young women, drinking endlessly with fans and admirers, dancing with whomever he could find, and finally slowing down a bit because of a kidney disorder, which Dr. Saviers was nearby to treat. Soon Mary developed a fever and a respiratory infection that led to a severe cough.

The Davises and others found it hard to understand how Mary tolerated Ernest's abuse, him being Ernest Hemingway notwithstanding. However, no matter how much in shambles their marriage appeared to be, Mary had kept them together through even more trying times than his infatuation with Valerie. Some years earlier, Ernest had developed even stronger feelings for Adriana Ivancich, an aristocratic young Italian woman with whom he had fallen in love, and he had invited her to stay with them in Cuba. Some believe she was the muse who inspired Hemingway's creative period that gave rise to *The Old Man and the Sea*.

Adriana was the sister of Ernest's friend Gianfranco Ivancich, a man twenty years younger than Ernest whom he had met at a Venice bar in January 1949. Both of them had suffered serious leg wounds during war, and Ivancich later found work in Cuba, staying with the Hemingways at their house. When Ivancich's job failed, Hemingway even gave him money to buy a Cuban villa of his own. By then, Ernest's relationship with Adriana had developed into a love affair, though there is some question about whether it ever went beyond platonic love. "What happened when we met is a little more than a romance," Adriana wrote in her 1980 memoir, *The White Tower*. "I broke down his defenses; he even stopped drinking when I asked him to. I'm proud to remember I led him to write *The Old Man and the Sea*. . . . He said words flowed out from him easily thanks to me. I simply uncorked the bottle." Adriana Ivancich was the beautiful daughter of a Venetian aristocrat who had died in World War II, shot to death in an alley, where his son discovered the body. She had been raised by a mother who was a severe disciplinarian, and her childhood had been divided between a Venetian palazzo and a sixteenth-century villa in the countryside. Her friendship with Hemingway became the talk of Venice society where it was said that the great American author had been captivated by her long-necked, swanlike beauty, her obvious intelligence, and her romantic history.

Ernest had been on a hunting trip in northern Italy with a friend of the Ivancich family when he first set eyes on Adriana in 1948. She later portrayed the image of herself as bedraggled from a sudden rainstorm when the attentive Hemingway broke his comb in two and gave her half. Ernest had been forty-nine when he met Adriana, who was soon to turn nineteen. Their close friendship gave rise to a love affair, and Ernest cemented those rumors when he appeared to have used her as a model for Renata, the heroine of his 1950 semiautobiographical novel, *Across the River and Into the Trees*. "Then she came into the room, shining in her youth and tall striding beauty," Ernest wrote of Renata in a description that seems to fit Adriana at that age. "She had pale, almost olive-colored skin, a profile that could break your, or anyone else's heart, and her dark hair, of an alive texture, hung down over her shoulders." The book includes a scene in which the young Renata makes furtive love in a gondola to a middle-aged colonel close to Ernest's age. He aroused even more suspicions by forbidding the publication of *Across the River* in Italy for ten years, reportedly to spare Adriana's reputation. There was still a scandal, however, which she bore stoically for almost two decades after Hemingway's death. "I let the scandal freeze into oblivion and my sons grow up," she explained. "But I owe this book to Papa. This was a responsibility I had to face. I am the missing link in his life."

But exactly what was that link? Lovers? A father-daughter relationship? Adriana was a talented artist, and Ernest had encouraged her to write, giving her his Royal typewriter and his Rolleiflex camera and even convincing his Italian publishers to hire her to illustrate the dust jackets of his books. His collection of correspondence included seven years' worth of unusually long, effusive letters. In her book, however, Adriana denies that she and Ernest were ever lovers and maintains that they never indulged in anything more than occasional kisses, which they concluded to have been "mistakes."

"Never did he do the slightest thing that might oblige me to be defensive," wrote Adriana, who nevertheless claimed that Ernest once asked her to marry him, disregarding that he was married to Mary. They were in Paris at the Café Deux Magots, where she said Ernest told her he loved her but couldn't do anything about her—and that he and Mary had grown apart. "From his voice I knew that he was terribly serious and suddenly I felt paralyzed," she remembered. "It was like waiting for an avalanche, an avalanche that would break from the mountain at any moment . . . 'I would ask you to marry me,' [Hemingway said], "if I didn't know that you would say, 'No.'"

"He was too old," Adriana wrote, claiming she never seriously considered the proposal. "He was married. It was unthinkable." The proposal, though, did ruffle some feathers with Mary at the time of the book's publication. "That's nonsense," she said in interviews at that time. "Ernest was fond of her, as he was fond of quite a few young women. He certainly didn't make this one a problem for me."

In Ernest's own letters to Adriana, he refers to her as "daughter," suggesting that while he may have wanted her, there had not been anything sexual between them. In 1954, after being in two plane crashes in two days that left him with severe internal injuries, he wrote from Nairobi: "I love you more than the moon and the sky and for as long as I shall live. Daughter, how complicated can life become? The two times I died I had only one thought: 'I don't want to die, because I don't want Adriana to be sad.' I have never loved you as much as in the hour of my death." Of course, there was a connection to violence and death that Ernest and Adriana shared of which neither of them may have been aware. In 1983, three years after the publication of her memoir, Adriana killed herself. Henry Fonda's fourth wife, Afdera, who was a lifelong friend of Adriana, later confirmed to author Jeffrey Meyers that "Adriana's suicide in 1983 was somehow connected to her involvement with Hemingway. Afdera explained that Adriana had had a nervous breakdown, drank heavily, quarreled with her second husband, was estranged from her sons, and was deeply depressed by the failure of her book about Hemingway—a sad attempt to revive the past in order to compensate for the present."

For Mary, having endured Ernest's fascination with Adriana Ivancich and having held on to her marriage undoubtedly emboldened her to deal with Valerie Danby-Smith in Ernest's life. Mary had suffered abuse in both instances. At their Cuban finca, in front of Adriana and her visiting family, Ernest had thrown a glass of wine at Mary, missing her but hitting the white wall of the sitting room. What had Mary done to anger Ernest? She had been typing up a visa application for Gianfranco so that he could visit the United States. It seemed apparent that Ernest was trying to cause a marital breakup with Mary, who had threatened to leave him at other times but now was going to make a stand. "No matter what you say or do—short of killing me, which would be messy," Mary wrote in her own memoir, "I'm going to stay here and run your *Finca* until the day you come here, sober, in the morning, and tell me truthfully and straight that you want me to leave."

Ernest never took Mary up on her ultimatum, even as he continued to abuse her. Friends and guests wherever the Hemingways happened to be were often embarrassed for Mary when they witnessed Ernest's mistreatment of her. Mary took to calling herself "the Short Happy Wife of Mr. McPapa." In Cuba, it was not unusual for Ernest to talk about his sexual adventures in Mary's presence, leading some guests to wonder if this was nothing more than his example of masculine bravado. Once, according to biographer James Mellow, Ernest arrived at the Finca Vigía with a prostitute he called Xenophobia. And still, Mary curiously put up with the behavior, suggesting that this was some kind of running antic she participated in to help her husband save face, presenting the aging writer as a virile sexual animal still, a front that Ernest undoubtedly sought to present to his public. This, after all, had been Hemingway's sexual pathology, as it were, throughout his life, as Nancy W. Sindelar concludes in *Influencing Hemingway: People and Places That Shaped His Life and Work*: "The parallels between Ernest's lifelong interest in hunting and his quest for the youthful Adriana also were not lost on the critics. Many believed that the bases of his pleasures when hunting were the rituals and satisfaction associated with conquest, and that to some extent Ernest's relationships with women were based on the same needs and his desire to collect trophies."

Left unresolved, however, is what role Hemingway's romances with Adriana, Valerie, and numerous other women in the last dozen years of his life actually played in his true sexual life. "Hemingway was a silly old fool who liked employing young country girls as maids and was always feeling them up," remembered Pilar Osborne, who lived in Churriana, not far from La Consula, and observed Hemingway often during the summer of 1959. So typically Hemingway of that age, it would seem, flirting on dregs from his early years. There is a possible telling sentence in Mary Hemingway's autobiography, *How It Was*, where she writes that she and Ernest were "androgynous" in bed. What did she mean by that? Was it another sign that Hemingway was impotent in those last years, perhaps longer? Or was it, as some critics have suggested, that Ernest's attitudes and mistreatment of his wives had been a veiled revenge against Grace Hemingway, his mother. Her son blamed her for imposing her will on his father, who never stood up to her, and Ernest never forgave her—not even attending her funeral when she died. When Ernest was a little boy, she dressed him in girl's clothing, and who knows what that might have done to his young psyche. "I hate her guts," he wrote about her when he became famous, "and she hates mine. She forced my father to suicide." So had Hemingway in the last third of his life been on an altogether different kind of hunt? In his *New York Times* review of Bernice Kert's *The Hemingway Women* in 1983, writer Aaron Latham raised a point that even the author had failed to note. "Martha Gellhorn, the third Mrs. Hemingway, was eight years younger," Latham wrote. "By now the bearded writer was calling himself 'Papa.' And he seemed—at least as I see it—to have given up his mother search to begin a daughter search. He had hoped to have a daughter but never did and so began calling younger women, including his wife, 'Daughter.'"

Had not a single one of those romantic relationships ever been consummated? Did Hemingway, after the affairs that had contributed to three divorces and lusting for young women a third his age, face some moral dilemma? Or was there something more basic at play? Was all that speculation true, that because of injuries, age, and liquor, Hemingway was impotent by that point of his life? "His sexual boasting," as Jeffrey Meyers put it in his biography, "was directly related to his fear of impotence and his declining sexual powers in middle age."

Impotence, the fear of it as well as the reality, had long been part of Hemingway's work and life, most notably with his character Jake Barnes from *The Sun Also Rises*, who has been rendered impotent by a war wound and suffers a hopeless love for Brett Ashley, a promiscuous and exciting English aristocrat. According to Jeffrey Meyers, "Hemingway had become impotent, for psychological and physical reasons, with Pauline just after their marriage in May 1927, with Jane Mason during their crisis in January 1936, and with Mary after his two concussions during August–November 1944. Now his diseased liver, badly damaged by heavy drinking, caused a high concentration of estrogen in the bloodstream, reduced his libido, and contributed to his [being] impotent."

Ernest had been suffering from high blood pressure, which at one point had forced his hospitalization at the Mayo Clinic. The side effects of the medications, among them reserpine, that he was taking for hypertension might have also contributed to his severe depression and sexual dysfunction. Hemingway was also diabetic, something that was not fully diagnosed until 1960. That same year in Cuba, a doctor told him he was also suffering from chromatosis, a rare and fatal form of diabetes that "makes you blind and permanently impotent."

It was this Hemingway, then, the famous Hemingway at war with the obscurity of the Hemingway few, even he himself, knew that he sought to reach again in that summer, for all that life had been in the years in Spain that had launched his literary power. And at La Consula, with each return from one of the *corridas* and surrounded by his worshiping *cuadrilla*, the Hemingway that Ernest perhaps might not have wanted to make public became more visible, as if by a sequence of exposures on film.

"He was noticeably cold and distant and indifferent to [Mary] at times, as if though he were a stranger at her side," observed Spaniard José Luis Castillo-Puche, the novelist who befriended Hemingway in the late 1950s. "He made excuses for not making love to her."

"[Hemingway] treated Mary like a goddamned dog," said a disappointed Buck Lanham, who was also disgusted when Ernest one day bragged that his wife "would be more amenable [because] he had irrigated her four times the night before."

Mary, though, may have had the last word about her famous husband's sexual prowess when after Hemingway's death, Buck Lanham asked if Ernest had indeed been a tremendous lover in his golden years.

Her words may have been the best pessimistic autopsy of a resigned and wistful generation: "I wish to hell it were true."

8

Who Was Bill Davis?

The man who has begun to live more seriously within begins to live more simply without.

—ERNEST HEMINGWAY

As TRANSPARENT AS ERNEST HEMINGWAY WAS TO THE WORLD IN THE late 1950s, his image as much an open portrait of the famous artist in his later years, Bill Davis was equally his enigmatic host, as wealthy as he was mysterious. Even Hemingway, in their friendship that spanned more than two decades, didn't know what Davis did for a living, much less how he had made his fortune. To Ernest, William Nathan Davis existed almost as a character he had created for one of his novels. Negro, he called him, a name none of Hemingway's biographers were ever able to figure out the meaning or origin of. It could just as easily have been given to Davis because his role with Hemingway was that of his Man Friday, his male personal assistant who had once driven a cab for him in Mexico, much as Davis drove him around Spain in 1959.

Davis's friends and neighbors in Churriana had even less of an inkling of who he was. What they knew about him was a portrait created for them by his brother-in-law Cyril Connolly, who even long after his divorce from Annie's sister remained the family's best friend and the chronicler of what at best could be called the legend of Bill Davis, if descendants of those neighbors were to be believed. They had heard that the rich American expatriate who owned the area's most extravagant villa had a heroic past, according to some reports having covertly provided guns and other weapons to the Loyalists during the Spanish Civil War. It was this deed that made Davis an admirable figure among the locals, especially in the bars like Pedro's along the coast, where Bill wasn't known, though the stories about him abounded: in addition to the story that he was a gunrunner, there were rumors that he had been a friend of Spain's most beloved poet and playwright Federico García Lorca, who was shot to death by General Francisco Franco's Nationalists at the start of the civil war. To these locals, many of them sympathizers of the old Spanish Republic, Bill Davis was an outlaw who could not return to America for mysterious reasons and a rebel who managed to stay ahead of Franco's death squads.

Years later, Davis's son, Teo, shook his head in disbelief at the suggestion that his father had been a gunrunner helping the Spanish Republicans in the 1930s, a real-life version of *Casablanca*'s Rick Blaine with La Consula his Café Américain. "I don't think that's true," Teo said from a hospital bed in Pasadena, California. "I've never heard that." But by his own admission, Teo had little more than a passing relationship with his father, a man who may have been as much of a puzzle to his children as to his friends. In her memoir, *My Life as a Wife: Love, Liquor and What to Do about Other Women*, Elisabeth Luard quotes Annie Davis as saying this about her husband: "Bill adores writers. He'd never been good with babies, not even his own."

Hemingway, of course, ate it up as if he were dining on *Magret de canard à l'orange* (duck breast in orange sauce) at Les Deux Magots café in Paris—that was how much La Consula had ingratiated itself that summer. For the Davises' villa had become Hemingway's sanctuary during what would be the most pivotal months of the last years of the Nobel laureate's life.

It was a perfect fit for Hemingway. Bill Davis was a fellow adventurer, reportedly a Yalie who survived the Depression running arms to the losing Loyalists in the Spanish Civil War, something Ernest might have done—and he had spent much of his life looking for Hemingway, eventually finding and befriending him. That Ernest Hemingway was staying with Bill and Annie did not surprise anyone who knew them. Kenneth Tynan, the English critic, had become Davis's foremost endorser with writers who might get an invitation to La Consula over the years. "Bill's your man," Tynan would tell those who called him for a reference. "He's a shit. But a hospitable shit. He adores writers. His wife has money, and Bill knows how to spend it."

Of course, the bit about Bill spending Annie's family money wasn't true. That was something that Cyril Connolly spread around, having been the recipient of handouts from the Bakewells for years and probably under the impression that Bill was, too. Bill himself may have found it better for Cyril and others to think that it was Annie's fortune that was behind their extravagance than to inquire too diligently into the source of his own wealth.

For starters, the trail to Bill Davis's money began on the walls of La Consula and the contemporary artwork of abstract expressionist Jackson Pollock, which eventually would be worth a king's ransom. Davis had become acquainted with Pollock and his work through Peggy Guggenheim, the American art collector, bohemian, and socialite. According to her biographer Anton Gill, Guggenheim had a voracious sexual appetite and had "slept with 1,000 men" while living in Europe. It was in 1946, after the end of her marriage to her second husband, German artist Max Ernst, that Guggenheim is believed to have had a brief but intense affair with Davis in New York and encouraged him to invest in Pollock's paintings. According to Guggenheim's auction records, Davis purchased at least two Pollocks—*Shimmering Substance* and *The Tea Cup*—from an East Hampton show before it even opened and also added the brief note to the sales catalog that the artist was "working in a somewhat gayer mood." Guggenheim already represented Pollock and helped Davis secure some of the artist's famous "drip" paintings produced in the postwar era. Those Pollocks have included a painting identified as *The Comet*. Provenance records for yet another Pollock painting, *Water Figure*, shows that its ownership was passed from "Mrs. Graydon (Emily) Walker, Ridgefield, CT, c.1947–1959" to "Mrs. Anne Bakewell Davis (Mrs. William N. M. Davis)" in a Sotheby sale in London. Davis's daughter, Nena, confirmed years later that "my father Bill did own one of the largest, if not the largest Pollock collection." Davis also owned at least one Mark Rothko painting—*Olympian Plan*—which he loaned to a Rothko watercolors exhibition at the

Mortimer Brandt Gallery in 1946, according to an exhibit catalog. At the time, Davis was married to his first wife, though there is some question as to her identity. Long after her father's death, Nena believed his first marriage had been to Isabel Peabody, who appears to have been as mysterious as her husband, assuming she was the first wife. There appears to be some public documentation that Davis's first wife was a Colombian American socialite named Beatriz Diaz. Other documents, including correspondence from Hemingway, indicate that in the 1940s Davis was married to a woman named "Emily," possibly the Emily Walker listed in Sotheby's auction records. According to her family, Diaz showed up in Málaga, Spain, in the summer of 1959 looking not so much for Bill Davis but for her share of the Jackson Pollocks, which her ex-husband had apparently run off with when they split up. Canadian art collector Thomas Ranco believes Davis and his wife may have owned at least seven Pollock paintings between them. When Diaz arrived in Málaga, it was three years after Pollock's death in 1956, and his artwork began moving upward in value. Bill Davis's multiple paintings would eventually be worth at least tens of millions of dollars. "I remember Annie but it might have been Mary Hemingway, telling me that Bill could not return to the U.S. because he had absconded with all paintings although his ex-wife was entitled to a share of them," Valerie Hemingway wrote in a 2014 e-mail to Thomas Ranco. "He never returned to the States again because he would have been apprehended." Diaz, who died in 2006, apparently left Spain without any of the Pollock paintings, though possibly with a settlement or arrangement.

For when he wanted to be, Nathan "Bill" Davis could convincingly hide all the gruffness and ragged edges of his personality that so many saw in him and present himself with what A. E. Hotchner called his "misleading jolly Pickwickian face." In fact, what Davis put on was the urbane, sophisticated manner of an aristocrat, which according to some is the story he often told about himself. Booth Tarkington, according to a Christie's auction catalog, used Davis's family as the basis for *The Magnificent Ambersons*, his 1919 Pulitzer Prize–winning novel, which contrasted the decline of the "old money" Amberson dynasty with the rise of "new money" industrial tycoons in the years between the American Civil War and World War I. In this version of the family history, the Davises, like

Tarkington, were said to have been from Indianapolis and caught in the grips of America's turn-of-the-century transition, which soon eroded their fortune and influence in their midwestern community.

Born in 1907, Davis grew up in a privileged environment, as the family still lived in a grand old mansion but faced a life of reduced circumstances in a city where the Davis name no longer carried any weight. Davis traveled extensively with his father, including trips to Europe, developing an appreciation for art and literature while exposed to the American expatriates living in Paris in the 1920s. According to this history of the family, Davis was a freshman at Yale when *The Sun Also Rises* was published, and he became enamored with the romantic expatriate life in Spain that Hemingway created. Before graduating in 1929, Davis came to epitomize the consummate Ivy Leaguer: on the staff of the *Yale Banner*, the nation's oldest college yearbook, as well as achieving memberships in Phi Beta Kappa, the Literary Society, and Chi Delta Theta. His focus, all the while, though, was Hemingway.

"My father spent a lifetime as a student and admirer and finally as a friend of Hemingway," Teo Davis said in a 2014 interview. "I think any number of people envied him for being who he was and having that kind of access to Hemingway and just as many, if not more, resented him for it. Because, of all the people who became close to Hemingway during his lifetime, my father may have been the only one who never wrote a book about Hemingway and their friendship. My father, above all, was the consummate confidant, and he took all of that with him to his grave."

How Davis befriended and managed to maintain his long friendship with Hemingway was merely a sampling of how he could engage with and win the trust of anyone he chose, trading on a genuine sincerity that he hid well under a hard-nosed veneer. It was a trait that Davis had reportedly told friends he had acquired while residing in Mexico, where he had gone to live in the late 1930s and from where he apparently helped secure arms and weapons for the Spanish Loyalists. It was while in Mexico that Davis, through painters Diego Rivera and Frida Kahlo, also befriended Leon Trotsky, one of the fathers of the Russian Revolution, in the late 1930s after Trotsky was granted asylum and took refuge in Coyoacán on the outskirts of Mexico City.

In early March 1942, Davis received a letter from Hemingway and third wife Martha Gellhorn, who were in Cuba, telling him that they would be visiting him on "the 18th of this month (I hope)," with Ernest adding "hope to see some bullfights and have no publicity and see Mrs. D. and yourself. Let us know what we ought to bring, coming from here by plane and where to stay. It will be swell to see you both again. E.H." It appears that another reason for Hemingway's visit was to meet with disillusioned communist Gustav Regler, a German novelist he had known in the Spanish Civil War, according to an FBI memorandum in his file. As he would later do for Hemingway in Spain, Davis drove Hemingway and Gellhorn around the Mexican capital as he tried to persuade Regler to return to the Communist Party, which he had left in protest of Joseph Stalin allying himself with Adolf Hitler. A literary figure himself, Regler in his memoir "remembered Hemingway's passionate plea for communism because it was still the best hope for beating the Nazis." As Regler recalled in his book *The Owl of Minerva*:

> *Hemingway came from Cuba to see the bullfights. . . . At one point he clapped his hand on my shoulder and thrust me against the marble façade [of the Tampico Club]. "Why did you leave them [the Communists]?" . . . [H]e would not let me go; he was in an alarming state of emotional confusion.*
>
> *"Why did you believe [in] them in Spain? There has to be an organization, and they have one. Go back to them! . . .*
> *The Russians are the only ones doing any fighting."*

This was a year after Ernest had accompanied Martha on an assignment to China for *Collier's* magazine. It was also a time when, according to the 2009 book *Spies: The Rise and Fall of the KGB in America*, Ernest worked for a while for Soviet intelligence under the name "Agent Argo." Cowritten by John Earl Haynes, Harvey Klehr, and Alexander Vassiliev, the book is based on notes that Vassiliev, a former KGB officer, made when he was given access in the 1990s to Stalin-era intelligence archives in Moscow. The Hemingways had returned to Cuba before the declaration of war by the United States in December 1941, and Ernest convinced the Cuban government to help him refit his boat *Pilar*, which Ernest intended to use to ambush German submarines off the Cuban coast.

The story that Hemingway put out—and which several biographers used without verifying—was that Davis had been a cab driver he befriended, but that apparently was not true and had been part of an elaborate ruse to try avoiding publicity. With Davis's help, Hemingway did manage to keep a surprisingly low profile on the Mexico trip, though not without coming to the "attention of the FBI because, according to a confidential informant, the author was residing in a hotel in Mexico City 'under an assumed name,'" according to FBI files. Of Hemingway's meeting with Regler, the FBI files reported that "Hemingway said that he had visited Regler in Mexico, and that to hear him talk, one might have thought that 'Spain was only [about Soviet intelligence] torture cells.' Yes, men had been executed, 'many times wrongly,' but that was only 'the smallest part of what went on.' It was more important to remember the cause that they were fighting for."

Meanwhile, Davis had rented the taxi from a member of the communist and socialist movement in Mexico at the time, according to a Communist Party member's descendent who was familiar with the account, and he chauffeured Hemingway during his stay. Davis himself was never a member of the Communist Party nor of the socialist movement within Mexico at that time, although his sympathies appear to have aligned with both organizations dating back to the Spanish Civil War. Davis evidently was in Mexico during the Spanish civil war in his role of helping arm the Spanish Loyalists, who received weapons and volunteers from the Soviet Union, Mexico, the international Marxists movement, and International Brigades, according to English historian Antony Beevor. Unlike the United States and major Latin American governments, the Mexican government supported the Spanish Republicans, providing $2 million in aid and material assistance that included twenty thousand rifles—"good Mexican rifles," Hemingway called them—and twenty million cartridges. Davis was apparently among those involved in delivering the arms, as well as helping transport some of the fifty thousand Spanish refugees, including intellectuals and orphaned children, from Republican families who were given sanctuary in Mexico.

It was a selfless act that Davis seemingly chose not to share with too many, though Hemingway may have been aware of his role, since Gustav Regler and his socialist associates were among those who had worked with Davis in transporting weapons to the Spanish Republican forces. The refugees included intellectuals, writers, and artists—exactly the people Davis most enjoyed being with—and this was a glorious time for them in Mexico. It was a time when Mexico had been swept away with socialist popularism. Diego Rivera, whom Davis befriended, and other artists had come to oppose the idealization of the Mexican Revolution and the Stalin socialism as well. When Mexican president Lázaro Cárdenas granted sanctuary to Leon Trotsky in January 1937, the exiled revolutionary became symbolic of the political divisions within Mexico's left. Davis's own friendship with Trotsky placed him uncomfortably in the middle of that feuding, a position complicated all the more by Hemingway's involvement with Gustav Regler. However, by the time of Ernest's visit to Mexico, the country's romance with socialism had waned. Once a fixture in the Rivera-Kahlo bohemian household, Trotsky lost his welcome there over an affair with Frida that ruined his friendship with Rivera and hastened the end of his status as a luminary of Mexico's left even before his assassination in August 1940, when he was stabbed with an ice pick in the head by an undercover Stalinist agent.

Even in Mexico, Davis had shown the "obsessive interest in the very rich and their 'arrangement'" that American publisher Ben Sonnenberg later observed in Málaga. In Mexico, he became a regular at Rivera and Kahlo's home, known as the Blue House—La Casa Azul—for the structure's cobalt-blue walls, which had been where Frida was born, where she grew up, where she lived with Rivera for a number of years, and where she eventually died. The house was a meeting place for intellectuals and artists, especially those with communist ties, and it was where Davis visited Trotsky, who lived and worked there from 1937 to 1939. In 1942, being driven around Mexico City by Davis, Hemingway called on the painters at La Casa Azul because he hoped he could secure the help of Rivera and Kahlo with Gustav Regler, whose politics the artists shared. For Hemingway, it was also a reunion with Kahlo, whom he had first met in Paris. It had been in 1939, when Kahlo was in Paris for a problem-plagued exhibition of her work that left her with bitter memories that she shared in a letter to New York photographer and lover Nickolas Muray:

I have decided to send every thing to hell, and scram from this rotten Paris before I get nuts myself. You have no idea the kind of bitches these people are. They make me vomit. They are so damn "intelectual" [sic] and rotten that I can't stand them any more. It is really too much for my character—I rather sit and sell tortillas, than to have any thing to do with those "Artistic" bitches of Paris. They sit for hours on the "cafés" warming their precious behinds, and talk without stopping about "culture" "art" "revolution" and so on and so forth, thinking themselves the gods of the world, dreaming the most fantastic nonsense, and poisoning the air with theories and theories that never come true. Next morning they don't have anything to eat in their house because none of them work and they live as parasites of the bunch of rich bitches who admire their "genius" of "Artists." Shit and only shit is what they are. I never seen Diego or you, wasting their time on stupid gossip and "intelectual" [sic] discussions. That is why you are real men and not lousy "artists." Gee weez!

Davis could not have agreed more, and this was a window into the surrealist artist he came to know in her native Mexico. Ultimately, for Davis it was also choosing art over politics, as his friendship with Rivera and Kahlo proved to be stronger than with the exiled Russian Bolshevik revolutionary. After a failed attempt on Trotsky's life in May 1940, led by the painter David Alfaro Siqueiros, Rivera left Mexico for San Francisco, where he stayed with friends of Davis in the Bay Area. In August, when Trotsky was assassinated, police questioned Kahlo because she knew the assassin as well as the Russian revolutionary. A month later, Frida left Mexico and joined her ex-husband in San Francisco, where they remarried and lived until her father's death forced their return home.

Not long after Hemingway's visit in the spring of 1942, with World War II in its first months and Frida Kahlo's deteriorating health shutting down salon life at La Casa Azul, Bill Davis left Mexico and joined his wife in San Francisco.

9

Silencio, Por Favor

There is nothing to writing. All you do is sit down at a typewriter and bleed.

—Ernest Hemingway

As memorable as the Hemingways' arrival at La Consula was, Teo Davis's most vivid memory of the family's famous guest was the next morning when he ran down to the indoor veranda on the second floor overlooking the courtyard below, as the sound of his quick, small footsteps reverberated off the reddish Spanish-tile floor and echoed along the stucco-walled corridor. On most mornings, Teo and his younger sister, Nena, were awake early and played within the villa until they were called for breakfast. They were children, though—Teo had recently turned seven, Nena was almost two years younger—and they had forgotten their parents' admonition that they were to be unusually quiet in the mornings while they had company.

Down the long veranda, Teo spotted a tall wooden desk that hadn't been there the day before but had now appeared outside one of the bedroom doors. He slowed down as he approached it and then stopped, wide-eyed and startled, as their father's friend jumped out from inside the room, crouching with outstretched arms.

"Timoteo!"

The white-bearded old man bellowed his playful greeting, smiling and delighted, as he had caught Teo off guard. "Timoteo. Timoteo. *Vamos a desayuno, no?*"

Teo said he was sorry for making so much noise so early, but Ernest dismissed the apology. He had been awake for hours, long before anyone else was awake, he told the youngster. He showed Teo the unique desk that Teo's father had found for Ernest and the adjoining table for his papers. Hemingway was impressed by the special high desk because at home in Cuba, he had simply used a cluttered bookcase that was almost chest high, and his typewriter there was permanently set up on top of it.

"Anyone who can't write here," said Hemingway, motioning to the wide balcony overlooking the garden in the courtyard, "can't write nowhere."

Now, however, he was ready to take a break, but he appreciated Teo's concern. On most days in the future, Hemingway said, he would sometimes work again for a few more hours after breakfast, and it would be then that he would treasure the children's silence. At those times, he said, "*Silencio, por favor.*"

That first morning after breakfast, Hemingway took a walk to check out this fabulous estate, which reminded him of his own Cuban finca, though La Consula was larger and older. "The house was enormous, magnificent and fresh, of spacious rooms and carpets of esparto in each of them and in the corridors," Hemingway would write of La Consula. "Everywhere they were finding many books, old maps and good pictures adorning the walls. They were having fireplaces for when it has been cold. There was a swimming pool that they were filling with water from a spring of the mountain and did not have telephone." The house would be perfect, it must have occurred to Hemingway as it did to Davis—the next best thing to working at home. Ernest walked through the gardens and then out to the sixty-foot swimming pool before strolling down the long graveled driveway to the gate, where a guard was on duty.

On that first day at La Consula, Hemingway began working on the preface of a new school edition of his short stories. He also wanted to provide background about the origins of those stories, but the first draft was so overwritten that he soon discarded it. Writing about "The Short Happy Life of Francis Macomber," acclaimed as one of Hemingway's most successful artistic achievements, the writer maintained that he had created Macomber's cheating wife and African safari big-game hunter based on the wild and beautiful Jane Mason, his mistress in the 1930s. In the short story, Macomber kills a charging buffalo while at the same time the domineering Margot fires a shot from the car, missing the animal but hitting Macomber in the skull, killing him. "I invented her complete with handles from the worst bitch I knew [then] and when I first knew her she'd been lovely," wrote Hemingway about the story, which had originally been published in the September 1936 issue of *Cosmopolitan* magazine. "Not my dish, not my pigeon, not my cup of tea but lovely for what she was and I was [while with] her all of the above which is whatever you make of it."

Hemingway's writing desk was just outside his large corner bedroom on the second floor, adjoining Mary's own bedroom. It was customary at La Consula for visiting couples to be assigned separate bedrooms, a custom that Bill Davis had implemented from the start. Usually they were adjoining bedrooms, although it was not out of the ordinary for the husband to be assigned a room in the main villa while his wife would be relegated elsewhere.

"La Consula, it transpired, was not baby friendly," Elisabeth Luard wrote in her memoir. "Bill was exactly as Ken [Tynan] had described him, a big, shambling balding New Yorker who didn't look as if he much liked women, let alone women with babies. His wife Annie, who came out to greet us, was slant-eyed, flat-faced, brown-skinned and mercifully child-friendly. She was, it transpired, half-Mexican. 'I've put you in the annex,' said Annie. 'It'll be quieter for you both.' Us both? Was my husband billeted elsewhere? Indeed he was. Nicholas, it transpired, was already installed in the main house. His reputation, Annie explained, had preceded him. Ken had sent down the reviews for Nicholas' first novel, *The Warm and Golden War*, a thriller loosely based on his experiences in Hungary. The book had received favourable attention in the literary heavyweights. So Bill, my husband explained, had insisted Nicholas occupy Hemingway's old room in the main house. 'Bill adores writers,' [Annie] explained."

Hemingway appeared happy those first days at La Consula as he roughed out the preface. He felt surprisingly well and rested, and his moods so often hinged on how he felt physically. Ernest had been hoping to recapture glimmers of the past in revisiting Spain for an extended period, and he thought this experience could at least take him back to the high he had felt after the publication of *The Old Man and the Sea*. When the novel became an instant success, topping the best-seller list and immediately hailed by many critics as a classic, Hemingway felt that it validated the ultimate exhibition of his writing, with his sparse, subtle, streamlined prose resonating with power. Then, being awarded the Nobel Prize for Literature in 1954, Hemingway found himself at the high point of his writing career, his legacy ensured for generations to come.

"I think he would not be the celebrity he is still today," Hemingway scholar Dr. James Nagel said in an interview, "were it not for *The Old Man and the Sea* and the two prizes."

At the height of his career, Hemingway could not attend the official Nobel ceremony, as he was still recovering from the near-death experience that seemingly began his downward spiral, which culminated in his death seven years later. In 1954 while on safari in Africa, Hemingway was almost killed in two successive plane crashes. As a Christmas present to Mary, he had chartered a sightseeing flight over the Belgian Congo, which crashed, leaving Hemingway with injuries that included a head wound and Mary with broken ribs. The next day, going for medical care in Entebbe, Uganda, the Hemingways boarded a second plane, which exploded on takeoff. All of the plane's passengers survived the crash, although around the world newspapers erroneously reported that Hemingway had been killed. Hemingway later joked about how he enjoyed reading his obituaries, but the crashes' impact on his life was no laughing matter. Following the second crash, Hemingway suffered burns and another concussion, this one serious enough to cause leaking of cerebral fluid. He also sustained the permanent loss of almost all kidney function for the rest of his life, which Hemingway blamed for causing his high blood pressure condition. Often he was in tremendous pain, making him withdrawn and moody, as well as delusional from some of the medication. Sadly, in Hemingway's mind, the near-death experience along with the outpouring of sympathy also may have taken off some of the sheen of winning the Nobel Prize. According to biographer James R. Mellow, "There must have been a lingering suspicion in Hemingway's mind that his obituary notices had played a part in the academy's decision."

Still suffering pain from the African accidents, Hemingway decided against traveling to Stockholm for the award presentation, instead sending a speech to be read, defining the writer's life: "Writing, at its best, is a lonely life. Organizations for writers palliate the writer's loneliness but I doubt if they improve his writing. He grows in public stature as he sheds his loneliness and often his work deteriorates. For he does his work alone and if he is a good enough writer he must face eternity, or the lack of it, each day."

With the Nobel Prize, Hemingway had reached the top of the mountain from which there was nowhere to go except down. From that time in the mid-1950s, Hemingway was never again the same writer, and his frustration only intensified as his problems grew in finishing any of the books he had been working on. In all, Mary Hemingway would later find 332 works that Ernest left behind at his death, more than she ever imagined. As those final years crept up on him, Hemingway found himself swamped with novels and short stories that would have inundated even younger, healthier writers. From the end of the year in 1955 to early 1956, Hemingway was bedridden, drinking to excess against his doctor's orders while dealing with the pain and recovery of his plane-crash injuries, which were more extensive than he had let be known publicly: two cracked discs, a kidney and liver rupture, a dislocated shoulder, and a broken skull. When he felt well enough to continue writing, he was inundated with what he had planned as well as with a pleasant surprise. In 1928, he had stored trunks filled with notebooks and writing from his Paris years, which he had never retrieved and were now discovered. The most notable of those finds was the memoir that eventually would become *A Moveable Feast.* Among the other manuscripts on which he worked in those years from 1957 to 1959 were *Islands in the Stream,* Hemingway's first posthumously published novel, in 1970; *The Garden of Eden,* his second posthumously released novel, published in 1986, forty years after he began writing it; and *True at First Light,* about his ill-fated 1953–1954 African safari with Mary, released posthumously in 1999, commemorating his hundredth birthday.

If Hemingway slid into depression from which he was unable to recover, as biographer Michael Reynolds maintained, it may have been also fueled by the uncertainty of Cuba's politics and the future of his beloved home, Finca Vigía, where life had already become unbearable because of the hordes of guests and tourists. Ernest stored the manuscripts to *The Garden of Eden*, *Islands in the Stream*, and *True at First Light* in a safe-deposit box in a bank in Havana, of all places, and delayed any additional work on them by setting off with Mary to find a new home in the United States, eventually settling in Ketchum, Idaho, overlooking the Big Wood River, just weeks before the 1959 trip to the south of Spain. Clearly, it was a time when Hemingway's life was at a crossroads. His physical health and emotional condition were plainly deteriorating, though he would have been the last to acknowledge this and his friends and loved ones may have been in denial. As James Michener wrote in his introduction to *The Dangerous Summer*: "In 1959 Hemingway went back to Spain and during that long, lovely summer . . . he was already beginning to suffer the ravages which would in the end destroy him—monomania about being spied upon, suspicion of his most trusted friends, doubt about his capacity to survive."

Spain, though, seemed like a literary elixir for Hemingway, who had learned in 1953—his first return to Spain since the Spanish Civil War—that the country that had been the source of his first triumph still regarded him as an adopted favorite son. He had expected some hostility because he fought against Franco but found a surprising welcome at the Spanish border, where a guard asked him, "Are you any relation of Hemingway the writer?" Hemingway answered, "Of the same family." The border guard gave Ernest an enthusiastic greeting and told him he had read all of his books.

A similar homecoming sentiment swept over Hemingway that first full day at La Consula, and he later recalled those days fondly:

In May it was cold and the moccasins were turning out to be more adapted for the stairs of marble. We were eating marvellously and were drinking well. We were leaving . . . others alone some, and when on having got up in the morning it was going out to the balcony that was crossing the whole front of the second floor and was looking over the pines of the garden it was doing the mountains and at the time that one heard the sea whistling to the wind between the trees, then I understood that I had never been in a more beautiful site [place]. It was ideal to work and I began to write immediately.

Hemingway and Davis spent that first night after the writer's arrival catching up on old times, overindulging in drinks before dinner, which in the Spanish tradition was late, often 11 p.m., at La Consula, as Mary Hemingway was to quickly learn. It concerned her because it meant that Hemingway would get even less sleep than usual before waking up between 5:30 and 6:00 a.m. each day to begin writing, which was his custom. The early morning hours especially offered him the tranquil atmosphere and solitude he was always looking for in a working environment. It was in that quiet that he sought to make sense of his noisy and compelling outer life, with the frenetic activity and social interaction with which he surrounded himself. Gabriel García Márquez, the Latin American Nobel laureate, would later write that he imagined Hemingway working in a room so austere that no woman would disturb him. Not surprisingly, that had been exactly how Bill Davis asked his housekeeper to set up Hemingway's bedroom at La Consula, making the furnishings as sparse as possible. Of course, this was contrary to the image of the young Hemingway writing at the cafés in Paris in the 1920s, which had come to be associated with him. However, that had been a practice he had taken up when it was too cold to work in the room he kept for himself overlooking the rooftops of the city. He had even written about such a café in the rough draft of the memoir he had brought with him to La Consula: "It was a pleasant café, warm and clean and friendly, and I hung up my old waterproof on the coat rack to dry and put my worn and weathered felt hat on the rack above the bench and ordered a *café au lait*. The waiter brought it and I took out a notebook from the pocket of the coat and a pencil and started to write."

At La Consula, Hemingway had arranged to have café au lait brought to him at his desk on the veranda at sunrise and again at midmorning. There the maids would find him standing in unfettered concentration in front of his tall desk, occasionally shifting his weight from one foot to another and perspiring heavily as the morning warmed. American journalist and writer George Plimpton had seen him working in Cuba and said that "when the work is going well, [Hemingway was] excited as a boy, fretful, miserable when the artistic touch momentarily vanishes—slave of a self-imposed discipline. . . . He stands in a pair of his oversized loafers on the worn skin of a lesser kudu—the typewriter and the reading board chest-high opposite him. He keeps track of his daily progress—'so as not to kid myself'—on a large chart made out of the side of a cardboard packing case set up against the wall under the nose of a mounted gazelle head."

In a 1958 interview, Plimpton had asked Hemingway about his process of writing, and Hemingway had been as explicit as ever:

When I am working on a book or a story I write every morning as soon after first light as possible. There is no one to disturb you and it is cool or cold and you come to your work and warm as you write. You read what you have written and, as you always stop when you know what is going to happen next, you go on from there. You write until you come to a place where you still have your juice and know what will happen next and you stop and try to live through until the next day when you hit it again. You have started at six in the morning, say, and may go on until noon or be through before that. When you stop you are as empty, and at the same time never empty but filling, as when you have made love to someone you love. Nothing can hurt you, nothing can happen, nothing means anything until the next day when you do it again. It is the wait until the next day that is hard to get through.

At La Consula, Hemingway followed this routine faithfully, with the household quickly becoming aware that the mornings were his alone, unless he wanted to come downstairs, when his presence alone would signal that he was done working for the time being. Hemingway usually wrote his initial drafts in pencil—"Wearing down seven number-two pencils is a good day's work," he often bragged—on onionskin typewriter paper, which Davis had ordered specially for him, along with a clipboard that Hemingway always kept on the left side of his typewriter.

An examination of those handwritten pages shows that his scribbling at times was almost childish, with little regard for punctuation and using an X instead of a period at the end of a sentence. When he had several hand-written pages that he liked, he would take that draft and type it on his stand-up desk, where the Swedish-made Halda typewriter was at chest height. Hemingway's goal was to write five hundred words a day, and he would post his daily output on the chart that he had pinned on one of the walls of his bedroom. For the first few days at La Consula, Ernest would remain in his bedroom when the maids came by to clean after he had finished working, just to keep close watch that they didn't move his papers or touch his work chart.

"*Este es el cuento de mi trabajo,*" he told them each day until he trusted them completely, "*y es como el cuento de mi vida.*"

10

Bullfighting as Art

Bullfighting is the only art in which the artist is in danger of death and in which the degree of brilliance in the performance is left to the fighter's honor.

—ERNEST HEMINGWAY

ERNEST HEMINGWAY'S FRIEND AND BIOGRAPHER A. E. HOTCHNER ONCE said that in Spain, Ernest used bullfighting as his way to cool out from his writing—bullfighting and everything surrounding bullfighting, from the drinking and eating to the touring and the ambiance of the *corridas*. Mary Hemingway, much like his three former wives, could never fully understand Ernest's obsession with a sport, if it were that, that could be so brutally cruel to animals. But for some reason, Hemingway became obsessed with bullfighting from the moment he attended his first *corrida*—the glorification of blood, the matador's artistry of passes with the cape, and finally, the sword and the art of the kill. For Hemingway, it seemed to be working out some personal philosophy about death, which he explored in *The Sun Also Rises* and again in *Death in the Afternoon*. Would Hemingway, if he had been able, have chosen to become a matador over a writer? Had this been part of the death wish—rushing into war, even if only as an ambulance driver, when he had been denied admission as a soldier, or the heroics beyond reporting in the Spanish Civil War and again in World War II?

Never was the kinship between obsession and the need for diversion in Hemingway truer than during the summer of 1959 in Spain, following the *mano a mano* between Antonio Ordoñez and Luis Miguel Dominguín. Hemingway was there to write about their much-anticipated showdown in the bullring, and it would prove to be both the inspiration and the distraction that his withering talents needed. It was more than three decades since he had first ventured to Spain from Paris, where he lived with Hadley on the Left Bank at the Hotel Jacob, 74 rue Cardinal Lemoine, and later at 113 rue Notre Dame des Champs. That had been the young, supremely confident Hemingway without much more than newspaper bylines and short stories to his credit. He had become arguably the world's greatest man of letters of the twentieth century up to that time, though he was now simply an old luminary, increasingly struggling to make his way through the mental cobwebs of time.

In 1923, sitting at Gertrude Stein's flat at 27 rue de Fleurus, Hemingway had been urged to go to Pamplona, as she enticed him with stories of how the locals ran with the bulls through the streets in the morning, then partied with the matadors before they killed the bulls in the evening. It took only one visit to Pamplona for it to become an obsession that Hemingway would never be able to shake, nor would he want to. In 1923, though, Pamplona was barely in its infancy compared to what it would become. Now it has become the famous home of the *Feria de San Fermín*, largely because of Hemingway and the incredible fame it gained from *The Sun Also Rises*. Pamplona in 1923 was little more than an obscure citadel, the capital of the Navarre region, hemmed into the northeast corner of Spain. In all, Hemingway visited Pamplona on nine occasions, traveling there every year from 1923 to 1927, with his journey in the summer of 1925 producing *The Sun Also Rises*, which transformed what had once been a provincial party into a global event and a famed fiesta of bullfighting and brutality, drink, and song. Ernest had been immediately smitten by the drunken, spirited celebrations of the *Feria de San Fermín*, sitting in bars and watching the locals risking injury running with the bulls stampeding half a mile to the bullring. But none of this had quite the hypnotic effect on Hemingway as did the image of the *corrida* itself, the sight of a matador seemingly out of a Goya print standing his ground against a wild, half-ton animal unleashed in what was at best not so much symbolic of a national sport but of a cultural tragedy. In Hemingway's mind, he came to see it as the purest form of courage.

"In Spain bullfighting is written about in the cultural pages of newspapers, not the sports section," bullfighting historian Alexander Fiske-Harrison would write of the Spaniards' national obsession half a century after Hemingway's death. "Even Hemingway in *Death in the Afternoon* wrote that 'the bullfight is not a sport.'" It likely never occurred to Hemingway that someday parts of Spain would ban bullfighting, as Catalonia did on July 28, 2010. He would have undoubtedly condemned Catalonia's action as an assault on Spanish history and culture and even as a threat to Spanish identity, as many Spaniards did. In a clear provocation to its great rival Barcelona, Spain's capital city of Madrid responded by officially elevating bullfighting to the status of a protected art form, as matadors, philosophers, and politicians became embroiled in a furious dispute over the country's bloody but emblematic sport. Painters such as Pablo Picasso and Francisco Goya and poets and playwrights such as Federico García Lorca were among those who had long considered bullfighting to be an essential part of Spanish culture. Hemingway, too, saw bullfighting as an art, comparable to theater or dance, joining a mind-set cultivated for centuries in serious works of art and literature in which bullfighting lived as a stylized "dance of death," a morality play, and a metaphysical drama that, as Manolete had once put it, "ennobles both man and bull, because through it their virtues of bravery and courage are realized." As Hemingway wrote, "A death will occur this afternoon, will it be man or animal?"

Hemingway had once boasted to have seen fifteen hundred bulls killed on the field of honor, and he acknowledged in *Death in the Afternoon* his indebtedness to some 2,077 "books and pamphlets in Spanish dealing with or touching on *tauromania*," all as testament to his expertise on the art of bullfighting. No one challenges that he became the American literary expert on bullfighting—not that he had much competition. For Hemingway, who had experienced a personal baptism of sorts in war, bullfighting had taken on a special significance in his understanding of human nature and life and death.

"The only place where you could see life and death, i.e., violent death now that the wars were over, was in the bull ring and I wanted very much to go to Spain where I could study it," Hemingway wrote by way of explaining his reasoning for undertaking *Death in the Afternoon*. "I was trying to learn to write, commencing with the simplest things, and one of the simplest things of all and the most fundamental is violent death."

It was a personal manifesto that seems all the more remarkable when you consider Hemingway's first exposure to what would become a life's passion.

Ernest Hemingway saw his first bullfight in 1923 in Pamplona, and he did not expect to like it. "Most people who wrote about it condemned bullfighting outright as a stupid brutal business," he recalled, admitting that even its supporters "were apologetic about the whole thing." And the politics were all wrong. For the better part of a century, Europe's left-wing reformers had been crusading against bullfights—they thought them inhumane and needlessly cruel and distrusted the public bloodlust. In the Spanish Civil War, General Francisco Franco would become the great protector of the *toreros*, the bullfighters. The Republican armies, like the Socialists before them, would storm farms that raised bulls for fighting, massacring the ranchers. "One less *torero*, one less fascist," proclaimed the left-wing newspapers.

Ernest Hemingway wrote about his first bullfight for the *Toronto Star Weekly*, which had given the young author freedom to write and roam, as well as to develop his craft, and published that story on the front page with the headline "Bullfighting Is Not a Sport—It Is a Tragedy," words that would forever be linked with Hemingway. "That piece in the *Toronto Star* was his first working out in print of that material which would show up in his first major novel, *The Sun Also Rises*," Professor Sandra Spanier, a Hemingway expert at Penn State University, said in a report about the Hemingway Letters Project of which she was lead editor. "Being a foreign correspondent for the *Toronto Star* allowed Hemingway to get out and see contemporary postwar Europe in a way he wouldn't have had he simply been traveling as a tourist. And he wrote things up for the *Star* that he later worked into fiction."

The Hemingway letters published by that project include a poignant one dated February 15, 1922, in which the young author explained to his mother the unique pull of Paris on his heart. "Paris is so very beautiful," he wrote, "that it satisfies something in you that is always hungry in America."

Writing about the bullfights also offered Hemingway an opportunity to earn more money from the *Star Weekly*, with which he had a deal that offered an obvious incentive to travel because it paid more. Assigned to Paris, Hemingway earned only modest per-word rates, starting at a half a cent a word and earning $5 for a one-thousand-word story. However, for out-of-town assignments he made $75 a week plus expenses. At the time, it was cheap to live in Paris, writing one story in which he detailed how it was possible to live "very comfortably" there on $1,000 a year. In 1923, he and his first wife, Hadley, were paying $20 per month for a small, cold-water flat near the Pantheon and boasted that they could live on as little as a dollar a day. So Hemingway's out-of-town travels to Spain to cover the bulls gave him the financial freedom to write his short stories, his poetry, and his fiction.

"I am not going to apologize for bullfighting. It is a survival of the days of the Roman Colosseum," Hemingway wrote in that first story about bullfighting. "At any rate bullfighting is not a sport. It is a tragedy, and it symbolizes the struggle between man and the beasts. . . . A popular *espada* gets $5,000 for his afternoon's work. An unpopular *espada* though may not get $500. Both run the same risks. It is a good deal like Grand Opera for the really great matadors except they run the chance of being killed every time they cannot hit high C."

By 1959, Hemingway's name in Europe was synonymous with Spain, both the Spain from his youth and the country of a generation later, the Spain that he had called "the last good country left." James M. Markham, who would later serve as the Madrid bureau chief for the *New York Times*, observed that a quarter of a century after his death, Hemingway and his image still cast a long shadow over Spain. "One could not get around him, or even avoid some of the carnage he'd left behind," he wrote. "Hemingway drank and ate in as many places as George Washington slept in." Perhaps, Markham said, it was because there was the perception, especially among other writers, that Hemingway "had done so much to fix Spain in the contemporary imagination. He wrote things that one was tempted to steal, or pilfer from around the edges . . . heartland that he encountered, and reinvented in literature, a tragic Spain of impassioned living and violent dying, a nation of Goyas and García Lorcas that seemed cast to his own virile, existentialist morality."

Great Fortune

To be a successful father . . . there's one absolute rule: when you have a kid, don't look at it for the first two years.

—ERNEST HEMINGWAY

FROM EXPERIENCE WATCHING THE CHILDREN OF WEALTHY PARENTS, Bill Davis knew that often great fortunes can have disastrous effects upon heirs, swamping them with too much money at an early age. Balzac, after all, had once said that "behind every great fortune lies a great crime." In Bill Davis's case, though, that crime perhaps may not have been any felonious method in how he had acquired his fortune as much as in the social misdemeanor that he took in parenting. Some would say that he and his wife Annie were guilty not only of not looking at their kids in the first two years but in not looking at them much at all after that as well. For the story of Davis's fortune is essentially the story of his mysterious life and why his children seemed to have mattered so little in it.

In 1959, the Davis children were at that young, impressionable age when the slightest neglect might cause irreparable harm in a most delicate and crucial period of life—childhood. They had seen their parents' incredible hospitality toward famous friends and strangers but never on the scale as what they showed the Hemingways, whose extended stay in 1959 made it seem as if they, not the Davises, were the rightful owners of La Consula. Ernest and Mary had virtually made the Davises' estate their own, and it wasn't just the Hemingways who made themselves at home in La Consula for months at a time that year. Most of the Hemingway entourage was housed there, as was much of Antonio Ordoñez's *cuadrilla* as he made La Consula his personal rehab facility while he recovered from a serious goring in the bullring.

"Why the hell do the good and brave have to die before everyone else?" became a mantra that came out of Hemingway's mouth frequently as he personally tended to Ordoñez's wound.

For Teo and Nena Davis, the children of special, glamorous U.S. expatriates who in the words of some were more European than American, life was almost like that of the upper class out of the Victorian era: stuffy, conventional, and routine, not to mention quite lonely at times. Bill and Annie Davis were rarely around to be seen by their children as they led almost totally separate existences. Victorian children like Winston Churchill later recalled such "cold relations between their selves and their mothers that [they] would be able to count how many times in [their] life they had been hugged." Sir Osbert Sitwell, the English writer and friend of Queen Elizabeth, once argued that some "parents were aware that the child would be a nuisance and a whole bevy of servants, in addition to the complex guardianship of nursery and school rooms was necessary not so much to aid the infant as to screen him from his father or mother, except on some occasions as he could be used by them as adjuncts, toys or decorations." Children like Teo and Nena, in short, were a convenience to their parents—and had only the best of toys, clothes, and education; and it would seem absurd to suggest that they were neglected. However, according Elaine Dundy, the mother of the children's friend Tracy Tynan, they "lived on the other side of the villa in a nursery where the doorknobs were placed too high for them to open the door leading out."

As for the Davises themselves, Bill and Annie loved each other, enjoyed their own company, and had the gift of making life enchantingly pleasurable for those who were fortunate enough to be their friends. Their children? That was another matter, as Elisabeth Luard wrote in her autobiography, discovering that she and her baby were relegated to La Consula's annex when they accompanied her writer-politician husband to the Davis villa. "Next morning I woke early and found my way around to the servants' quarters for breakfast in the kitchen," she wrote in *My Life as a Wife: Love, Liquor and What to Do about Other Women*. "As I had expected the pair of us were greeted with delight. Andalusians—all Spaniards and everyone in the land of the Latins—adore babies and for the first time since I had become a mother, I began to feel welcome." Years later, while hospitalized in South Pasadena, California, Teo Davis's eyes would light up when he was shown an old photograph that included him and Nena with Ernest and Mary Hemingway. Davis, however, hardly paid any attention to the Hemingways in the photo. Instead, he immediately identified some of the servants who were also in the picture—especially a gardener, a nanny, and the cook—and he began recounting stories about his time with them.

The early days of Hemingway's visit in 1959, when he played with young Teo as housekeepers straightened up the villa from the previous late night dinner and drinking, soon gave way to a crazed bustle whenever Ernest, Bill Davis, and others departed for wherever the bullfighting schedule took them for the next *corrida*.

For Davis, his travels with Hemingway became a firsthand journey to the past, as he was able to relive *The Sun Also Rises*, a book he had reread numerous times over the years. Now, incredibly, he had the author as his own personal travel guide. In Pamplona, once he had entered its square, like many Hemingwayphiles before and after, Davis likely couldn't have avoided Jake Barnes's first impressions: "The square was hot. The flags hung on their staffs, and it was good to get out of the sun and under the shade of the arcade that runs around the square." The warmth is inevitably always there during the fiesta, and once in the plaza there is no avoiding what Davis couldn't have missed: seeing the distinctive low overhang of the architecture that still flanks the historic Spanish plaza on four sides.

Davis joined Hemingway for coffee at the Café Iruña, sitting in the comfortable wicker chairs undoubtedly similar to those described by Hemingway in the novel because it hadn't seemed to change over the years, down to the polished mirrors on the walls, Arabesque pillars rising to ornate ceiling, and the scuffed black-and-white tiled floor. At their rounded table, Ernest and Bill were surrounded by aging matriarchs, relaxing with their own *café con leches*, waiting for a nod to strike a note. The hotel where Jake Barnes stayed in *The Sun Also Rises*, the Hotel

Montoya on the southeast corner of the Plaza del Castillo, had actually been the Hotel Quintana, which disappeared in the post–Civil War 1940s and had been converted into apartments. Later, Ernest and Bill had slipped into the nearby Bar Txoko, where Davis looked on and admired his famous guest drinking himself into a personal oblivion, as if it might have been the mid-1920s again.

This momentous trip to Spain had begun in April, but it had been almost a year in the planning. A. E. Hotchner remembered Ernest talking about it in March 1958 while on a motor trip from Hemingway's home in Ketchum, Idaho, to Key West. They drove through Las Vegas, through the American Southwest, across Texas to Corpus Christi, where Hotchner first heard about Hemingway's friend Bill Davis who lived in Spain and had invited him to visit. Ernest said he hadn't seen him in twenty years.

"Would be a beauty summer," Hotchner recalled Hemingway telling him in *Papa Hemingway: A Personal Memoir.* "Would do Pamplona, which I visited briefly in '53 but haven't done properly since *Sun Also Rises,* and all *ferias* where Antonio and Luis Miguel will fight *mano a mano.* Might be the most important summer in the history of Spain."

So the Pamplona of 1925 still lingered.

The Hemingway who returned to Pamplona on this trip was only a shadow of the writer who had fallen in love with Spain as a young man. The years of hard living and hard drinking had taken a toll on his body and his spirit. However, the memory had enough fumes in it to give Hemingway a whiff of why he had come. As he had once written to Edward O'Brien, an editor who dedicated an annual anthology of stories to him: "Do you remember me talking one night at the pub up on Montallegro about the necessity for finding some people that by their actual physical conduct gave you a real feeling of admiration. . . . I have got a hold of it in bull fighting. Jeesus [*sic*] Christ yes."

In 1959, at Pamplona and elsewhere in Spain, Hemingway himself was sometimes as much of a popular figure at the *corridas* as the matadors, especially to aficionados who, like Davis, were there because of the romantic lure from *The Sun Also Rises.* The young Irish journalist Valerie Danby-Smith, who was traveling with the Hemingway *cuadrilla,* recalled in an interview with author James Plath that often young people would look to Ernest for insight into that day's *corrida*. "So if Antonio [Ordoñez] were fighting there'd be speculation as to what he might do with that particular bull," she said. "There would be various serious discussions, but all the time there would be the interruptions, because young Americans, old Americans, and sometimes Spaniards, Europeans, and all sorts of people would come up and interrupt, constantly. Then we would have lunch before going off to the bullfight. In some ways, it was fairly sedentary. Ernest would go—because bullfighting is essentially a man's sport, and women really don't hang around the bullring or the pen where they keep the bulls—especially if Antonio were fighting, he would want to go and actually look at the bulls. Often he would go off and talk to the other matadors. He would go and busy himself with that sort of thing."

Danby-Smith, who would later marry into Hemingway's family, also happened to be in the unique position, as a journalist within the *cuadrilla*, to observe the privileged members of Hemingway's entourage, which had taken over La Consula for the most part, and how they fit into his personal and literary life. She told Plath in their interview:

Then, of course, there was the infamous [A. E.] Hotchner, who was invited as a friend. I think Ernest really enjoyed his company and did feel he was a friend. I mean, my only quarrel with Hotch was his writing a book when it was totally understood that friends did not write books. I mean, it was more than understood. You were told that if you want to be a part of this cuadrilla, *then there were no books. So Hotch was there as a friend, and he was pretty much like the court jester. Ernest would bounce things off him. Ernest would say something and Hotch would counter it, and we'd all laugh. He had his position there. Then Dr. George Saviers and his wife, Pat, came from Idaho, and again it was something that Ernest wanted to show them. It was part of his teaching. I don't think they'd ever been to Europe before—certainly not to Spain—and they hadn't seen bullfights and he loved to teach them. A lot of people who came to Pamplona and who were there most of the summer were personal friends who had been invited to the birthday party. But obviously, only people who had a certain amount of money and leisure time were able to do that.*

Hotchner had met Hemingway in 1948 when he edited one of his novels, *Across the Rivers and Into the Trees*, and later had adapted numerous Hemingway stories for television and film. The two would remain close friends until Ernest's death in 1961. Like Bill Davis, Hotchner became a favorite foil of Hemingway, with whom he also had shared several life adventures, among them fishing for marlin and hunting birds in Idaho. When Hotchner arrived in Spain that year, he had joined the *cuadrilla* for the *mano a mano* in Valencia and then gone to Málaga for the *mano a mano* there, which ended with a drunken celebration, by which time he had become a favorite of Ordoñez, who had nicknamed him *"Pecas"*— Spanish for the freckled one. That night, Ordoñez told Hotchner that he had to join him in the bullring at the next *corrida*, and Hemingway went so far as to tell him he would act as his manager. "I'll put you in one of my suits," Ordoñez said to Hotchner, who soon forgot about the drunken dinner proclamations. However, days later, when Hotchner went to wish Ordoñez luck at his next *mano a mano*, he found an unexpected surprise—his own bullfighter suit of lights awaiting him.

"Antonio came over to me and said, 'I thought you'd like the color of this,'" Hotchner would recall in telling the story for public broadcasting's *The Moth Radio Hour*. "It was ivory and black with a touch of red. He said, 'I think it goes with your complexion.' I said, 'My complexion right now is white and getting whiter!' Now I'll tell you, a bullfighter's costume is no laughing matter. The undergarment is put on you, and it's like new skin. Then they give you your outer garments. They weigh approximately like an anvil being put on your back. So I was dressed up in my suit. There was no way to really move around in any direction. I was mummified. You have to be suited like this because if you go in a ring, and there's a breeze, a little wind, and you're wearing anything that moves, the bull is going to go for you instead of the cloth that you're waiving [*sic*] out here. So therefore I'm now am [*sic*] put together, and I thought this was one of those biblious jokes: They get me dressed up. They go to the ring, and they leave me here in the room. Ha! Ha! I'm not going to be in a bull ring."

But as the time for the *corrida* to begin approached, Hotchner said, everyone left the hotel room except for Ordoñez and himself. Ordoñez then begins his ritual of praying to some religious objects on a makeshift altar.

"I'm over in my corner wishing I had something to pray over," said Hotchner. "The door opens. It's for real. I'm now down in the van, and we're on our way to the bullfight. And I'm sitting next to my manager, Mister Señor Ernest Hemingway, and he said to me, 'You know, this is my first time as a matador manager, and I'm rather nervous.' He said, 'I'm rather nervous. How about you?' And at that moment, the van is going by the bullring, and outside near the entrance to the bullring is a poster bigger than this room and at the top it says, '*Mano a Mano*' and it's Dominguín v. Ordoñez and underneath: '*Espada Siguiente*: El Pecas.' Now I want to tell you what an *Espada Siguiente* is. It's a matador who only goes into the ring if the other two matadors have been blasted off the face of the sand, either by a goring or whatever. Obviously a joke."

It is no joke to Hotchner, though, who soon is in the bullring's opening ceremony with Dominguín versus Ordoñez, all three holding their capes in similar fashion. Ordoñez then cautions Hotchner to take the ceremony seriously, especially when they parade over to salute the dignitaries. He tells him that once someone else posing as an *Espada Siguiente* had been exposed as a fraud and had spent a week in jail.

"I thought: Now's the time to run," Hotchner said.

Earlier, while in the van, Hemingway had given his friend three pieces of advice for how he should behave in the bullring: "Number One: Look tragic. . . . Number Two: When you get to the ring, people are watching you. Don't lean on anything—it's ugly for the suit. And number three: If the photographers come toward you, put your right foot forward; it's sexier."

Now, with Hotchner in the *callejon*, the corridor just off the bullring, Hemingway leans over with more advice.

"There's something I forgot to tell you," he tells Hotchner. "There's a fourth thing. You have to show yourself to this crowd."

This Hotchner did inadvertently while Ordoñez was fighting his second bull. As part of the showmanship, Ordoñez had stopped the bull in its tracks—he had "fixed" the bull in a spot, in *corrida* parlance—and walked over to Pecas. However, the bull charged the two of them, with Hotchner frozen in horror, only to have Ordoñez wave the animal away from Hotch with his cape. Soon, Ordoñez killed his third bull in such spectacular fashion that, with the crowd waving white handkerchiefs, he was awarded the bull's two ears and a hoof, demanding that the matador parade around the ring. Ordoñez obliged and insisted that Hotchner join him in the celebration as aficionados rained the ring with hats, flowers, wineskins, shoes, and anything they could throw.

"Pecas, pick up the ladies' shoes," Ordoñez whispered to Hotchner as he waved to the crowd. "My men will pick up the rest."

Soon Hotchner's arms are full of women's shoes as a group of men lifted Ordoñez on their shoulders to parade him out of the bullring, with a band playing, toward the street and back to his hotel.

"And left alone in the center of the ring," recalled Hotchner, "is the *Espada Siguiente* with his arms full of shoes."

Back at the hotel, Ordoñez asked Hotchner to toss the shoes on his bed and to join him and Hemingway for wine and tapas.

"I went over, had a glass of wine, Ernest was enjoying himself and there was a knock on the door," said Hotchner, continuing his story. "He said 'Pecas, could you get that?' I open the door, and there is the most gorgeous señorita you've ever seen. She's in stocking feet. She's holding one shoe. She says, 'I've come for my shoe.' So I ushered her to the bed. I helped her put the shoe on her dainty foot. And Antonio and Ernest come over and invite her for wine, and we all have a glass of wine, and there's a knock on the door. And another knock on the door. And another knock on the door. And in they came. They reclaimed their shoes. They joined the party. It was wonderful! They stayed until the wee hours. And the next day the photographer of *Life* magazine who had been with us and taking pictures of the day before . . . came with his prints of [us] and there was a big 8x10 of El Pecas with the two great matadors of the world on his right and left. And Ernest comes over."

"Ah, that's wonderful, Hotch, you found your true profession," said Hemingway, examining the photograph.

"Just a minute," Hotchner shot back. "It may be wonderful to you. But look at the front of their pants. Those significant bumps. And look at the insignificant thing that I have."

"How many handkerchiefs did you use?" Hemingway asked.

"Handkerchiefs?" asked Hotchner. "You're my manager. You didn't tell me to use handkerchiefs."

"You've been to a lot of bullfights with me," said Ernest. "Didn't you see that a lot of these matadors have nice humps in the front of their pants?"

"The subject," said Hotchner, "never interested me until now!"

"Look, I can make it up," Hemingway assured his friend. "Antonio has his next fight in Ronda. He wants you to be his *Espada Siguiente* again, and this time we'll make a level playing field out of it."

"Fine," said Hotchner, who maintained that Hemingway then paid him one of the biggest compliments of his life.

"I'll tell you what we're going to do," said Ernest. "While [Dominguín and Ordoñez] are dressing, they'll be using two handkerchiefs, but, Pecas, you only need one."

Ernest and Mary Hemingway on the grounds of La Consula with young Teo Davis (seated on the wall, left), his sister Nena (embraced by Mary) and the household staff. (PHOTO FROM THE TEO DAVIS COLLECTION)

Ernest and Mary Hemingway enjoy a late afternoon lunch with host Bill Davis (far left) and guests on the balcony of the Davis family La Consula villa in Spain. (PHOTO FROM THE TEO DAVIS COLLECTION)

Ernest Hemingway at his standing work desk outside his bedroom at La Consula villa. (PHOTO FROM THE TEO DAVIS COLLECTION)

Ernest Hemingway greets actress and close friend Lauren Bacall before a *corrida* during the 1959 *mano a manos* between matadors Luis Miguel Dominguín and Antonio Ordoñez. (PHOTO FROM THE TEO DAVIS COLLECTION)

Ernest Hemingway strolls dripping wet just moments after slipping out of the pool following his daily swim at Bill and Annie Davis's villa outside Málaga, Spain. (PHOTO FROM THE TEO DAVIS COLLECTION)

Ernest Hemingway is about to hop into the salmon-pink Ford, with Bill Davis behind the wheel, that Davis rented to drive his famous guest around Spain early in his visit. (PHOTO FROM THE TEO DAVIS COLLECTION)

Ernest Hemingway reads a telegram in the privacy of his sparsely furnished bedroom—which was the way he wanted it—during his long stay at the La Consula estate in 1959. (PHOTO FROM THE TEO DAVIS COLLECTION)

Ernest Hemingway with friend and host Bill Davis (on the author's left) as they watch a bullfight during the summer of 1959. (PHOTO FROM THE TEO DAVIS COLLECTION)

Ernest Hemingway was always on the lookout for pretty young girls to add to the entourage who traveled around with him following the *mano a mano* bullfights in Spain in 1959.
(PHOTO FROM THE TEO DAVIS COLLECTION)

Ernest Hemingway hangs out with friends around the swimming pool at La Consula. They included hosts Bill Davis (seated far left) and Annie Davis (to Mary's right). (PHOTO FROM THE TEO DAVIS COLLECTION)

Ernest Hemingway has a pre-*corrida* talk with Antonio Ordoñez, the matador he championed in his series for *Life* magazine, which ultimately became his posthumously published book, *The Dangerous Summer.* (PHOTO FROM THE TEO DAVIS COLLECTION)

With host Bill Davis's back to the camera, as he appears to take photos himself, Ernest Hemingway whiles away the minutes before a *corrida* with Spain's two great matadors of that time, Luis Miguel Domínguín and Antonio Ordoñez, with Hemingway biographer and confidant A. E. Hotchner between the bullfighters. (PHOTO FROM THE TEO DAVIS COLLECTION)

12

The Well Runs Dry

Happiness in intelligent people is the rarest thing I know.

—ERNEST HEMINGWAY

THE BEST THING ABOUT HAVING ERNEST HEMINGWAY LIVING AT YOUR home for months, as he did at La Consula in 1959, may not even be the stories the hosts would later tell—but the yarns that the celebrated writer himself spun each evening as the wine pumped through his veins or until it got the most of him in the wee night hours. Those tales captivated everyone within earshot and, according to one anonymous account, "were frequently so grand and full of wild incidents that those who listened were often left questioning whether one man could really have experienced so much in a single lifetime." Perhaps a better question at that time in Hemingway's career was whether his writing on the grandiose assignment for which he was then in Spain equaled the talented wit of the oral stories that delighted his faithful entourage with each telling.

The sad, tragic answer is that apparently it didn't—not even close.

In the past and throughout his career, Hemingway had always been able to call upon his talent or his muses whenever he felt himself blocked or unable to write as he knew he could. "Do not worry. You have always written before and you will write now"—the line Hemingway had famously advised himself as a young man standing and looking over the roofs of Paris in *A Moveable Feast*. "For luck," he had added, superstitiously, "you carried a horse chestnut and a rabbit's foot in your right pocket." More fabled still was this: "All you have to do is write one true sentence. Write

the truest sentence that you know." Or: "If I started to write elaborately
. . . I found that I could cut that scrollwork or ornament out and throw it
away and start with the first true simple declarative sentence I had written." Hemingway, it seems, had legions of mantras, mottos, and self-help
tips that he often called upon, though perhaps the one he needed most as
his summer in Spain wore on was not a lucky charm as much as a nugget
of wisdom, a warning almost of what could happen to the writer if he had
used up all his marvelous skills: "I had learned already never to empty
the well of my writing, but always to stop when there was still something
there in the deep part of the well, and let it refill at night from the springs
that fed it."

Now, there in Spain at what was supposed to be his last hurrah,
Hemingway was experiencing what happens to a creative mind when
that well, which had once seemed inexhaustible, finally sputters, having
run dry, with nothing more left from which he could refill it at night. The
magazine article for *Life* on the bullfighting *mano a mano* had spun as out
of control as Hemingway's own life in Spain that summer. What was to
have been an article of perhaps ten thousand words had become longer
than *The Old Man and the Sea* and was still growing but hardly a work of
literature, though Ernest thought it to be. So he talked about it as if it
were, each night bringing the most recent *corrida* back to life with minute
details of what Antonio Ordoñez and Luis Miguel Dominguín had done,
their kills, their awards of ears and hooves, the triumphant celebrations,
and, of course, Hemingway's role as friend and adviser to Ordoñez, as well
as the hilarious escapade of Hotchner as the *Espada Siguiente*, the Sancho
Panza in the exploits of the *mano a mano* matadors.

Away from La Consula, Hemingway often continued this same oral
storytelling, sometimes even meandering into an anecdote told best in
Spanish, even in his imperfect use of it, and continuing in his adopted
language. "[I] am considered a Spanish author who happened to be born
in America," Hemingway had written in a 1956 letter to American poet
and playwright Harvey Breit. Two years earlier, Ernest had said—in what
was more braggadocio than truth—that Spanish was "the only language I
really know. If I had been born in Spain like your defunct friend [philoso-
pher and writer George] Santayana I would have written in Spanish and

been a fine writer." According to the Spanish journalist-novelist José Luis Castillo-Puche, Spanish was a tool and Hemingway "liked to use it very much. He felt proud talking in Spanish to waiters, hotel maids, people in the bullring, and everyone."

Ernest had become proficient in Spanish while living in Cuba, where the household staff at Finca Vigía were all Spanish-speaking, and a seamstress in the nearby pueblo would come to the villa to give Mary Spanish lessons.

"Papa spoke primarily in Spanish to the *Finca* staff," said Rene Villarreal, who with his son Raul wrote the memoir *Hemingway's Cuban Son*. "Once we had Jamaican maids, the Richards sisters, and they spoke English, but for the most part even Miss Mary learned Spanish. At first when she arrived in 1945, she tried to speak a lot to my little sister, who was very eager to teach at the young age of nine. Then Papa eventually hired a Spanish teacher, who taught *castellano* Spanish, which Hemingway thought would be wiser because that way one would be understood in any Spanish speaking country."

All these oral stories, however, may have been partly at fault for the trouble Hemingway was now having writing well, as he may have been exhausting the life out of his valuable anecdotes, exchanging the admiring, fawning praise from his guests and *cuadrilla* each evening for the guarding care the writer must do with his material. Ernest himself had often warned other writers of how dangerous it was for a writer to talk about a work in progress. He had spoken of this in his 1954 interview with George Plimpton for the *Paris Review*. Plimpton had asked Hemingway why he feared talking about his work, when writers like Mark Twain, Oscar Wilde, James Thurber, and Lincoln Steffens used to polish their material by testing it on listeners.

"I cannot believe Twain ever 'tested out' *Huckleberry Finn* on listeners," Hemingway told Plimpton. "If he did they probably had him cut out good things and put in the bad parts. Wilde was said by people who knew him to have been a better talker than a writer. Steffens talked better than he wrote. Both his writing and his talking were sometimes hard to believe, and I heard many stories change as he grew older. If Thurber can talk as well as he writes he must be one of the greatest and least boring talkers. The man I know who talks best about his own trade and has the pleasantest and most wicked tongue is Juan Belmonte, the matador."

Five years after that interview, a struggling, sometimes disoriented Ernest Hemingway found himself less like a literary giant and more like his character Harry, the dying writer in *The Snows of Kilimanjaro*, lamenting his wasted talent, skills diminished by drink, women, wealth, and laziness. His time in Spain was highlighting Ernest's increasing problem with writing the clear, effective prose that made him famous, along with his physical deterioration, which had become obvious during that summer. For the first time in his life unable to organize his writing, Hemingway's magazine article grew out of control and into a book-length manuscript while in his last weeks at La Consula—and it would grow even longer, to almost 130,000 words, once he left Spain.

All the while that summer, following the bullfighters at a hectic pace from arena to arena around Spain and becoming absorbed in the high drama, Hemingway drew closer and closer to Antonio Ordóñez in what his friend Buck Lanham described as "Ernest's unhealthy nostalgia for his young manhood." Hemingway insisted to those around him that Ordóñez was unable to perform in the bullring without him nearby.

"Antonio needs me," Ernest said in those moments, according to the *Life* magazine story, apparently believing this and with no one to treat it more seriously than it being a famous old man's vanity. "Antonio wants me with him all the time . . . as we are a winning combination."

Photographs from that summer show Hemingway looking like a man twenty years older than the sixty he had just celebrated. His physical health and emotional condition were plainly deteriorating, as described in detail by Michael Reynolds in *Hemingway: The Final Years*. Ernest was increasingly despondent and experiencing mood swings, worsened by his heavy drinking of up to a quart of liquor a day. James Michener, in his introduction to *The Dangerous Summer*, summed it up this way: "In 1959 Hemingway went back to Spain and during that long, lovely summer . . . he was already beginning to suffer the ravages which would in the end destroy him—monomania about being spied upon, suspicion of his most trusted friends, doubt about his capacity to survive."

The collapse of Hemingway's physical and emotion health—and with it his ability to write—was evidenced in the months after his return to Cuba and then to Idaho in late 1959 and 1960. Ernest became a prisoner of a giant mound of handwritten and typed manuscript pages, notes written on *corrida* flyers and scraps of paper, and Spanish newspapers and magazines that exhausted him just thinking about it. Editors at *Life* in New York had only hints of Hemingway's deterioration, but the presentation of a run-on, out-of-control manuscript caused enough vexation and panic that the magazine hired Hotchner to edit the first draft down to seventy thousand words. It would be another quarter century before the manuscript could be reedited into shape to be published in book form as *The Dangerous Summer.* James A. Michener, himself a bullfighting aficionado who wrote the introduction for the book, could not be constrained from being forthright about the manuscript's inherent problems.

"No magazine could have published the entire version," Michener wrote. "No book publisher would have wanted to do so either because it was redundant, wandering in parts, and burdened with bullfighting minutiae. . . . I doubt if there will ever be reason to publish the whole, and I am sure that even a reader who idolizes the author loses little in the present version of the book."

What Hemingway had produced, in essence, in that summer of 1959 on a quixotic quest to recapture the Spain of his youth and document the historic bullfighting *mano a mano*, fell far short of being what he was most famously known for—it had failed to be classic Hemingway. Sadly, the ultimate paradox may have been that those closest to him, from his hosts to everyone bidding to be near him in his *cuadrilla*, had all been unable to recognize that Hemingway, in his obsession with dying and courage, had become irrevocably entangled in that summer's dance of death. Perhaps it took someone who knew Hemingway but was not selfishly involved in the adventure, someone such as Rene Villarreal, a longtime member of the Hemingway household at Finca Vigía in Cuba, to see the devastation of the man he saw as an adoptive father.

"The only time I noticed a different routine [in Hemingway] was when A. E. Hotchner arrived at the *finca* to assist with *A Dangerous Summer*," Villarreal said in a 2012 interview. "That was the first time ever I saw

Papa need someone's assistance with his work in that capacity. During that time Papa was edgy, agitated and very nervous. He was not himself at all."

But that was still in the long months ahead. In Spain in 1959, the series of *mano a manos* had blurred into an ongoing adventure of trips to and from the *corridas*. It also seemed that if anyone could make sense of it to form a clean, almost novelistic narrative, it would have been Hemingway. He had all around him in his *cuadrilla* the people who would figure into the book in addition to the matadors—from the Davises and wife Mary to Hotchner and the friends who had come for his birthday party and had stayed on, as some did. It was perfect for Hemingway, who, according to biographer Jeffrey Meyers in an essay for the journal *VQR*, "always tended to exaggerate and embroider the events of his life. He wrote about his personal experience and could not invent without it."

Because of his tendency to obscure the distinction between his fiction and his life, he was temperamentally primed for corruption by publicity and wealth. The boy who boasted in infancy that he was "'fraid a nothing," that he had once caught a runaway horse, began to establish his public persona while on the editorial board of his high school newspaper. He was not a great athlete or scholar but constantly reported his own minor exploits in the Oak Park Trapeze. *He inflated his genuine heroism in war through newspaper interviews and public speeches while he was still in his teens. As a foreign correspondent, he learned how to create a romantic image and generate publicity. He had a literary reputation among expatriate writers before he had published a word of fiction.*

Not everyone, though, saw Hemingway and his entourage's summer in Spain in the favorable light in which they would be seen in America. Eventually, Spaniards would take great exception, especially later, after the publication of Ernest's *Life* serialization. Foremost among them was José Luis Castillo-Puche, who believed that by time of this 1959 trip to Spain and a second brief visit in 1960, "Ernesto was no longer a fascinating figure to people in Spain—he had become a sort of joke, in fact."

He especially took issue with the roles of A. E. Hotchner and Bill Davis around Hemingway. "Two ridiculous figures hung around Ernesto every minute," he wrote of them in *Hemingway in Spain*, the English translation of *Hemingway: Entre la Vida y la Muerte*. "Davis the jealous watchdog of his fame and fortune and Hotchner the exploiter of his reputation." His unkind characterization of Hotchner as "a hypocrite, a sickening toady, an obsequious bore, a clever exploiter," led to Hotch winning $125,000 in damages, though his libel case was subsequently thrown out by a federal appeals court.

Other Spanish writers questioned whether even Hemingway's perceptions of Spain as a young man might not have been, as author and Fulbright scholar Jeffrey Herlihy-Mera put it, "limited to repeated 'honeymoons' allowing him to imagine the place as a perpetual paradise." They also question Hemingway's understanding of Spaniards beyond those with whom he socialized or wrote about—all from one social demographic: male, upper-middle-class individuals who often represented the conservative part of Spanish society. In an essay for Academia.edu, Herlihy-Mera wrote:

> At times, Spaniards were also critical of Hemingway's mannerisms during bullfighting rituals. In 1959 Hemingway followed Antonio Ordoñez and Luis Dominguín on the bullfighting circuit; his chronicle of that tour would become The Dangerous Summer. At a bullfight in Nîmes, France, where Ordoñez was performing, Hemingway stood at attention as the band played the Marseillaise, his right hand at his cap in military salute. After a few moments, seeing no one else was saluting, Hemingway put the hand in his pocket. Picasso, watching this scene, remarked "Quel con" ("What an idiot"). While it is unclear whether Picasso made this remark to Hemingway's face, the author was sensitive to the opinions Spaniards had of him throughout his life.
>
> Moreover, while Death in the Afternoon had enjoyed a largely positive critical reception in Spain, The Dangerous Summer was almost universally derided. Even Ángel Capellán, a scholar often uncompromisingly enthusiastic about Hemingway, called some of the text "foolish" and went on, "It is hard to understand how a man of

Hemingway's experience and knowledge of Hispanic character could publicly condemn" bullfighters he had never seen perform.

Or had Hemingway touched a raw nerve in the sensitive Spanish psyche, one that couldn't accept or didn't know how to understand his observations and pronouncements? For in America, hadn't perhaps the most poignant perceptions come from a Frenchman, Alexis de Tocqueville, and an aristocrat at that from an old Norman family with ancestors who had participated in the Battle of Hastings in 1066? His observations from the nineteenth century, when he spent about as much time in the United States as Hemingway ever did in Spain, remain part of the bedrock about the philosophy and thought of America and democracy even today. America's egalitarian penchant for civil rights, especially, for it was de Tocqueville who correctly observed that "Americans are so enamored of equality that they would rather be equal in slavery than unequal in freedom."

Yet it had been Hemingway who had done so much to fix Spain in the contemporary imagination. In *Death in the Afternoon*, his sentimental description of Madrid had a priceless finality and wonderment of seeing someplace you love for the last time: "If it had nothing else than the Prado it would be worth spending a month in every spring, if you have the money to spend a month in any European capital. But when you can have the Prado and the bullfight season at the same time with El Escorial not two hours to the north and Toledo to the south, a fine road to Avila and a fine road to Segovia, which is no distance from La Granja, it makes you feel badly, all questions of immortality aside, to know that you will die and never see it again."

A Spanish friend once asked Hemingway if he had ever come to Madrid without visiting the Prado.

"Never," Ernest replied, "except during the Civil War, because in those days you didn't go to the museum to see Goya—you went out on the streets."

Why had Hemingway fallen so head over heels for Spain, notwithstanding the slaughter of the country's civil war or murderous reign of Francisco Franco, that he would now in 1959 see it as a place for his much-anticipated literary valedictory? It was more elementary perhaps than just the fact that Spain had made his early career, and he had fallen back on it time after time. His four-decade love affair with Spain put its mark with major works from each decade of his career: *The Sun Also Rises*, *Death in the Afternoon*, *For Whom the Bell Tolls*, *The Dangerous Summer*, and *The Garden of Eden*. Hemingway's only full-length play, *The Fifth Column*, and his civil war documentary, *The Spanish Earth*, were also inspired and set in Spain—as was some of his greatest short fiction, including "Hills Like White Elephants" and "A Clean, Well-Lighted Place."

Over and over, Hemingway famously calling Spain "the country that I loved more than any other except my own" is found in the thousands of essays written on the topic of Hemingway and Spain, a country he said was the place where he should have been born, as well as the place of his spiritual rebirth. However, could the answer for Hemingway's attachment to Spain have been something more fundamental and basic in his psyche? Could it, in fact, have been that Spain and bullfighting had been the landing place of his rebellion, if not from his motherland, then from his overly civilized, demanding mother, whom he resented, while clinging to the untamed wilderness of an America he had known with his father? He had left America at an impressionable age with a deep dissatisfaction with the suburbanization of the West and what he saw as its effete, insincere 1920s high society.

That summer, after a stop in Madrid for that leg of the Domínguín-Ordóñez *mano a mano*, Hemingway and his pals A. E. Hotchner and Bill Davis had traveled on some twenty-eight miles northwest to the Royal Site of San Lorenzo de El Escorial, commonly known as El Escorial, a historical residence of the king of Spain. But with its grand basilica, it is also a monument to Spain's role as a center of the Christian world. Hemingway had loved visiting El Escorial because it was also an enormous storehouse of art, with the library containing thousands of priceless manuscripts. He knew it, too, as having been the burial site for most of the Spanish kings of the last five centuries, Bourbons as well as Habsburgs. The royal pantheon there contains the tombs of the Holy Roman Emperor, Charles V (who ruled Spain as King Charles I), Philip II, Philip III, Philip IV,

Charles II, Louis I, Charles III, Charles IV, Ferdinand VII, Isabella II, Alfonso XII, and Alfonso XIII.

Late that afternoon, Hemingway stood for one last time on the heights of El Escorial, looking out over the golden panorama of wheat fields and autumn trees, a view that had always captivated him.

Hemingway took one last look at the spectacular views and the sun about to set, then, turning to Hotchner and Davis, said, "I always feel good here, like I've gone to heaven under the best auspices."

13

Needing a Death in the Bullring

To quote an old Cheyenne Indian chief: Long time ago good, now heap shit.

—ERNEST HEMINGWAY

DEATH IN THE AFTERNOON HAD BEEN A CLEVER TITLE FOR ERNEST Hemingway's book-length essay on bullfighting, and dying was certainly on the writer's mind in 1959, though he was never clear on whether he feared a tragedy in the *mano a mano* he was covering that summer or if he was brooding about the possibility of his own demise. Hemingway had missed Manolete, Spain's greatest bullfighter, not just failed to catch him at his prime but hadn't been there for Manolete's fatal goring. His death had plunged Spain into national mourning and made a saint of Manolete in the minds of many Spaniards. A great death in the bullring for a bullfighter of Manolete's stature demanded a great writer's rendering of the moment and the event, like Homer at the heroic *mano a mano* between Achilles and Hector. What would that have been worth? What was the price tag on a real death in the afternoon and its chronicling the way only Hemingway, the Homer of the *corrida*, would inevitably write it?

Was $30,000 enough for human tragedy in the bullring that summer? Or could Hemingway drive the price higher? The thirty grand was what *Sports Illustrated* was offering Hemingway for a personal essay on the *mano a mano* for an article of up to four thousand words. . . but only if either Antonio Ordoñez or Luis Miguel Dominguín were killed or

127

permanently disabled, according to a cable Hemingway had received from the magazine. Ernest could almost bank on it. "By August, he fully expected [that] to happen," author Michael Reynolds wrote in *Hemingway: The 1930s through the Final Years*. "With Luis Miguel and Antonio taking more and more risks, there was excitement and tension every time they entered the ring. Something tragic or magnificent or both might happen that day."

For Hemingway's mind was still working well enough to believe he could parlay his experience writing about the *mano a mano* far beyond what *Life* magazine was paying him or the amount he would get for an update of *Death in the Afternoon*. Hemingway and his friend A. E. Hotchner had set up H&H Corporation, and they had grandiose plans. Hotchner had already secured a fabulous deal of almost a quarter of a million dollars for a four-story deal with CBS, with Buick agreeing to sponsor four live shows on the network.

This was early on in the schedule, after Ordóñez had been gored in the bullfight in Madrid and faced a recovery that eventually would be overseen by Hemingway at La Consula. Antonio had no idea that he was being helped to return to the bullring as soon as possible by a friend who had a financial stake in either he or his brother-in-law Luis Miguel suffering grave harm. Making no attempt to hide his belief and bias that Ordóñez was the greater matador, Hemingway was obviously betting that it was Dominguín who would take the fall.

By August, the *mano a mano* was at a fever pitch, and Hemingway had convinced almost everyone sitting with him that it was a matador duel destined to be won by Ordóñez. At the *mano a mano* in Málaga, Hemingway and Bill Davis insisted that newsman Eric Sevareid sit with them. Afterward, this was Sevareid's dispatch:

Luis Miguel Dominguín is the world's second greatest bullfighter . . . when he was lifted like a willow wand on the horns of the fifth bull for what seemed an eternity, classic Greek tragedy seemed to have reached its climax. . . . A great bullfighter like Dominguín is in command of the bull because he knows the bull. Ordóñez, the master, is in command of the bull because he is in command of himself. It is the difference between talent and genius, between what a great man can do for himself and what the gods can do for him with their touch.

Of course, if anyone knew personally the dangers involved in a *mano a mano*, which could seduce matadors into risking death and injury, that person was Luis Miguel Dominguín. For *mano a manos* were rare, as rare as there being two great matadors who are contemporaries. They happen about once a generation, and the last one had occurred when Dominguín was a young bullfighter who was every bit as charismatic and exciting as Antonio Ordoñez was in 1959. That previous *mano a mano* had taken place twelve years earlier as the young Dominguín sought to establish himself alongside the great Manolete.

Manuel Rodríguez Sánchez, who would be known as Manolete, was born in Córdoba, Spain, in 1917, seemingly destined for bullfighting greatness. He was fighting bulls in his childhood and at the age of thirteen made his public debut, then joined an itinerant bullfighting show called "Los Califas." By the time the Spanish Civil War ended, he was already on the road to becoming a national hero, with a serious, somber style in facial appearance and technique. He increasingly wowed the crowds with the uncanny courage of standing as still as a statue as bulls passed so dangerously close to his body that goring seemed inevitable. Then, instead of making his passes of the bull separately, as other matadors did, he would remain glued to one spot in the ring while linking four or five consecutive passes together into an exciting, compact series.

Outside the bullring, Manolete had endeared himself to General Francisco Franco as he carried the banner for Spain's greatness and had sworn allegiance to the post–civil war government, something that Hemingway never forgave. Then in 1946, during an unprecedented triumphant tour in Mexico, Manolete created a political uproar when he protested the presence at one of the bullrings of the flag of the now defeated Spanish Republic, which Mexico still recognized as the ruling government of Spain. Manolete proved to be such a magnetic draw in Mexico that promoters had to schedule additional *corridas* to satisfy fans' demands. Carlos Fuentes, one of Mexico's greatest literary figures, said that "people sold their cars and pawned their mattresses" to buy tickets to see Manolete in the bullring. "If Manolete was the unconscious incarnation of the philosophy of Seneca," Fuentes wrote after the matador's death, "he was also the heir . . . to the unmovable appearance of Greco's Spanish gentlemen and the foreshadowing of the mortal poetry of Federico García Lorca."

Hemingway, however, couldn't stand Manolete or his elevation to the status of "Spain's greatest matador." Nowhere does the author offer any reasonable explanation for his opposition to Manolete, leaving independent readers and students of Hemingway to wonder how much of it was ego—certainly it always entered into Hemingway's conclusions or feelings about anything or anyone. How much was that the self-proclaimed arbiter of bullfighting hadn't been the one to proclaim Manolete's brilliance nor, for that matter, had he had the privilege of being an insider to the matador the way he had been to Cayetano Ordoñez in the 1920s and now to his son, Antonio Ordoñez, in the 1950s. So instead, Hemingway now saw his role not unlike an embittered sportswriter—he was writing about the Spanish national pastime for *Life*, after all, and working out a deal with *Sports Illustrated*. It can be argued that Hemingway, in this instance, was behaving less like a Nobel laureate and more like the fictional Max Mercy, the slimy sportswriter in Bernard Malamud's baseball novel *The Natural*, who believes it's his God-given role to "protect the game." So, presumably, to that end—to protect bullfighting—Hemingway used his position to attempt to diminish Manolete. In his *Life* article and in what became *The Dangerous Summer*, he accused Manolete's managers of shaving the horns of the bulls he faced and of using cheap, crowd-pleasing tricks in the bullring. Of Domínguín, Hemingway was equally dismissive, and his bias against the other matador is obvious throughout both the article and the book, starting with the way he first introduces him: "Luis Miguel was a charmer, dark, tall, no hips, just a touch too long in the neck for a bullfighter, with a grave mocking face that went from professional disdain to easy laughter." Then there was the way he wrote about the bronze, life-size statue of Domínguín in the matador's own home. "I thought Miguel looked better than his statue," he wrote, "although his statue looked just a little bit nobler."

Dominguín felt much the same way about Hemingway. In a 1972 biography, he told author Keith Botsford that Hemingway was "a commonplace bore . . . a crude and vulgar man" who "knew nothing about fighting bulls," and he dismissed Ordoñez as a "cowardly fighter" with "feet of clay all the way up to his brain."

In his heyday, Dominguín's fame had opened up extraordinary adventures: the love affair with Ava Gardner while she was married to Frank Sinatra, the showdown with Ol' Blue Eyes when he tracked down his faithless wife to Spain, the string of discarded women, and his marriage to an Italian actress, Lucia Bose, with whom he had three children. Dominguín was close to Pablo Picasso, who was living in France because Franco considered him an enemy of the state. Even so, Picasso became the godfather of Dominguín's youngest child, Paola, and the family regularly visited the artist at his home without incident.

Dominguín's almost familial ties with Picasso also had an impact on Hemingway, whose own relationship with the artist was, as Bill Davis once said, twisting a line of Shakespeare's, "a little less than kin and even lesser than kind." Picasso and Hemingway had been close in the 1920s, having been paired by Gertrude Stein in Paris, and even traveled together to Pamplona the first time Hemingway visited. Picasso later said that on that initial trip for the running of the bulls at the *Fiesta of San Fermín*, Hemingway had "behaved as if his *afición* went deeper than anyone else's." What had especially miffed Picasso was an incident two decades later, when Hemingway called on him at his apartment at 7 Rue de Grands Augustins in Paris after the liberation from Nazi occupation. Told that Picasso wasn't home, Hemingway had asked the concierge if he could leave a note for him. When the concierge wanted to know if the author wanted to leave a gift, as many others had, Hemingway excused himself to go to his car. He returned minutes later, frightening the war-weary concierge by handing him a case of hand grenades, scrawling "to Picasso from Hemingway" across its label. "What do I want a hand grenade for?" Picasso later said he told Hemingway. "I'm a painter!"

"That's Hemingway for you," the artist told biographer John Richardson, who wrote that "as an Andalusian, Picasso found Hemingway's appropriation of Andalusian machismo offensive."

Incidentally, it was that time in Paris with Picasso, Jean-Paul Sartre, and other writers and artists at the St. Germaine cafés and at Gertrude Stein's home that Hemingway stumbled across the label—"the Lost Generation"—that would forever be associated with him and American expatriates in Europe. Hemingway attributed the name to Stein, but how it came about was possibly a better story. Stein had taken her Ford automobile to a garage in Belley in 1924, where it was serviced and repaired surprisingly quickly by a young mechanic. When she mentioned his efficiency to the proprietor of the Hotel Pernollet, where she was staying, the owner made a remarkable comment. "He said that every man [like the young mechanic] becomes civilized between the ages of eighteen and twenty-five," Stein later wrote. "If he does not go through a civilizing experience at that time in his life, he will not be a civilized man. And the men who went to war at eighteen missed the period of civilizing, and they could never be civilized. They were *une génération perdue.*"

"When Hemingway heard the story at the rue de Fleurus," author Christine Graf wrote in *The Cafés of Paris: A Guide,* "he decided to use the sentence 'You are all a lost generation' [attributing it to Gertrude Stein] as an epigraph for his first novel, *The Sun Also Rises,* a story about the 'uncivilized,' aimless lives of the very people M. Pernollet had in mind. Due to the book's tremendous success, the phrase was guaranteed enduring fame."

The story that Stein told had a profound effect on everyone who heard it but especially on Hemingway. "In those days we did not trust anyone who had not been in the war," he would write in *A Moveable Feast,* "but we did not completely trust anyone."

What neither Hemingway nor Stein may have known was that the term *lost generation* had a long history dating back to 1834, when Russian czar Nicholas I said in a speech in Warsaw that "the current generation is lost." The *New York Mirror* headlined the news story on the czar's speech "A Lost Generation."

Hemingway became the most emblematic figure of the Lost Generation, and he also popularized it. Later, F. Scott Fitzgerald was considered the leader of the movement, which within the literary crowd grew to include T. S. Eliot, Waldo Pierce, Alan Seeger, Erich Maria Remarque,

Ezra Pound, John Dos Passos, E. E. Cummings, Archibald MacLeish, Hart Crane, John Steinbeck, Sherwood Anderson, and Sylvia Beach. Picasso and Salvador Dalí led the names of painters in the group, who shared disillusionment over the large number of casualties of World War I and who were cynical and disdainful of their elders' Victorian notions of morality and manners. That scene flourished in Europe between the two world wars and became symbolic, in a sense, of the changing psyche in America.

"The late 1920s were an age of islands, real and metaphorical," observed author Malcolm Cowley in *Exile's Return: A Literary Odyssey of the 1920s.* "They were an age when Americans by thousands and tens of thousands were scheming to take the next boat for the South Seas or the West Indies, or better still for Paris, from which they could scatter to Majorca, Corsica, Capri or the isles of Greece."

Or Málaga, as Bill and Annie Davis chose to do after the next world war, when they followed brother-in-law Cyril Connolly's urging and eventually bought La Consula. There, the most obvious prize for the salon that they developed would have been the most famous painter in Europe and native of the Andalusian province.

Pablo Picasso had been born on October 25, 1881, in Málaga and lived there until he was ten years old. The story in his hometown is that he started painting and drawing before he could even speak and that his first word was *piz,* short for *lapiz,* the Spanish word for pencil. He was the son of a painter, José Ruiz y Blasco, who was probably a better teacher than artist. José was a professor in Málaga's School of Fine Arts and curator of the city's Museum of Arts. When Pablo was thirteen, the story goes, his father allowed his son to finish a painting of his and made the astonishing discovery that it was superior to what he had begun. Pablo's father vowed never to paint again. The Picassos then moved around Spain as José took on better teaching positions. Pablo would become the titan of twentieth-century art, but he would live most of his life in France, self-exiled from his homeland after 1939, when Generalissimo Franco defeated the Republican government of Spain in the three-year civil war. Picasso was a proud Communist until his death in 1973 and always had a succinct reply to those who asked him why. "When I was a boy in Spain," he said in more than one interview, "I was very poor and very aware of how poor people had to live. I learned that the Communists were for the poor people. That was enough to know. So I became for the Communists."

Perhaps fittingly, Picasso's most famous painting was *Guernica*, a mural-sized painting completed in 1937 showing the horrors of the Spanish civil war. A major focus is the bombing of Guernica, a Basque Country village in northern Spain, by German and Italian warplanes. Picasso had been deeply affected by the bombing of Madrid and the attack on Guernica itself, as well the bombardment of the Málaga-Almería road in 1937, when there were enormous civilian casualties among those who were desperately trying to get away from Málaga. Picasso mourned the losses in his homeland, even if he had not lived in Spain since 1904.

"He was a man wholly Spanish. . . . This view of himself that he was not only an artist—but a Spanish artist—continued to impact his life until his death," Lael Wertenbaker wrote in *The World of Picasso*. "He lived as close to Spain as his political views would allow. But, even in his self-imposed exile from his homeland, Picasso continually emphasized the one aspect of himself that was immutable: his Spanish heritage."

That heritage included bullfighting, something apparently seeded so deep in Picasso's cultural soul as to transcend where he lived. Even while living in France, Picasso was aware of the bullring heroics of the incomparable Manolete in the 1940s and of the young Domínguín: the cold, analytical matador whose fearless tactics, like putting his lips to the horns of a wounded bull, to Picasso smacked of artistic bravado but to many others rang of conceit, loftiness, and reckless danger. Then there were Domínguín's torrid love affairs with some of the world's most beautiful women—Ava Gardner and Rita Hayworth among them—which obviously played to the vanity of Picasso, who in his sixties was carrying on romances with women four decades younger.

Picasso came to see the young Domínguín as his incarnation in the bullring. He also didn't have to return to Spain to see the sensational young matador, who became a popular figure in Arles in southern France, where Picasso had a home. There in Arles, Domínguín appeared in a setting that only the arenas of France could offer. The bullrings throughout the South of France were not typical *corrida* sites but great stone amphitheaters, similar to the Colosseum in Rome, left behind by the Romans twenty centuries ago. For a few hours, Picasso could forget his self-imposed exile and lose himself in the drama of watching the bullfights but especially in Dominguín, eventually connecting with him artistically. Picasso could not enter the bullring with Dominguín, but his artistic vision could. Nothing is more personal to a matador than his traditional *traje de luz*, his flamboyant "suit of lights" made up of rhinestones, beads, sequins, and reflective threads of gold or silver. The custom dated back to the eighteenth century, when no less than the famous painter Francisco de Goya created the suit of lights for many of the great bullfighters of that time. During their friendship, Picasso would create dozens of suits of lights for Dominguín, including a new outfit he wore on the fateful date of his *mano a mano* with Manolete.

It was barely a month after Manolete had celebrated killing his one thousandth bull in a *corrida* at San Sebastian, looking much older than someone who had recently marked his thirtieth birthday. "They are asking for more than I can give," Manolete told an interviewer minutes after the *corrida*, talking about the demands of his fans in a somber voice. "Always more and more. All I can say is I wish the bullfighting season was over."

Manolete had been thinking about retiring and was about to call it a career in 1946 but held out for one more bullfighting season. His longtime girlfriend, Spanish actress Antonia Lupe Sino, said Manolete's rabid fans had a cult-like obsessive hold on him that made her afraid. "They'll never let him go," she said, "until they see him dead."

Antonia's worst fear was well founded. Trying to please his fans, Manolete was fighting too often and possibly drinking too much. He had turned thirty on July 4 of that year, with promoters still offering money he didn't need, but it was no longer about the money. It was about the fame and his place in history—and about those young matadors like the twenty-one-year-old Dominguín who wanted to replace him on his bullfighting throne. The claims Hemingway later maintained that Manolete had been fighting bulls with shaved horns that made them less deadly did have some foundation, although the writer seems to have overstated the allegations. Promoters, wanting no harm to come to their big box-office draw, had reportedly shaved the horns of bulls for his *corridas*, though there was no proof Manolete or his manager knew about the practice. In fact, there were reports in Spanish newspapers of Manolete berating promoters when he suspected that the horns of some of his bulls may have been ground down.

That fateful afternoon, August 28, 1947, in Linares, Spain, there was no question about the bulls for the *corrida*, nor of the condition of their horns. The bulls were of the Miura breed, considered the fiercest and most unpredictable fighting bulls in the world, and Manolete was aware of how deadly they were. Miura bulls had killed Manolete's great-uncle and many other famed Spanish matadors. There was a third matador involved in that day's *corrida*, so Dominguín and Manolete shared only four of the six bulls on that day's card. As it turned out, Manolete was on the defensive almost immediately. He was unimpressive in handling his first bull, while Dominguín began with a spectacular kill. As Manolete prepared for his second bull—a Muira named Islero who was said to have bad eyesight and a quirk of chopping with his right horn—he could hear boos among the applause in the arena.

Manolete then gave his last great performance in the bullring. He was brilliant, even in the kill, going dangerously over Islero and driving his sword in classic fashion between the bull's shoulders to the hilt. Islero, though, had chopped upward, driving a horn into Manolete's upper thigh, into his femoral artery, and throwing him aside. As Manolete clutched the wound with his hands, Dominguín and other bullfighters rushed to his side, carrying him to safety as Islero staggered and fell dying at the edge of the ring.

"Is the bull dead?" an ashen-faced Manolete asked in the infirmary as he lit up a cigarette and waited for the first of a series of transfusions of dry plasma.

14

The Ghost of Manolete

That is what we are supposed to do when we are at our best—make it all up—but make it up so truly that later it will happen that way.
—ERNEST HEMINGWAY, LETTER TO F. SCOTT FITZGERALD

IN THE DAYS AND WEEKS AFTER ERNEST HEMINGWAY'S SIXTIETH BIRTH-day party, Spain faced the most important moment of its national pastime in almost a dozen years. It had been that long since Manolete, its greatest matador, whose following was almost that of a Spanish saint, had been fatally gored in a bullring in Linares, near the ancient village of Castulo, where the Carthaginian general Hannibal had married the local Iberian princess Himilce on the eve of the Second Punic War. Even as he lay dying in the bullring infirmary, the mournful-faced, hawk-nosed Mano-lete was awarded two ears for his brilliant kill of the Miura bull Islero, who with a sword deep inside him had at the last moment swung his head upward and dug a horn into the matador's right thigh. Doctors were unable to stop the bleeding even after he was transferred to a hospital that night. By dawn the next day, Manolete was dead, and a shocked nation had begun dressing for mourning.

"He died killing and he killed dying!" a Madrid newspaper headlined its story on Manolete's death.

It was no coincidence that a pivotal figure involved in the tragedy of Manolete's death on August 28, 1947, was also now in 1959 a major player in the drama unfolding in Spain's bullrings. In 1947, a young mata-dor named Luis Miguel Gonzales Lucas Dominguín, two months and some days shy of his twenty-first birthday, was the widely proclaimed future of bullfighting, as ambitious as he was brave and talented—and he wanted Manolete's crown. The great Manolete, born Manuel Laureano Rodríguez Sánchez, was from Cordoba, Spain—the heart of bullfighting country—and matadors ran in the family. His mother was the widow of a matador before she married the man who would be his father, who was also a matador. In post–civil war Spain, Manolete became arguably the most famous sporting figure in the world, perhaps even more heroic and admired in more countries than the greatest baseball player of his age, Joe DiMaggio, or heavyweight boxing champ Joe Louis, who held that title throughout most of the 1940s. Manolete became a professional bullfighter as a teenager and rose to such prominence that he assumed the place of the legendary Juan Belmonte, considered by many to have been the greatest matador of all time. During World War II, already acclaimed in Spain, Manolete's astounding successes in the bullrings of Mexico, Peru, Venezuela, and Colombia made him the most celebrated bullfighter in the world.

"*Amigo*, you call it a sport as many do," Manolete once said to actor Johnny Weissmuller, talking about bullfighting. "It is not a sport. It is a ritual. It is an art. It is a tragedy. But it is not a sport."

For almost a decade, Manolete served as Spain's leading cultural hero, becoming a millionaire and being adored by a nation buying dolls bearing his image, singing songs in his honor, even sipping a liqueur called Anís Manolete. A cottage industry grew up around him made up of agents, promoters, bull breeders, and advertisers, all having a vested interest in not wanting him gored or injured. It didn't take long for critics, including Hemingway, to claim that promoters were shaving the horns of the bulls Manolete fought in order to protect the matador.

Dominguín would become the toast of the bullfighting world, as well as an international celebrity, known as much for his hobnobbing with the rich and famous as for his bullfighting. In 1959, having retired from the bullring, the tables were turned on him when he was called out of his comfort by his brother-in-law Antonio Ordoñez, who had laid claim to being the greatest matador of his time but who wanted to meet Dominguín in order to prove it, much as Dominguín had met Manolete.

Spain also wanted to know, especially after the previous season, which man had been the best of their career and the *mano a mano* had split the country and bullfighting aficionados between *Ordoñistas* and *Dominguístas*. This is what had brought Hemingway back to Spain, and that summer he had become an integral part of their *mano a mano*, which had captured the imagination of the sports world outside Spain. Along with Hemingway, Bill Davis, and their own *cuadrilla*, writers from throughout Europe and abroad had been following the duel and introducing new readers to a new lingo of bullfighting terms and the rewards given matadors. *Life* magazine alone had dispatched two writers and as many photographers to document the summer's most anticipated event. *Sports Illustrated* reported as if it were a heavyweight prize fight: "At Zaragoza, Luis Miguel cut three ears, Ordoñez one. In Barcelona the result was the same, and again at Puerto de Santa María."

Coming at the time that it did, Hemingway's birthday party amounted to an intermission or seventh-inning stretch, allowing both Dominguín and Ordoñez to rest and heal. To be accurate, the *mano a mano* was but a part of Spain's bullfighting long season, which seemed as exhausting as, if not more so than, the major league baseball campaign of 154 games for each of the sixteen teams at the time. In 1959, the Spanish bullfight season began at the end of February and ended in the middle of October, totaling some 360 *corridas de toros*. According to Spanish news media reports, 2,000 bulls were killed, and 1,130 ears, along with hundreds of tails and hooves, were awarded to 63 matadors. For all the publicity and commotion over the Dominguín and Ordoñez *mano a mano*, their actual head-to-head actually lasted about two months, from June 27 to August 21. It was all of ten bullfights—little more than the seven games of a full baseball World Series—that involved forty-nine bulls from which the two matadors were awarded forty-seven ears, eleven tails, and four hooves.

"A *mano a mano* like that comes up maybe once every lifetime, and this was something we see rarely, like Tunney-Dempsey, if you're a fight fan, El Babe and his 60 home runs, or DiMaggio's hitting streak in '41," Roberto Herrera Sotolongo, personal secretary and good friend of Hemingway, said in an interview in Cuba in 1967. Herrera, who crewed for Ernest on his boat *Pilar* for eighteen years, was later appointed by Mary to act as conservator of the Hemingway estate and museum in Cuba. "It was as exciting as Ernesto thought it would be, and I don't think it would have been the same without him."

To read Hemingway's account of the *mano a mano*, one would think that Dominguín had been over his head and, at times, was an embarrassment to the legacy he had built over a long, illustrious career. Hemingway, though, was as subtle as a biased, small-town sportswriter reporting in one-sided fashion for the local high school team. He was unreserved in his criticism of Dominguín and seemed to see only the best in Ordóñez, his friend and partner—and his unapologetic alter ego. Hemingway would later write in his third *Life* magazine installment:

> *Too many things were piling up and he [Dominguín] was running out of luck. It was one thing to live to be the number one in the world in his profession and have that be his one true belief in his life. It was another thing to be almost killed each time he went out to prove it and to know that only his wealthiest and most powerful friends, a number of beautiful women, and Pablo Picasso who had not seen a bullfight in Spain in twenty-five years still believed it.*

Perhaps Hemingway was too close to the young Ordóñez to realize that in those words alone he had made a fabulous case for what he had always valued most—the incredible courage being displayed by Dominguín, confronting death in the bullring and in a more direct and braver fashion than the way Hemingway himself was now confronting his own mortality. Was Hemingway projecting his own death wish onto Dominguín? Was this behind his almost pathological dislike of a man who had shown him no animosity to speak of? Wasn't it almost the same as his unreasonable dismissal of Ordóñez's father, Cayetano, who had inspired the handsome, heroic Pedro Romero character of *The Sun Also Rises* only to be cast off for being cowardly in no one's eyes but Hemingway's? Could it also help explain how over his life Ernest had repeatedly rejected his wives as they grew older, always for a younger woman, it seemed, and sometimes for a woman, like Adriana Ivancich or Valerie Danby-Smith, young enough to be his granddaughter?

It was a self-delusion that was part of the Hemingway personal and literary persona, according to biographer Jeffrey Meyers. "Hemingway not only helped to create myths about himself but also seemed to believe them," Meyers wrote in a 1984 issue of the literary journal *VQR*. "In the last decades of his life, the Papa legend undermined the literary reputation and exposed the underlying fissure between the two Hemingways: the private artist and the public spectacle. When his writing slacked off and he attempted to live up to and feed on the legend, his exploits seemed increasingly empty."

Understandably, the events of 1959 showed how much Hemingway had lost his sense of judgment, perspective, and fairness. His coverage of the *mano a mano* had turned into a protective, biographical profile of Antonio Ordoñez, whose exploits and relationship with Ernest soon dominated what became an excessively self-absorbed diary of that summer, growing eventually to book length, far beyond what *Life* magazine intended to publish or would publish. His central, real-life characters became, at points in the account, Ordoñez and A. E. Hotchner, who had been an aspiring writer when he met Hemingway in 1948. Hemingway and Hotchner would become close, especially during that time in Spain. At Hemingway's urging, it would be Hotchner who taught Ordoñez the intricacies of baseball during those weeks of the matador's recuperation at La Consula. In turn, Ordoñez groomed Hotchner in the ways of a matador, even outfitting him in one of his suits of lights and insisting he parade with him and Dominguín into and around Madrid's Ciudad Real bullring, pretending to be one of the entourage of bullfighters. "It was a little irregular but Antonio had invited him," Hemingway wrote of Hotchner's role parading as if a matador. "In keeping with his dignity as a *sobresaliente* he neither threw back hats nor kept cigars. Few that looked at him could doubt that he, 'El Pecas' [Hotchner's nickname], would have been capable of taking over the *corrida* if it had been necessary."

Even Hotchner would later say that Hemingway had been using his relationship with Ordoñez and his time in the summer of 1959 to project himself back in time, at least in his own mind. In his biography, *Papa Hemingway: A Personal Memoir*, Hotchner wrote, "I felt that Ernest was, in effect, transporting himself back to that happy time when he roamed

Spain with the true-life counterparts of Lady Brett, Bill, Mike, and Robert Cohn, attending the bullfights, drinking the rough Spanish wine from goatskin *botas* and dancing the *riau-riau* on the streets of Pamplona."

In his defense, it was Hemingway's presence that had turned the centerpiece of Spain's bullfighting season into an international spectacle. In a postwar era in which the world had little to watch beyond the early Russian-U.S. space race, symbolic of the East-West Cold War, Ernest Hemingway's open presence and seemingly last hurrah in Spain offered a rare cultural phenomenon. In New York, Time Life had agreed to not only pay Ernest his king's ransom for his reportage on the *mano a mano* in the pages of *Life* magazine but had also approved paying thousands to Mary Hemingway for her *Sports Illustrated* story on Ordóñez's rehabilitation at La Consula from a goring in early summer. Then, trying to capitalize even more on the story, *Sports Illustrated* assigned writer John Blashill to spend weeks chronicling the *mano a mano* and Hemingway, with Hemingway taking Blashill under his wing and insisting he stand or sit next to him at each *corrida*. Could it be that pack journalism never had it so good?

In his book *Literary Journalism in the Twentieth Century*, University of Massachusetts professor Norman H. Sims argues that serious, unbiased bullfighting experts have universally agreed that "Dominguín was not as outclassed as Hemingway maintains nor destroyed as a major torero as a result of the head to head contests. Dominguín himself stoutly resisted Hemingway's characterization, claiming that the writer had deliberately heightened his rivalry with Ordóñez into deadly competition." As Professor Sims goes on to maintain:

> *[Hemingway's] journalism was always a form of anti-journalism, emphasizing his own reacting presence and mingling observation with invention, always making more than describing. He sought to shape what he observed and experienced into an account of universal value, something that would hold up as the truth of art long after the truth of events had faded from memory.*

Those close to Hemingway would never have challenged him on his version of events. In an interview with author James Plath in 1999, Valerie Danby-Smith Hemingway conceded that, though Ernest had an "amazing memory . . . I don't know if he was accurate, because I can't remember those things pass by pass. If he made it up, it was exceptional, and nobody said, 'That isn't the way it was.'" What would make Hemingway's memory all the more amazing, assuming his recollection was accurate, is that with all his late-night reveling and early-morning risings, he was usually working on only three or four hours of sleep. He was also dealing with a new kidney disorder for which he was fortunate to have an old friend, Dr. George Saviers of the Sun Valley Hospital in Idaho, as part of his *cuadrilla*, able to check on Ernest's condition regularly.

As for reporting, Hemingway perhaps was also pioneering ahead of Truman Capote, Gay Talese, Tom Wolfe, and others of the New Journalism that sprang up in the 1960s—what Capote would call "the non-fiction novel"—using the technique novelists had long used of dialogue instead of interviews, descriptions of setting, and so-called interior monologue of what characters were thinking but doing it while writing nonfiction. In the *mano a mano* involving life and death, heroism and courage, Hemingway could not have picked more dramatic material than what was whirling around his own life.

Nine days after Hemingway's birthday party, the *mano a mano* reached its first critical point in Valencia, which had been the capital of Republican Spain during the civil war, as some twelve thousand spectators packed into the Plaza de Toros de Valencia with greater anticipation than ever. Not far from where Hemingway was standing, one aficionado jabbed his fist in the air, yelling what was on everyone's mind: "*¡Ya ha llegado la hora de la verdad!*"—"The moment of truth has finally arrived!"

Until then, Ordoñez's breathtaking skill and artistry displaying dangerous, classical passes had slowly given him a slight advantage over the older Domínguín, who was still impressive though lacking some of his opponent's showmanship. It put the pressure on Domínguín, who seemed up to the challenge through the first four bulls of the afternoon, though his second bull gave him trouble when he went in for the kill. Domínguín's sword hit bone three times before he finally succeeded.

"Too many bones today," Hemingway said to Dominguín as he approached the *barrera*, the edge of the ring where the author had been sitting.

"I'm surprised I have any left in my sword hand," Dominguín said back playfully.

If the *corrida* was close to even, Dominguín's third bull, the fifth of the match, changed all that. He was a big, strong black bull who knocked both the *picador* and his horse on their side just as the wind picked up in the ring. Dominguín tried to wear down the bull's strength with several passes and even watered down his *muleta* as he prepared for the kill. But then, just as suddenly, Dominguín was on the ground, gored as screams erupted in the crowd and other bullfighters rushed in to distract the bull long enough for others to lift the matador and carry him quickly out of the ring to the infirmary.

Ordoñez quickly stepped in to dispatch the bull, but the ghost of Manolete had risen its tragic head as it was apparent that Dominguín had been gravely wounded.

15

The Ordoñez-Dominguín Feud

There's no one thing that is true. They're all true.

—ERNEST HEMINGWAY

LAUREN BACALL HAD WONDERED WHETHER IT HAD BEEN A MISTAKE TO agree to meet a young writer at her Manhattan apartment for an interview arranged by her old Hollywood friend, famed celebrity columnist James Bacon. He had become an institution himself in Tinseltown, a close friend, and a chronicler over the years of entertainment's biggest names and couples during Hollywood's Golden Age: Frank Sinatra, Marilyn Monroe, and John Wayne; Spencer Tracy and Katharine Hepburn; Humphrey Bogart and Lauren Bacall. Jim and I had later become desk mates at the *Los Angeles Herald Examiner*, where he often had been generous in opening doors to friends and sources, such as Lauren Bacall. He had asked her to see a friend who now worked for a sports magazine, so she was mystified as to what interest someone who wrote about football, baseball, and tennis might have in an actress whose best films he likely had never seen. She was in her early sixties, and her last starring role had been in the 1981 forgettable horror film *The Fan*.

She was pleasantly surprised, however, to find that the writer had not been that young and knew her best films, plus thanked her graciously for agreeing to meet with him by bringing her a dozen of her favorite roses, as their mutual friend Jim Bacon had suggested. He helped her arrange the flowers in a vase, and the actress insisted they have tea in the library, which led to a Juliet balcony that looked out over the treetops of Central

Park. There she showed me the view and touched my shoulder to point to two young lovers in the park.

"You should be there with your lovely wife enjoying the day than cooped up here," she said. I had told her I was a newlywed, and she had asked to see a photograph of my wife, who was back in Los Angeles.

"She is gorgeous," she said, and just then, as her eyes sparkled looking at the photo, I was star struck, realizing that I was standing there talking to the Lauren Bacall who had melted the hearts of men of all generations in roles like Marie Browning in *To Have and Have Not* and that line: "You know how to whistle, don't you, Steve? You just put your lips together and . . . blow . . ."

"I am just curious," she said, bringing me back to earth, "as to why you wanted to meet. I haven't ever done anything I can imagine would be of interest to *Sports Illustrated*."

"Hemingway," I said.

It was a magical word. I was new to the magazine, and I was hoping to resurrect stories about the author—his hunting, his fishing, his time in Florida, and, of course, the bulls. Jim Bacon had told me some of the stories he had heard over the years from Bacall, but I wanted to hear them firsthand from her. I would soon learn that she was witty and funny, personable and helpful, but she wasn't much of a storyteller. She was an actress, and perhaps if I had wanted stories about Humphrey Bogart, she could have told me plenty, though I don't think I was the person she would have wanted to confide in about the love of her life. However, she helped me with stories of her visit to the Hemingway homes in Cuba and Key West, as well as to his birthday party in Spain—though once she said she sometimes wondered if she had been at the party or promised to be there "and then I couldn't bear telling Ernest I skipped it . . . because as much as I wanted to go, I wondered if I should . . . too much champagne, does that ever happen to you?"

What could you say to that? It was Lauren Bacall, and she could do as she pleased is what you say.

I would come away from an afternoon with her with a dramatic change of heart about the great *mano a mano*, which I had read about years earlier in the *Life* magazine serialization, which had been published posthumously as *The Dangerous Summer* several months earlier. The two matadors, Antonio Ordoñez and Luis Miguel Dominguín, had been brothers-in-law. It was difficult to believe they were bitter enemies simply because each wanted to be recognized as the world's greatest bullfighter when, in fact, they each had been recognized as such in their own time, about a decade apart. So what had been the real story; how could Hemingway turn a rivalry into a family feud without ever explaining the reason for the breakup? I hadn't really expected Lauren Bacall to have an answer. Was I ever wrong.

"I told Ernest—he just didn't want to believe it, or maybe he believed it but didn't want to write about it—but that *mano a mano* was never about Luis Miguel and [Antonio] and who was the greatest matador," she said that afternoon, after changing our tea for brandy. "Seriously? Seriously? That was foregone. Luis Miguel knew it. He told me that because I was with him that summer. He played it down, but Luis Miguel had had his day. He just wouldn't have told anyone about it. His brother-in-law, Ordoñez, was the new king of the bullring, and he was all right with it, I believe. Luis Miguel had retired. He had a good life. He lived well. He didn't need all the money and gold they had offered him to come out of retirement. For damn sure, he already had half the gold in Spain, or close to it. So money couldn't bring him back into the bullring, but pride, it's always about pride, with you Hispanics, isn't it? Pride, machismo. Pride could. Family pride. His own pride. His manhood. That's all it took. What finally lured Luis Miguel back into the bullring was someone gossiping. Most likely someone close to Antonio starting the story that Antonio and I had been lovers, and then counting on that gossip pushing the right buttons with Luis Miguel who had a nasty, awful temper. So someone put that little thought in his ear: That Antonio was being unfaithful to his wife [Carmen], who was Luis Miguel's little sister. Luis Miguel would have been livid, and he was. That's all it took for this Spanish novella to explode. Luis Miguel wanted to show that brother-in-law of his a thing or two. He still thought he had the *cojones* to get in the bullring. Luis Miguel was fearless. He thought himself immortal in the bullring, and he was. He once said to me, 'I saw Manolete die in the bullring from a bull. That's not me. I'm not meant to die from a bull. Picasso told me so.' *Picasso told him so!* I wanted to laugh. As if Picasso was God! And maybe to Luis Miguel he was. Oh, I still remember the day he told me that, and I'm thinking, 'If I laugh, I know I die here and now.' So I held it in. For Luis Miguel, Antonio cheating on his sister and cheating was bad enough, but then to be cheating with me, that drove him over the line, because I think in his own Spaniard mind, with Luis Miguel, once you were his, you were always his. What can I say, he was an incredible man who knew the secrets of killing bulls and taking the hearts of women, and who knows which he was the best at."

I sat in her library flabbergasted and in need of another brandy, which she was kind enough to pour. Her sultry looks might have aged, but she had told it all in that distinctive, throaty voice, and then sat there, cross-legged on her sofa, looking incredibly satisfied that she had left me looking visibly stunned.

"So you're saying," I finally managed to ask, "the *mano a mano* was about you?"

"Well," she said, looking up at me from under her brows, "it sure as hell wasn't about the bulls."

It was one of the most memorable interviews of my *Sports Illustrated* career, and it sure as hell wasn't about sports either. Bacall insisted that there had never been anything sexual between Hemingway and her, and that the gossip about Ordoñez and her had not been true. But she would offer no similar denial about Dominguín. She also explained something I didn't know: that some of the early *corridas* in the summer of 1959 that had featured Dominguín and Ordoñez had not technically been *mano a manos* because they involved a third matador, no matter how Hemingway described them as such in the *Life* articles and in *The Dangerous Summer*.

"Luis Miguel said those weren't *mano a manos*, and that showed how much Ernest knew about bullfighting," Bacall said. "He said the *corrida* with Manolete, the *corrida* where he was killed, hadn't been a *mano a mano*, that a *mano a mano* was two matadors in the ring, not three."

By Bacall's definition, the first *mano a mano* in 1959 hadn't come until Thursday, July 30, in Valencia, where Dominguín was gored badly while handling his third bull of the *corrida* when a gust of wind tore his red cape to one side and he caught a bull's horn in the stomach. Then while Dominguín was healing, Ordoñez had been gored. Meanwhile, Bacall recalled, she had stayed discreetly in the background, especially since Dominguín's sister Carmen had ensconced herself in Spain. She traveled with Ordoñez from *corrida* to *corrida* and even to La Consula while he recuperated from one goring and then stayed for Hemingway's sixtieth birthday party. Bacall met with Hemingway several times away from La Consula and the bullfights for lunch and drinks, and she said she tried to impress upon the writer two important points she thought he should know. The first was that to observers listening to his regular retelling of the bullfights, his apparent dislike of Dominguín had become obvious and appeared to cloud his fairness of how he talked about the *mano a manos*. Second, Bacall wanted to impress upon Hemingway that someone—possibly a member of one of the matadors' *cuadrillas* or one of the promoters—had circulated the vicious gossip about Ordoñez having had an affair with her as a ploy to anger the overly protective, jealous Dominguín out of retirement and into the bullring.

"There were only two parties who wanted [the *mano a manos*], and Luis Miguel wasn't one of them," Bacall said. "Antonio, who was younger and on top of the [bullfighting] world, wanted to show off and show up Luis Miguel—and the promoters, they wanted the biggest paydays they would ever have in Spain. Ernest didn't want to believe this. I hate to say he had a vested interest that got the best of him, but who knows? I might have done the same thing if I had been in his shoes. It was a fabulous story and a fabulous adventure, and Ernest lived for both."

Of course, there was also more to the Dominguín-Ordoñez feud beyond just women. Their family connection had once extended to business, and Dominguín's father had managed Ordoñez until the young bullfighter fired him, alleging "dishonesty."

"My father found him and made him into a torero, but I gave him his career," Dominguín told biographer Carlos Abella. "I took him from nowhere to as near the top as he could get with his talents. . . . He knew that I couldn't give up while he was still trying to take my place as Número Uno. He knew that I was too proud to allow shit to follow on the real thing. All through the years before Hemingway got into the act, it had been one long story of provoking me, cheating me, lying, trying to get ahead, climbing on people's backs."

The personal animosity between the two matadors, involving family and women, created an intense rivalry between Dominguín and Ordóñez, but Bacall said in our interview that she feared for a time in the summer of 1959 if Hemingway himself hadn't intentionally provoked the two bullfighters into a duel to the death.

"I wondered if Ernest hadn't just added more fuel to the fire," she said, "challenging Antonio and Luis Miguel, too, with his crazy 'death in the afternoon' bull that played right into the machismo mentality of two matadors who I don't think ever intended to take it to that level. But Ernest shined and shamed them on. By then, Antonio was like a little kid hanging on every word that came out of Ernest's mouth, and Luis Miguel still had enough respect left for him and for what the Hemingway name meant in Spain. Luis Miguel thought Ernest had been magnanimous and courageous taking an interest in Spain during the Civil War. It was only what he knew second hand because Luis Miguel had been a youth and in his early teens during the Civil War. But he was familiar with Ernest's books about bullfighting [*The Sun Also Rises* and *Death in the Afternoon*], and he thought what Ernest really knew about bullfighting was superficial and that he had tried covering that up by dropping in every bullfighting term that existed. 'That damn Ernesto,' he used to say. 'He's a clown and a fake' because Luis Miguel believed Ernest made more of his knowledge of bullfighting than what he really knew, to make himself the American expert on bullfighting. Luis Miguel said Ernest was just a tourist who loved *corridas* and knew more about bullfighting than most Americans, who knew very little."

Those words were mild compared to what Dominguín said in his biography, calling Hemingway "a drunkard, liar and bore . . . vulgar, childish and slightly mad." Dominguín also claimed that Hemingway had threatened to destroy him. "I'm going to ruin you for life, Miguel," he quoted Ernest as saying. "I'll have you kept out of the ring."

It was a sad disintegration of their onetime friendship. Luis Miguel had spent time with Hemingway in Cuba, where in 1953 he had met Miroslava Sternova, and they became ill-fated lovers the next year when they were together in the United States. In 1955, the Czechoslovakian-born Mexican film actress who appeared in thirty-two films took her own life by overdosing on sleeping pills. Her death shocked Mexico, the film community, and fans around the world, as well as others who knew her, which included Bill Davis. While living in Mexico, he had befriended her through Frida Kahlo and Diego Rivera, who had become close to Miroslava, an avid painter.

"Dominguín had a hypnotic impact on women that was beyond belief—something about the eyes and the way they focused on you," actor and Hollywood insider Skip E. Lowe said in a 1990 interview. Lowe said he heard that summation of the matador from both his onetime lover Ava Gardner and Cecil Beaton, the Oscar-winning costumer and photographer. In 1952, Beaton shot a famous photograph of Dominguín in one of the suits of lights designed by Picasso and later told Lowe that he had been "the most charismatic figure I met in a lifetime of charismatic figures." Until his death almost three decades later, Lowe said, Beaton still spoke of the bullfighter as if he were one of the famous films stars in Hollywood. "Cecil believed he could have been a leading man in films. You couldn't take your eyes off him, and he said he could see how women might feel he could undress them with a look. He was that seductive in person. . . . And Ava. Ava didn't mince words. She once said that spending a night with [Dominguín] felt like she'd spent the night with the entire 5th Cavalry."

A far more discreet Lauren Bacall would not go into her own romantic relationship with Dominguín. In 1959, the actress was seeking an escape from the life she had known in Hollywood during her twelve-year marriage to Humphrey Bogart. But after Bogart's death in 1957, Bacall's personal life in Los Angles would never be the same again, especially after a relationship with Frank Sinatra had gone sour. Her friend Susan L. Schulman said Bacall felt "spurned" by Hollywood after Bogart's death. "Nobody wanted her without Bogey," said Schulman. So she left Hollywood for New York and, while waiting for her starring Broadway play *Goodbye, Charlie* to begin in December, took off for Europe.

"Chemistry," was almost all Bacall would say about what had attracted her to Dominguín. "We had great chemistry."

She was more effusive about Hemingway and how there had been no chemistry between them, no matter how much people said otherwise. Lauren also scoffed at accounts that in 1959 Mary Hemingway had interrupted a conversation between her and Ernest to show Lauren a bullet she kept for anybody who made a move on her husband.

"Oh, please, Mary had the patience of a saint when it came to Ernest," said Bacall. "I saw her put up with more in just a few days visiting in Cuba that would have driven any other woman away. She loved Ernest to a fault. If she were going to pack a bullet for any woman who made a move on Hemingway, she would have been wearing bandoleers across her chest."

16

The Cost of the Softhearted Man

Fear of death increases in exact proportion to increase in wealth.
—Ernest Hemingway

Money was never far from Ernest Hemingway's mind all that summer, especially since learning from his lawyer that his tax liability had increased more than $40,000 because of his accountant's error. Although he was far from broke, Ernest could only see the negatives of his finances, which just heightened his increasing paranoia. He knew he would have paychecks coming from *Life* magazine, from the ventures of his business partnership with A. E. Hotchner, and from his past and future book royalties. At various times, Hemingway was also getting unexpected news of additional sums of income that balanced out his short temper and orneriness. Typical of this was the day that, while waiting for a *corrida*, Ernest received a telegram from New York restaurateur Toots Shor. "Ernie, where shall I send the four thousand bucks, you bum!" the telegram read.

Days earlier in Málaga, Hemingway had left La Consula and had Bill Davis drive him to a bar so that he could place a call to Shor to ask what the odds were on the upcoming heavyweight boxing championship fight between title-holder Floyd Patterson and Swedish challenger Ingemar Johansson. "When he said the boys were laying four to one on Patterson, I told him to put down a G on the Swede, but he tried every which way he could to talk me out of it," Hemingway told Hotchner, according to his memoir. "I don't bet much on fights any more. Have a new rule: Never bet on any animal that talks back—except yourself."

Johansson had entered the fight that summer a five-to-one favorite but stunned the boxing world with a savage knockout of the popular champion, knocking him down six times in the third round. Patterson felt so humiliated that he left the arena in a disguise to avoid the crowd waiting for him. In Spain, Hemingway was $4,000 richer and fattened his earnings with a second telegram in which Hollywood producer David O. Selznick wrote with good news that surprised Ernest even more. Selznick's actress wife, Jennifer Jones, had just starred in his remake of *A Farewell to Arms*, which Ernest had not been enthusiastic about because he wasn't getting paid anything for it. He had sold the rights to the book when it was published back in 1929 without any provision for payment upon a remake. Selznick, though, was so happy with the remake and the boost to his wife's career that he had decided that he was going to pay Hemingway $50,000 from the 1957 film's profits, should there be any. Ernest was thrilled, but he would never see the money. According to David Thomson's biography *Showman: The Life of David O. Selznick*, the film made a little money, although not enough for Selznick to recover his costs and pay Hemingway.

In 1959, however, illusion mattered as much to Ernest as reality. In fact, it may have even been more favorable. Like all men who worry about money, he felt better if he was secure in the thought that he had a lot of money coming in, especially since he spent it so freely. Hemingway had had a taxable income in 1958 of $153,800, and he lamented that it placed him in the eighty-first percentile tax bracket with a tax bill for the year of $95,000. How could that be, he bitterly complained. Looking back, one can sympathize that someone with three mortgages and his expenses didn't have an accountant who could have found additional legitimate deductions. Was it a blessing or a curse that Ernest could be trustful of those around him? Hotchner and others in the Hemingway *cuadrilla* had been amused and surprised when they were joined by a young American named Mervyn Harrison who had no real business in the crowd except that he appeared to be a leech and had found a willing target in Hemingway. Harrison had tracked down Hemingway in Idaho the previous winter, supposedly to interview him for his English thesis. It sounded like a fishy story, especially when he squeezed Ernest for thousands of dollars so that he could go to Paris and learn French at the Sorbonne. Ernest, however, was not one to have anyone question his own expenditures, whether it was Mary or one of his friends.

Ernest also needed new income because he apparently had been so impressed with Bill and Annie Davis's estate that he had decided to buy his own villa in Spain, according to a letter to his son Patrick dated August 5, 1959. "The place where we stay is really lovely," he wrote Patrick. "Bill Davis is an old friend that you met at Sun Valley and we hunted rabbit together one time. Have been to your place along the coast going back and forth to Antonio's ranch which is north of Tarifa and this side of Cadiz within sight of Chiclana. That is a country that I never knew and you would love very much. We are buying some land on the coast in that area called Conil. It is like everything was in the old days before they spoiled everything."

Hemingway's letter to his son is also notable for being more forthright about Antonio Ordoñez's shortcomings and vulnerability than he ever let on in the *Life* magazine article or in the manuscript of his eventual book. "Antonio is wonderful, brave, consistent and unbelievable with both cape and *muleta*," he wrote. "His killing is rapid but still defectuous except *recibiendo*." It was an admission that Ordoñez's killing skills were one-dimensional and needed improvement. "But he does kill them decently and get them out of the way." Hemingway also told Patrick that he was having to "sweat him out all the time," alluding to Ordoñez's brushes with death and gorings. "He is spooked sometimes in the night the way we all are," Ernest wrote, "and prefers to sleep in the daytime which is smart but he loves his work truly and he loves his bulls."

It may have been Hemingway's fear that to be as candid in his writing about Ordoñez would somehow diminish the image he had helped create for the matador. In Ernest's mind, it may have seemed important to portray Antonio Ordoñez as the greatest bullfighter and the *mano a mano* as the greatest moment for Spain's greatest passion. It would have been as much, as Ernest sought to leave the impression that everywhere he happened to be was the pinnacle of that moment in history, which perhaps it was—but Ernest's flaw may have been to seemingly insist that it was all because of his presence. Literary scholar Matthew Bruccoli later wrote about "how difficult it is to establish the truth about virtually everything involving Hemingway" and how "difficult [it is] to differentiate the public Papa from the private writer."

And in the Spain of 1959, with the decade of his greatest triumph behind him—a Pulitzer Prize for *The Old Man and the Sea* and the Nobel Prize for his body of work—it was as if Hemingway had been given a blank literary canvas for something akin to the valedictory address that he was unable to deliver in Stockholm. Perhaps Hemingway sensed the challenge in the way others failed to understand. He had salvaged from his home in Cuba the manuscripts of several books that he hoped to finish, among them *A Moveable Feast*, along with countless short stories—all work that would never be published in his lifetime. However, he knew in his heart that he would see the *Life* article in print. In fact, he would see a serialization of three articles in *Life* that would be the basis for *The Dangerous Summer*. He might have also foreseen a big celebration on the publication of one of the other books he hoped to finish, but whether he thought he would be present for that fiesta is debatable. As James Michener said about Hemingway's undertaking of following the *mano a mano* in 1959: "This is a book about death written by a lusty sixty-year-old man who had reason to fear that his own death was imminent."

Hemingway's death almost happened that August, just weeks after his sixtieth birthday party as the series of *mano a manos* was about to take a break. In Bilbao, Dominguín was gored in the abdomen by one of his bulls' horns and almost killed. The next day, Hemingway, Hotchner, and Bill Davis climbed into a new Lancia that Ernest had just bought for $6,200 cash—it was the first new car Hemingway would ever own in his life. Davis drove them to Saint-Jean-de-Luz and nearby Dax, France, to see Ordóñez fight again. Without Dominguín on the *corrida* card, an uninspired Ordóñez gave a forgettable performance. Hotchner then hopped on a train to Paris, while Davis, Hemingway, and Valerie Danby-Smith were to drive on to Madrid after first stopping for a relaxing dinner before beginning the six-hour, five-hundred-kilometer drive.

However, sometime near midnight Davis fell asleep at the wheel, crashing the Lancia into several cement road markers and veering across a ditch and field near the town of Arando de Duero, north of Madrid. It was a miracle no one in the Lancia was hurt, much less killed. Later, other reports in newspapers blamed the accident on a blown tire.

"Absolutely can't blame Bill," Hemingway said to Hotchner when they spoke by phone the next day. "He's done all the driving all summer, and damn fine, and I shouldn't have pushed him on this. I should have known it was too late to start out.

"He feels awful about wrecking the Lancia."

Hemingway, of course, was used to flirtations with death, especially in the 1950s, when he had had medical problems and, of course, the plane crashes in Africa in 1954 that debilitated him so much that he had been unable to personally accept the Nobel Prize for Literature. "There is no lonelier man," he had written in a discarded draft of his acceptance speech, "than the writer when he is writing except the suicide. Nor is there any happier, nor more exhausted man when he has written well. If he has written well everything that is him has gone into the writing and he faces another morning when he must do it again. There is always another morning and another morning." There in Spain that summer, however, he was hardly a lonely man. In fact, this brush with death against the backdrop of Spain may have made him feel even closer to what he was witnessing: He, like Ordóñez and Dominguín, had stared down death and won the day. The close call also offered him the opportunity to show that death was not the ultimate fear: For the Hemingway hero, after all, knew how to confront death.

Hemingway took tremendous pride in his powers of rejuvenation, and he likely believed that he could muster up the physical, emotional, and literary strength to overcome the toll of time, just as he had walked away from this last near-death experience and had recuperated from his recent hardships. As he had said in a letter to his friend Archibald MacLeish: *"Dans la vie, il faut (d'abord) durer."*—"In life, one must (first of all) endure."

And to endure, for certain, was part of the challenge that summer, as the only constant seemed to be the *corridas* themselves, with the bull-fight as the metaphor for Hemingway's art. It would be overshadowed by the hurried packing and long, winding road trips of which they were now wary after the accident en route to Madrid, and the conflict and drama—often with Ernest and Mary at the heart of it—and the drinking and troublemaking. If there seemed to be parallels with the feuds and fights among friends in *The Sun Also Rises*, then perhaps this was the nostalgia that Hemingway also sought to capture.

However, in 1959, Hemingway had at his side someone the mythical Jake Barnes might have wished he had in *The Sun Also Rises*: Bill Davis. As that summer wore on, what became more evident with each week and every *corrida* was the close bond between Ernest and Bill. It was a friendship that biographers for the most part would see as a one-sided relationship, as it all seemed to be built around Hemingway, with the Davises serving his needs and complying with all of his whims. For Bill and Annie Davis, though, entertaining Ernest Hemingway for the better part of a year was not only a wish fulfilled but a validation of their standing among the narcissistic crowd of American expatriates in Europe.

Hemingway also understood the sacrifices and expenses incurred by his hosts, especially considering the lofty price tag that would have been rung up at hotels and restaurants for months of lodging not only for Ernest and Mary but also for Ernest's entourage of friends and admirers who lived extravagantly at La Consula as if it were their private residence.

And then the day came when Bill Davis presented his bill.

It happened when Davis's ex-wife showed up at La Consula without warning. Bea Diaz Davis had been trying to locate Bill for years. She maintained that when their marriage ended, Davis ran off with several Jackson Pollock paintings from their San Francisco home and that they were half hers under California's joint property ownership law. It is uncertain if Bea understood just how valuable the paintings were in 1959. She certainly should have. The Jackson Pollock paintings in La Consula were from the artist's drip period between 1947 and 1950, a style that rocketed to fame after *Life* magazine published a four-page spread in 1949 with a big headline asking, "Is he the greatest living painter in the United States?" While driving drunk in 1956, Pollock crashed his Oldsmobile convertible, killing a passenger as well as himself in a car accident that assured his immortality in world art circles. There is no indication that Bea had any legal papers with her when she appeared in Málaga and surprised Bill, who had a villa full of Hemingway's *cuadrilla*.

When Bea departed Spain a couple of weeks later, she apparently left on cordial terms with Bill Davis. There were no scenes of discord between former spouses and no angry recriminations that anyone was witness to. Bea had in her possession some incomparable memories, mementos, and souvenirs of her visit. However, they didn't include any of the Jackson Pollocks, nor any of the other valuable artwork that still remained on the white walls of La Consula. At Bill's villa, Bea Diaz Davis did meet Ernest Hemingway, who apparently showed he could be moved by all things Hispanic. Years later, when her estate was being sold at a Tennessee auction house, one of Bea's relatives claimed in interviews that while in Spain, the late Colombian socialite had carried on a torrid love affair with Ernest. The interviews were conducted on condition that the interviewer would not reveal Bea's identity, so the story seemed questionable to start with, not to mention the doubts about the aging author's own virility at the time. Her estate did include photographs of Bea at Ernest's side, along with Antonio Ordoñez, showing that she had spent time with them, and there were other items from her trip that might have been of interest to collectors. However, there was no sign of the Jackson Pollocks, whose whereabouts in future years would become a mystery.

For that time, though, they remained untroubled at La Consula.

What didn't go undisturbed, however, was the tranquility among Bill and Annie Davis's guests and friends. Kenneth Tynan, the illustrious critic, and his family had been frequent visitors to La Consula, as they were again that August. The Tynans were tight friends of the Davises, far closer and more intimate than the Hemingways. In addition to their literary work, the Tynans had the kind of Hollywood celebrity credentials the Davises loved. The Tynans were so connected to the Tinseltown crowd that their daughter Tracy, born in 1952, was named after Spencer Tracy and no less than Katharine Hepburn was her godmother. The Davis and Tynan children were friends, and the families continued to visit one another in the coming years, even after Kenneth Tynan and Elaine Dundy divorced and he remarried. The Davises' letters with the Tynans also were more entertaining to read than their correspondence with Hemingway. Six years after the summer of 1959, for example, Kenneth Tynan wrote

Bill and Annie about an upcoming visit and in that letter of July 26, 1965, offered gossip that must have been welcome rumor to the Davises:

> *A final flash, dead secret but (an unscrambled source assures me) dead true! Mike Nichols is having an affair with Jackie Kennedy. This has apparently made him quite insufferable and he preens about all day in dressing gown like Noel Coward in 'Present Laughter' and knows all the Secret Service men by their Christian names. More later as it reaches me. Can the tinsel and glitter of Broadway banish the grief that lingers in the eyes of the mysterious Woman in Black? Will she sacrifice her Wealth and Position to his Wealth and Position? What will become of Dan, the Secret Service agent who loves her? . . . etc. Love from both of us, Ken.*

The Davises were all too knowledgeable about Kenneth Tynan's dark secret, which has nothing to do with gossip. Tynan was a sadomasochist, as they came to learn during one of the Tynan's visits to La Consula at a time when Tynan and wife Elaine Dundy were trying to patch up their marriage. As Dundy wrote in her autobiography:

> *There being no Scott and Zelda, it was left to Ken and me to supply the fireworks. Our late night fights often shattered the well-organized serenity the Davises worked so assiduously to create to soothe the spirit of their guests in Shangri-La.*
>
> *Soon after we arrived Ken announced that he was reinitiating his sadomasochistic sex practices. He hadn't come back to me to be deprived of those, he said. For a week, after lunch, we retired for the siesta and he put me through his punishment routines. The night of the seventh day I got very drunk and we had a huge row at the dinner table, which ended with me overturning a plate of food on him in front of Bill, Annie, Cyril and other guests. The next morning Ken told me he'd apologized for my behavior to the Davises and said that we must leave. After packing I went weeping to Annie in her room and told her of Ken's sex acts so she'd understand what was going on. She was sympathetic.*

Tynan's sadomasochism became well documented years later. A story in the *Guardian* in 2001 discussing first-wife Elaine Dundy's memoir reported that, "During one of their apache dances, he laces into Dundy so hard she's left unconscious on the bathroom floor with a pair of black eyes and a broken nose. Tynan didn't mind when word got round about the fracas, she says. 'There was always part of him that gloried in his reputation as a lady-killer, the sinful, depraved Don Juan. The mad, bad, dangerous-to-know sadist.'"

However, as that 1959 summer with Hemingway showed, Kenneth Tynan wasn't as tough around men, especially men who could be as macho and neurotic as Ernest was in his final years. A. E. Hotchner's biography recounts a confrontation that exploded between Tynan and Hemingway that summer in which it was the critic limping away like a cowering bully who had been given a verbal beat down by an old man of letters of all people.

It happened over drinks after dinner at a Málaga restaurant one night when Tynan lavished praise on the performance of matador Jaime Ostos, who was the third bullfighter on the card of at least one of the ten meetings in *corridas* that season between Dominguín and Ordoñez. Not all their meetings in the bullring that summer had been true *mano a manos*, one-to-one confrontations splitting all six bulls of the *corrida*, though the issue of what was a *mano a mano* and what wasn't became convoluted in the widespread reporting in newspapers, as well as in Hemingway's own writings. On the day that Tynan happened to attend a *corrida*, he witnessed Ostos acquitting himself well, though he was overlooked in the hype and attention focused on Dominguín and Ordoñez. When Tynan praised one of Ostos's kill that evening, he didn't realize he had inadvertently stepped into Hemingway's own intellectual *corrida* and the danger that involved. Ernest immediately challenged him on his appraisal of the day's bullfight.

"You know, just because you wrote one skinny book doesn't make you an authority," Hemingway snapped, apparently dismissing Tynan's power as a critic and his work for the *New Yorker*. "On what authority do you make those statements?"

"On the authority of my eyes," Tynan shot back curtly.

"Fuck your eyes," said Hemingway. "You need glasses."

Incensed, Tynan stood up to leave. "There's no point to my staying at this table any longer."

"Maybe you'll stay long enough to pick up the check." Hemingway's tone was insulting.

"I'll make arrangements for that," said Tynan.

As he started to walk out, Bill Davis stopped him momentarily. "Why Ken," Davis said. "You look disturbed."

"I have just been insulted by a man with a white beard," said Tynan, "who doesn't have the wisdom to go with it."

Hemingway apologized effusively the next morning, but no one there forgot about it. The incident offered yet one more indication of the deterioration of Hemingway's mind with his mood swings and depression and how those closest to him, especially Davis and Hotchner, tolerated his abusive behavior. They were the apparent symptomatic signs of an inevitability ahead that perhaps no one wanted to consider. Hemingway's father, Clarence, had committed suicide, as had his father before him. Ernest's sister Ursula and his brother Leicester also committed suicide. The father of Hemingway's first wife, Hadley, committed suicide. In all, seven members of Hemingway's family would eventually die by taking their own lives.

"It is not likely that Hemingway was a brave man who sought danger for the sake of the sensations it provided him," Norman Mailer would later write in *Esquire* magazine. "What is more likely the truth of his long odyssey is that he struggled with his cowardice and against a secret lust to suicide all of his life, that his inner landscape was a nightmare, and he spent his nights wrestling with the gods."

17

The One True Sentence

There is nothing noble in being superior to your fellow man; true nobility is being superior to your former self.
—ERNEST HEMINGWAY

SOME THINGS ABOUT SPAIN NEVER CHANGE. ONE AUGUST DAY IN 1959, Bill Davis was reminded of that as he and Ernest Hemingway spent an afternoon, when there were no *corridas* to attend, in the cellar of the Museo Picasso Málaga and saw, still visible, the oldest architectural remains in the city—the walls of the Phoenician city, from the sixth century BC, when it was founded under the hegemony of ancient Carthage. Of course, Spain had changed profoundly since then, but its spirit in some ways felt unchanged to those who came to love the idea, if not the reality, of this country.

For Davis as for Hemingway, that was never more evident than as the days of this at times almost magical summer ebbed to an end. Spanish journalist-novelist José Luis Castillo-Puche called the Hemingway from that period "a pathetically lonely and a pathologically devious man." If so, that was only one side of the multifaceted author who otherwise appeared to be having the time of his life, even as his grumbling and nastiness at times was disappointing his loved ones and friends. Davis, however, was not among those who felt let down. "My father was non-judgmental when it came to Hemingway," Teo Davis would tell me years later. "I don't think there was anything Hemingway could have said or done to dissuade him from that. He was his undying friend. I don't know if Hemingway realized just how much my father cared for him, how high his regard was for him. I suppose, when it comes to friendship, you can't ask for much more." Perhaps at that time, Davis might have been equally moved by what Antonio Ordoñez told biographer Jeffrey Meyers: "Hemingway respected Davis more than [A. E. Hotchner] because he thought Hotchner was a poor writer."

Neither Davis nor anyone else, however, could keep tabs on Hemingway all the time. Hemingway had become careless in ways that he had never been before. It was unlike Ernest to lose things or misplace them. He usually left that to someone else. Perhaps the most famous of Ernest's losses were the manuscripts that Hadley lost on a train from Paris to Switzerland in 1922, or, more accurately, had stolen from her. "I was sure she could not have brought the carbons too and I hired someone to cover for me on my newspaper job," Ernest wrote in *A Moveable Feast*. At that point, Hemingway had not published any of his fiction. In a letter to Ezra Pound in January 1923, Hemingway wrote: "I suppose you heard about the loss of my Juvenalia? I went up to Paris last week to see what was left and found that Hadley had made the job complete by including all carbons, duplicates, etc. All that remains of my complete works are three pencil drafts of a bum poem which was later scrapped, some correspondence between John McClure and me, and some journalistic carbons. You, naturally, would say, 'Good' etc. But don't say it to me. I ain't yet reached that mood."

It was a different Hemingway in 1959, though, who himself had become an easy target for pickpockets and thieves who preyed on tourists, of which the writer now was one of thousands. Twice that summer he had his wallet lifted out of his pants pockets. The amount stolen was a couple of hundred dollars in Spanish currency, hardly enough to keep Hemingway up at night. The importance was the personal principle to Ernest, that he had become an easy mark. Then at a festival in Murcia, in southern Spain, on September 8, it happened again while Ernest was signing photographs of himself. If that wasn't bad enough, Hemingway brought attention to himself and the incident by making a public plea for his wallet's return. This wallet had sentimental value because his son Patrick had presented it to him as a gift after the theft of his previous wallet.

The police report of the theft and Ernest's plea for its return was widely circulated in Europe and in the United States. "Hemingway Asks Thief to Return His Wallet," the *St. Louis Post Dispatch* headlined its September 16 story. "As for the nine thousand pesetas (about $150) it contained, your skill deserves that prize as a reward," Hemingway said in his plea. A week later, not only was the wallet returned but the *New York Times*, on September 23, also published a story about it with the headline "Thief Heeds Hemingway."

For Hemingway, the *mano a mano* between Ordoñez and Dominguín, which was winding down in the bullrings of Spain, had become merely emblematic of the *mano a mano* that Hemingway was fighting within himself. Ordoñez had slowly but without doubt established his preeminence in the bullring, and both matadors performed brilliantly at times. The prizes at each *corrida* were the ears, hooves, and tails of slain bulls that were awarded to each bullfighter, often in an arbitrary fashion not unlike the way judges determine the scores in a figure skating or gymnastics competition. On that basis, savage as it may seem to the non-bullfighting set, by summer's end Antonio Ordoñez clearly held a decisive edge over Dominguín. There was no decisive knockout, as the *Life* magazine deal called for if the publication were going to pay Hemingway $30,000. "Bullfighting is worthless without rivalry," Hemingway had said earlier that summer. "But with two great bullfighters, it becomes a deadly rivalry." The summer, however, had failed to meet that great expectation. There was no tragedy, no death in the afternoon, nor was a matador wounded so badly as to be disabled. However, blood was spilled from both matadors, who were each gored during the long summer. Dominguín was first gored in Valencia, Ordoñez in Aranjuez and Palma de Majorca.

Leave it to Hemingway, of course, to put himself at the center of the action, figuratively, though to him it must have felt as if he were in the center of the bullring about to make the kill of the bull himself: As he wrote in *The Dangerous Summer*:

This was Antonio's regular appointment with death that we had to face every day. Any man can face death but to be committed to bring it as close as possible while performing certain classic movements and do this again and again and again and then deal it out yourself with a sword to an animal weighing half a ton which you love is more complicated than facing death.

For pure artistry, the *mano a mano* peaked fittingly enough, practically in Bill Davis's backyard, at the bullring in Málaga on August 14, 1959, as both Ordoñez and Dominguín put on perhaps the most memorable afternoon of bullfighting in Spain's history. Hemingway, like a small-town sportswriter rooting for his home team, saw it one-sided. "Antonio's first bull came out and he took him with the cape as though he were inventing bullfighting and it was going to be absolutely perfect from the start," Ernest wrote of the *corrida*. "It was how he fought all summer. . . . That day in Málaga, he surpassed himself again and he made poetry of movement with the hunting, seeking, pressing mass of the bull." Dominguín, though, was equally masterful that day, and he also had one thing going for him that Ordoñez couldn't match. Unlike some bullfighters, Dominguín also regularly served as his own *banderillero*, the fighter who plunges sharp sticks into the bull's back before the matador steps into the ring with the red cape and sword for the final passes and the kill. From the six bulls that they fought in Málaga, Ordoñez and Dominguín won ten ears, four tails, and two hooves as trophies, an extraordinary feat that Hemingway described as "one of the greatest bullfights I have ever seen . . . an almost perfect bullfight unmarred by any tricks." The dual triumph wasn't complete without the drama of one of the matadors almost being gored. It was Dominguín who flirted with death that afternoon, his heroics moving Hemingway to write in *Life* magazine:

He made two series of eight naturales [passes with a small red cloth] in beautiful style and then on a right-hand pass with the bull coming at him from the rear, the bull had him. . . . The horn seemed to go into his body and the bull tossed him a good six feet or more into the air. His arms and legs were spread wide, the sword and muleta *were thrown clear and he fell on his head. The bull stepped on him trying to get the horn into him and missed him twice. . . . He was up in an instant. The horn had not gone in but had passed between his legs . . . and there was*

*no wound. [He] paid no attention to what the bull had done to him
and waving everyone away went on with his faena [work].*

The fourth true *mano a mano* was at Ciudad Real, where Ordoñez
outdueled Dominguín, and the drama built up for their showdown in
Bilbao. It never developed into that as Dominguín suffered a near-fatal
goring in the mishandling of his second bull. While trying to maneuver
the bull toward a *picador*, the bull caught him against the *picador*'s horse.
The bull dug into Dominguín's thigh with a horn as the crowd gasped,
and Ordoñez and other bullfighters jumped into the ring to distract the
animal. Dominguín was quickly carried out of the ring, and Ordoñez
prepared to make a lasting statement.

In bullfighting, there is a rare way of killing the bull called *recibiendo*,
Spanish for receiving. The matador stands motionless with a sword and
receives the bull's charge. In *Death in the Afternoon*, Hemingway called it
"the most arrogant dealing of death . . . and one of the finest things you
can see in bullfighting." It is also extremely dangerous, and Hemingway
claimed to have seen it performed only four times in the almost fifteen
hundred kills he had witnessed. One of those times had been in 1956,
when Ordoñez killed a bull in that fashion and dedicated it to Hemingway, telling him, "Ernesto, you and I know this bull is worthless, but let's
see if I can kill him in the way you like it." Now, in Bilbao as he sought
to show up the wounded Dominguín, Ordoñez decided to dispatch this
fearsome bull in the most dangerous way known in the sport. It took
Ordoñez three attempts to kill the bull *recibiendo* style, and Hemingway
immediately began comparing his feat to that of the bullfighting icon
Pedro Romero, Spain's legendary matador of the late eighteenth century.
Hemingway, in *The Sun Also Rises*, gave that name to the heroic bullfighter
that he based on Cayetano Ordoñez, Antonio's father.

In the minutes after that *corrida*, Hemingway retreated, along with
Bill Davis and his *cuadrilla*, to leave the bullring as quickly as possible,
though there was some difficulty. Those who have written about him at
this time—both biographers and scholars—have almost unanimously
ignored this, not having been firsthand witnesses to the trouble Ernest
could often have moving around after sitting still for a while. There is a

moment for all of us to suspend reality with our heroes and world giants. Political writers, photographers, and editors in the 1930s and the 1940s certainly were culpable of this, and it was not until years later that most Americans realized that President Franklin D. Roosevelt had been crippled from polio and could barely walk, and then only with assistance. So, too, with Hemingway. The postwar America of the mid-twentieth century was like all societies, with the need for heroes not because they coincidentally made them up on their own but because heroes like Hemingway express a deep psychological aspect of human existence.

Ernest Hemingway was a figure through which an America profoundly affected by nuclear fear, by a dizzying plethora of atomic panaceas and proposals, and by endless speculation on the social and ethical implications of the new reality reconciled the conscious and unconscious aspects of the national psyche. People feared the bomb itself, yes, and such fears were probably overstated by authorities who wanted every new home to be built with fallout shelters. The bomb made midcentury Americans fear more acutely what they already had feared: that things that had been whole in their lives would now split and that such splitting could not be controlled. The evolution, or maybe revolution, in technology, race relations, and the very fabric of national culture, which Americans could whimsically reassure themselves of every time they looked at a Norman Rockwell painting on the cover of the *Saturday Evening Post*—all of that was changing; and it affected a nation that naively had believed its world had been made safe when Adolf Hitler had been defeated.

So in the moments after the *corrida*, perhaps the weight he had carried or maybe just the exhaustion from a long summer and its grand expectations came to bear on Ernest. "When the fight was over and people were leaving the plaza, we spotted Hemingway in the expensive seats below us, standing with a too-thin, wan-looking girl of seventeen or so," observed English scholar Terence Keough, who had been at the *corrida*. "He wore a brown and white checked pancake cap and a pair of sunglasses with yellow lenses. He carried his head angled slightly forward from his body, a slight compensation for the bad back that was caused by two consecutive small plane crashes in Africa."

In a sense, Hemingway had agonized over what he saw, what he had written about it thus far, and what he still had to write. Perhaps he hadn't intended to turn the experience into an introspection of what was still left of his life and his place in the literary landscape, but this is what had happened. Ernest had once told George Plimpton that "you make something through your invention that is not a representation but a whole new thing truer than anything true and alive, and you make it alive, and if you make it well enough, you give it immortality."

And yet here at the end of the summer, according to biographers, as Hemingway sought to find a fitting epilogue for his life and his art and made a glorious attempt for a glimpse back to his youth and heroism, what emerged more clearly was the sad reality of the great author dying, psychically and artistically—and, worse, he seems to have recognized that. Ultimately, if that was the case, Hemingway appears to have believed he would have not only the last word on who had won the series of *mano a manos* but also seeing his own legacy carried on by that winner, Antonio Ordoñez.

His standing in literature aside, however, Hemingway could not rewrite history, no matter how much he bullied the facts into how he wanted to see them. His dangerous summer had not decided once and for all who the greatest bullfighter was—not conclusively. In their first five meetings, Ordoñez and Dominguín fought to a virtual tie. "If you count the ears and tail and gauge Hemingway's description of the crowd reaction, it would seem that overall Luis Miguel got the better of Antonio in them," Edward Lewine concluded in a retrospective half a century later in *Death and the Sun: A Matador's Season in the Heart of Spain*. In the last five, Ordoñez had gotten the upper hand, though Dominguín had been clearly ailing from a goring, which hampered him the rest of the summer. "Antonio was the big winner in print," Lewine wrote, "but it was a pyrrhic victory because he was tarred as Hemingway's pet, which cost him credit with many in Spain."

It was as if Hemingway had now unwittingly become Santiago at the end of *The Old Man and the Sea*, left with nothing more than the bones of his latest adventure and having lost his chance to recapture something he wanted from the past, facing what was left of the future sadly alone.

18

Paris One More Time

If you are lucky enough to have lived in Paris as a young man, then wherever you go for the rest of your life, it stays with you, for Paris is a moveable feast.

—ERNEST HEMINGWAY

BILL AND ANNIE DAVIS HAD BEEN TO PARIS OFTEN, SO MUCH THAT THEY knew by heart the tourist ritual for following in the footsteps of the young Ernest Hemingway, strolling along the narrow, winding cobblestone streets. They had relived the Paris of the Lost Generation in the vibrant Left Bank and in the Latin Quarter and Montparnasse. Arm in arm, they had traipsed over the ancient stones, where Hemingway and friends had trudged, sometimes drunkenly after sitting at the same sidewalk cafés and restaurants where the Davises had gone to see if something of that time had been left to be conveyed to them decades later. They had bought books at Shakespeare and Company, though it wasn't Sylvia Beach's store on rue l'Odeon, the celebrated gathering place for writers of the Lost Generation. That bookstore closed in 1941 during the German occupation of Paris and never reopened, though another Shakespeare and Company opened a decade later. But along Boulevard du Montparnasse, Bill and Annie had experienced the legendary cafés with their timeless link to Hemingway's 1920s Paris: La Rotonde, La Coupole, Le Dome, Le Select, and La Closerie des Lilas.

However, the Davises had never been to Paris with Hemingway until that late September of 1959, after the last *corrida* of the *mano a manos* between Luis Miguel Dominguín and Antonio Ordoñez and with Ernest wanting to get away and perhaps catch yet one more whiff of the days that now seemed so long ago. Attempting to hold on to the feeling of being Ordoñez's alter ego, Hemingway had invited Antonio and his wife, Carmen, to Cuba, where he would soon be headed to clean out as much as he could from his finca estate before the new Castro government completely shut it down to him. He planned for the group to stay there only a few days and then move on to Sun Valley, where he was looking forward to the hunting season. But that was still weeks ahead. For now he said he had business that needed tending to in France, though that may have been only part of the reason.

Ernest arranged for Bill and Annie to drive him and Valerie Danby-Smith to France, along with Mary part of the way. It all seemed so civil from afar. Mary Hemingway was catching a flight back to America, and the story was that she was returning early to get the homes in Cuba and Idaho in presentable shape for their Spanish guests. Later, Mary left no doubt that she couldn't wait to get away from Ernest and had finally decided that she needed to divorce him, all her previous protests to the opposite notwithstanding. Ernest's long summer of amorous flirtations with almost every pretty young woman he met and his public mistreatment of her had finally gotten to Mary. In Madrid, she and Annie Davis chose to take the train to Paris, where they planned to meet up with Ernest and what was left of his *cuadrilla* at the Ritz.

In the long drive through northern Spain up into France, Hemingway enthralled Bill Davis and Danby-Smith, as she recalled in her memoir years later.

With prompting from Bill, he spoke of his old friend Scott Fitzgerald and what a shame it was that he had become a rummy, had sold out to Hollywood, and was no longer able to write. Gertrude Stein came in for her share of criticism, but she and Alice B. Toklas were [first son Jack] Bumby's godmothers, and there was a time when Ernest had respected her talent and opinion. He never spoke ill of "old Jim" Joyce, although he too might have been classified as a rummy; still Joyce never lost his ability to write, and for Ernest, that was the most important thing.

Hemingway had with him a worn leather briefcase he had brought that contained what he called "The Paris Sketches"—stories about Paris in his youth—which was the manuscript to that point of *A Moveable Feast*. It soon became obvious that this trip to Paris had a purpose beyond spending time with the young secretary with whom he had become infatuated. Hemingway was using the time to recheck himself on the scenes and places he had written about in the Paris of the 1920s. Ernest retraced his steps and entertained his friends from Spain, as well as others he collected on the drive. As he had done throughout the time in Spain, he ignored Mary, and the divide was growing ever wider between them. They also had an argument over money at Cartier's, where she had fallen in love with a pair of diamond earrings that Hemingway refused to buy because he felt they were too expensive. Within days, she departed for America while Hemingway returned to Spain and La Consula for the final weeks of his stay and prepared to complete the story of his adventure. According to Danby-Smith's memoir, Hemingway also used the time to declare his love for her and that he was considering taking his own life if she would not have him.

That account only added to questions about whether Hemingway might have found not only mortality but also madness in his quest for his youthful past in Spain. Perhaps this was just Hemingway being himself. He had always fallen in love with a future bride while still married to a previous wife, but he had not been sixty years old in those other instances. The Ernest Hemingway of Spain in 1959 was a walking advertisement of the great man of letters taking a literary curtain call but reduced as a writer to connecting labels with conjunctions and hoping no one would know the difference. Hemingway, however, did, and he could not fool himself. As Castillo-Puche remembered in writing in his memoir of that time: "I saw [Hemingway] get all confused, tear up whole sections of his manuscript, rip up photographs or fling them across the room in a fit of temper, swear at those present in the room and others elsewhere, and swear at himself."

It wasn't as if Ernest wasn't trying. In addition to this work of journalism on the *mano a mano* and the Paris stories for *A Moveable Feast*, he also had in that old briefcase the unfinished manuscript for the novel *The*

Garden of Eden. He was emotionally slaving over both books. No one—not Bill Davis or A. E. Hotchner nor any of the young women who had been the objects of his flirtation—knew the creative angst this had caused Hemingway. No one, that is, except Mary, whose determination to be the last Mrs. Ernest Hemingway had given her the strength and stomach to withstand his mistreatment.

When he boarded the *Liberté* at Le Havre for New York on October 27, Hemingway had two major priorities: making up with Mary and completing the bullfighting story for *Life* magazine. A part of Ernest may have underestimated the difficulty of both challenges. Hotchner met Hemingway when he arrived in New York on November 2 and noticed that the other man was preoccupied with how to reunite with his wife. He had already cabled her, telling her he didn't want the marriage to end and begging her to stay. "Still love you," he said. Before leaving Paris, he had even returned to Cartier's and bought a diamond pin for Mary. For whatever reason, however, he still wouldn't splurge on the diamond earrings she wanted.

"How did Mary seem to you?" Hemingway asked his friend.

"Well, fine," Hotchner told him, "but she was pretty upset about the summer."

"I know," said Hemingway. "Neglect. And she has a proper beef, you know. I was just having so much damn fun . . . well, it wasn't organized around her. There were us guys and the road and Antonio's fights and all that, and Miss Mary was mostly parked in various places. Pretty great places, but still and all . . . of course. I invited her on almost all of the trips, but she said they were too tiring or too dull. She didn't want to go, and she didn't want me to go."

Hemingway's remembrance of how he had treated Mary just months earlier bore little resemblance to the way most witnesses recalled it to have happened. That alone spoke volumes both about his memory and his inability to recognize how unfeeling and unreasonable he could be with loved ones. Ernest softened considerably by the time he joined Mary in Cuba and began entertaining Antonio and Carmen Ordoñez both there and then in Idaho. Hemingway, however, appeared to be in a dream-like state, according to documents in a collection of his papers at the

University of Virginia. "Hemingway moves as cheerfully as possible like in a Kafka nightmare," he wrote on November 8 to Hotchner, according to a digest of his letters. "He is bone-tired and very beat up emotionally. Wants to get back to writing. One of the big issues is that he expects others to subordinate themselves to his writing, and thus make them lead lives of drudges."

The writing that Hemingway wanted to get back to was the *Life* magazine story, of which he had lost control. Eventually, the piece grew to over 120,000 words, so excessively long for a magazine article that *Life* editors became concerned, threatening to do the cutting themselves in New York. Hired to help with the editing, Hotchner flew to Havana, where he discovered that Ernest had trimmed only 278 words in three weeks of work. He was surprised to find Hemingway "unusually hesitant, disorganized, and confused," as well as suffering badly from failing eyesight—but continuing to resist, asserting to Hotchner, "What I've written is Proustian in its cumulative effect, and if we eliminate detail we destroy that effect." Hotchner persisted and in less than a week's time had cut almost fifty-five thousand words. *Life*, which had hoped to publish the story in a single issue of the magazine, began making plans to serialize it—even Hemingway's correspondence to the editors defending the length is astonishing.

"There are no deaths, so had to build characters, feelings, etc.," Ernest wrote. "Can call whole thing off if hard to fit in during [1960] election year. Would have been easier if Miguel or Antonio had been killed."

Would have been easier if Miguel or Antonio had been killed.

There had been no death in the afternoon, in other words, just a dangerous summer.

It would take almost a year after the last *mano a mano* of 1959 for *Life* to publish Hemingway's account, and it would be no easier as the publication date neared than it had been to get the piece out of the author's hands. Ernest spent much of the first half of 1960 working on the article, complaining about *Life*'s editors, and making a word-count mockery of the initial assignment of a ten-thousand-word story. Then, as if he hadn't spent enough time in Spain in 1959, he insisted he needed to return in order to clean up loose ends. Mary refused to accompany him, fearing a repeat of the previous unhappy summer. Bill and Annie Davis welcomed him back with open arms but were shocked at the change of a year, as biographer Carlos Baker wrote: "He showed the symptoms of extreme nervous depression, fear, remorse, loneliness, ennui, suspicion of the motives of others, insomnia, guilt, . . . and failure of memory."

In the summer of 1960, what Hemingway found in his beloved Spain was disillusionment and despair, with his physical health declining as rapidly as his mental state. He wrote Mary repeatedly, telling her he feared he was "cracking up" and that he needed her. In the letter from August 19, Ernest wrote:

> *Kittner, I don't know how I can stick this summer out. Am so damned lonesome and the whole bullfight business is now so corrupt and seems so unimportant and I have so much good work to do. . . . Only this, I am afraid of, no, not only this, is complete physical and mental crack up from deadly overwork. . . . Would have given anything to have pulled out of here as soon as I saw how things were. Honey, I miss you so and our old lovely life. . . . I loathe this damned bull business now and I want to clean my work and get the hell out.*

When Hemingway returned to New York, there was little that could lift his spirits, least of all seeing his account of the summer of 1959 in Spain finally published in the pages of *Life*. It may also have been a sign that Ernest had little idea of his own real image, because his photograph on the cover of the magazine upset him. It was a picture of a handsome but elderly Ernest in Spain with a large bullfighting poster behind him, which photographer Loomis Dean had shot during his time with Hemingway that dangerous summer.

"The horrible face on the cover," Ernest said of his image, "made me sick."

Those stories in *Life* made the magazine issues collectors' items but little more. In 1985, the material was reedited and finally published almost a quarter of a century after Hemingway's death in book form as *The Dangerous Summer*. Reviewing the book for the *New York Times*, William Kennedy wrote, "I remember the articles. I looked forward to them but could not read them. I don't think I finished even one of the three. The great Hemingway had resuscitated all the boredom I'd felt in reading *The Green Hills*. This was also the response of *Life*'s other readers. The articles were a disaster."

They were the last words written by Hemingway that the public would read in his lifetime. When John F. Kennedy was elected president, Ernest was among the writers asked to contribute words of congratulations. He sat at his desk for hours trying to commit words to paper but could not. Later that month, he entered the Mayo Clinic for treatment of depression. Hemingway finally wrote President Kennedy a letter of congratulations four days after his inauguration.

On July 2, 1961, Ernest Hemingway, a writer preoccupied with death to the point of obsession and personal oblivion, committed suicide at his home in Ketchum, Idaho. The cause was a self-inflicted shotgun wound to the head. He was sixty-one.

The world mourned his death, no country more than Spain.

Epilogue

"Oh, Jake," Brett said, "we could have had such a damned good time
together."
Ahead was a mounted policeman in khaki directing traffic. He
raised his baton. The car slowed suddenly pressing Brett against me.
"Yes," I said. "Isn't it pretty to think so?"
—Ernest Hemingway, *The Sun Also Rises*

In the fall of 1974, after my wife had gone on a Lady Brett
Ashley–like wild spree and left me, I moved into a quaint, dilapidated cottage in an obscure rain forest corner of River Oaks in Houston where the
only amenity was being awakened each morning by a family of raccoons
rummaging through the kitchen. The address was fittingly pretentious,
8 Ashbury Place, and it belonged to a handsome playboy fashion writer
named Peter Heyne, who with his good looks helped by his connections
at *Women's Wear Daily* was forever entertaining young Houston debutantes
with double last names and lineages to names in Texas history books.

I was too depressed with self-loathing, pity, and half-baked plans
about moving to Paris in search of Ernest Hemingway or, at least, a reasonable facsimile of personal oblivion. To his credit, Peter didn't try to dissuade me and instead indulged my delusion. His previous roommate, who
had inhabited my bedroom, he enlightened me, had once sat on Hemingway's lap in some grand villa in Spain. His parents had been wealthy
American expatriates who entertained Hemingway and the group that
followed the world's most celebrated writer when he was there for his
last hurrah, and what better place to do it if not with the bullfights in the
splendor of their birthplace.

"His name is Teo Davis," Peter told me. "He was educated in Cambridge, married a contessa who later divorced him, and he moved in here with me."

"So where is he now?" Yes, I wanted to know, where do mending broken hearts go when they haven't shot their brains out?

"Teo? Teo's now in Hollywood. He's out there writing screenplays."

Having just seen *Sunset Boulevard* for the first time in my life, and with the image of slain screenwriter Joe Gillis in Norma Desmond's swimming pool swirling in my head, this was not what I wanted to hear.

Teo Davis, though, would remain indelibly on my mind, if for no other reason than that he had left behind notebooks and parts of what appeared to be a memoir or an unfinished novel. The most interesting of his notes were in Spanish: References to "Papa" and "Hotch" and "Málaga," I believe. His handwriting was so bad, however, that making sense of his ramblings proved to be an exercise in fiction and futility.

One afternoon after a considerable search, I found a library in Houston and checked out several biographies of Hemingway. To my surprise, what Peter had said was true. Bill and Annie Davis were rich, beautiful people in Málaga who, though they apparently may not have known Hemingway very well, had invited him and his fourth wife, Mary, to stay with them in 1959 at their elegant estate called La Consula. Their house was filled with a lot of servants and cars, and they were parents of a son and daughter. One of the biographies even mentioned Hemingway playing in the mornings with young Timoteo.

Peter didn't seem to know much more. "To be honest," he said. "I thought he might have been making it all up."

The social set in Houston, though, had bought it all, or at least they bought Teo—and it might not have mattered, according to society columnist Maxine Mesinger of the *Houston Chronicle*. "(Teo) was such an elegant young man," she remembered. "And single in a town where people couldn't find enough young single straight men to marry off their daughters. All it took was the name. Hemingway. It was magical. The rest was imagination gone wild."

It was a wonder considering that when he arrived in Texas, Teo was twenty-one years old, just three years removed from Eton and already capable of leaving a lasting impression that helped him make important connections. One of those was Harold Barefoot Sanders, a federal judge in Dallas who had been legislative counsel to President Lyndon B. Johnson—and at the time, one of the most influential men in Texas. It was through his connection with the Sanders family that Teo was hired as a reporter at the *Houston Chronicle*, according to Jack Loftis, the longtime editor at the newspaper.

"Teo was a friend of one of Barefoot's daughters," Loftis later recalled. "He was well spoken of by some very important people in Texas."

From there, his legend grew. Men as well as women, especially other writers, wanted to meet him. One of them even claimed to have an assignment to profile Teo for *Texas Monthly* magazine. Another wanted to write a book about him and his family and later offered to buy Teo's belongings that had been left in my bedroom. I'd already packed them up and mailed them to a return address on a letter from his sister in Southern California. If nothing else, he may have given some badly needed credibility to the dilapidated ranch-style house tucked away in an overgrown forest in Houston's tony River Oaks section, where he lived for a while with Peter Heyne. The house was beyond salvation, with holes in the roof and infested with raccoons. But River Oaks was the address to have, if you were a social climber, and Teo quickly became a regular in the city's social scene; no sweat for someone who had grown up surrounded by the wit and flamboyance of Sir Noel Coward, whose sense of personal style and flair had seemingly rubbed off on the scion of La Consula.

And Teo had a contessa in hand. That was the other story about Teo in Houston, that the debutantes there had little chance with someone who was already spoken for, and this was well before the *New York Times* announcement. Some there in River Oaks said she was a contessa, though she was apparently a marchioness-in-waiting, a British aristocratic title she presumably would inherit, and in Texas you would need a program on peerage to know the difference. She had been in a special spread in *UK Vogue* about young socialites going off into the world, photographed by the great fashion lensman and Oscar-winning costumer Cecil Beaton, no less, and that might have been more than the validation required in the

Lone Star State, where social climbing sometimes seemed like an event right alongside bull riding in a rodeo.

No one had reason to suspect, given the hoopla in the social fandango swirling around Teo in the mid-1970s, as he met Walter Hill and decided to split for Hollywood. But a few sensed something wasn't quite right about it all, though who would listen to them, and in a setting like that, they'd be fools to speak up. Watergate had just consumed America, so there was a dire need for something to believe in. Besides, if the perfect life that seemed to envelop Teo Davis's existence had the appearance of a fairy tale, there was good reason.

Then, almost as quickly as he had arrived, Teo was gone. He was in Houston only months, it seemed, and no one at the *Chronicle* could recall him working on any stories. Neither could Teo, for that matter.

"I couldn't tell you why I was hired," he said years later. "I was interviewed by a friend of a friend, and afterward, I had the job, and I can't tell you why. I couldn't even type. Anything I wrote, I wrote longhand."

Fifteen years passed. Instead of Paris, I went to Spain. I don't know whether I was searching for Hemingway or for Teo. I found neither. I wound up in Los Angeles. One day I finally sobered up. I was still alive, having written for an NBC cop show for producer Michael Mann in Tinseltown and sharing with writers an old office overlooking the fabled Sunset Boulevard. Peter had been right. When you've been to hell and back, you go on to Hollywood to make things up.

I moved into an old Spanish villa apartment in West Hollywood whose claim to fame was that F. Scott Fitzgerald had once lived there. I would soon learn that in Hollywood, someone famous has always lived where someone not so famous now lives. It's like reverse reincarnation: You were always someone famous in a past life. One day when we were in a story meeting at my office, a guy who looked like he had seen better days popped his head in the door. He was answering our classified ad in the *Recycler* for someone to paint our offices, but he was the most unusual-looking painter you could ever expect to find. He was wearing a rumpled, navy Armani blazer with soiled linen slacks that none of us could afford and a half-knotted Eton striped tie. He also had a slight English accent that was both unexpected and intimidating.

"My name is Teo," he informed us like some fancy waiter at LeDome up the Sunset Strip, "and I'm your painter."

This was the famous Teo Davis, the rising star of everything I'd heard so much about, having obviously fallen, if not from grace, then at least on some hard times.

"Like a cross between Churchill and Picasso," is how one friend later recalled Teo in that period before his life went awry and he walked through our office door. "The voice, the beautiful opinionated voice. Both grand and eloquent, hypnotic in its intelligence. We worked together both at MGM and Paramount. A man of a hundred shirts that he would dry clean in one shot once a month—a hundred boxes to cart up the steps of Pensione Paradiso . . . coming to work in his bashed up Cadillacs, his navy blazers and funky crushed linen pants with his old ties from Eton. We were impressed. We were intimidated. What's this on his desk? A bottle of Southern Comfort and Hemingway's typewriter! And there it was with his name on it this old Remington that sat there like a big spider."

Teo began working for us that afternoon, but I don't believe he ever finished painting the office. He spent most days chain-smoking unfiltered Camels on our terrace while we watched young actresses walking their composites and headshots to the talent agency across the street. Teo would often regale us with reminiscences of Hemingway in Spain that entertained us, though they seemed implausible considering he was barely eight when the Nobel Prize–winning writer had spent much of 1959 under the same roof.

But who was to argue with a man from Eton. As it turned out, Peter had been wrong on several counts. Teo had been educated at Eton, not Cambridge. At the time I moved into his former bedroom in Houston, Teo also hadn't yet married the contessa who would break his heart over and over again. They'd had an ongoing love affair for years and finally married in 1980. But there was no denying his vivid memories of the year Hemingway had visited.

"We called him Papa—everyone did," said Teo. "He was like a big teddy bear who was larger than life. When he was there, life revolved around him. Being around seven at the time, and a bit on the precocious side, I knew who Ernest Hemingway was—that he was an author of some importance—but just how important he was is something that I wouldn't even begin to comprehend until years later." For little Teo, the experience would forever influence his life. It appeared he became a writer because of Hemingway, whose few moments of fatherly-like attention lavished on Teo affected him enormously.

But I was almost as curious about the contessa as I was about Hemingway.

Like many first loves, Diana Radway epitomized all Teo had grown up both wanting and being told he should have if he were to achieve that place in society that his parents had so painstakingly planned for him. They had met as children, shortly before Hemingway's stay at La Consula, when Teo's parents had connected with Diana's mother, Lady Judith, the Marchioness of Linlithgow, and her husband Charles William Frederick Hope, 3rd Marquess of Linlithgow and, as befitting all peers of the United Kingdom at that time, a member of the House of Lords. The weighty title of English aristocracy could be enough to crush the confidence of most of non-noble bloodlines, and the Davises had been suitably impressed. If the perfect match for young Teo could be created, his parents felt, it would be someone like little Diana, a lovely girl full of sweetness, decorum, and breeding. There was never a contract of promise of marriage drawn up. That would have been too crass. These were not kingdoms, after all, that were at stake, but the possible matchmaking seemed advantageous to both families: Diana's lofty lineage of British peerage and the apparently incredible wealth, art collection, and estate that Teo would one day inherit.

"Was it all a bit much, a bit overwhelming? It wouldn't be accurate to say it wasn't," Teo was to remark one day in the future, looking back. "We were together since we were six years old. It was as if we were meant to be together. What did it feel like? It felt too good to be true. Like a fairy tale. Was I really worthy of her? I don't know. I suppose that at that time I had questions."

Ah, to be an American, albeit a wealthy one, but worthy of Lady Diana—that could indeed weigh on a sensitive soul, and Teo was certainly that. A friend from his youth in Málaga, Antonio de la Riva, remembered Teo as someone who could be easily hurt by even the suspicion of slights from other young Spaniards in Churriana. "Teo was an artist with an artist's sensitivities," recalled de la Riva. "He acted like things didn't bother him, but they did. They would get to him, and he would brood."

It may never have occurred to the Davises—why would it?—that there may have been an emotional and psychological emptiness in their pursuit or specifically in the social goals they had set before their son. It is also questionable how much they might have known about Diana's family, beyond what they had been told by Teo's uncle, their personal authority on English and European manners and society, Cyril Connolly.

The fairy tale, for Teo and for the Davises, too, would soon be over. The marriage between Teo and Diana lasted only a few months. "Of course he was not suited to marriage," Diana later recalled, "but we grew up together and shared homes and childhood and the '60s and New York and L.A."

Five years later, Bill and Annie Davis were history was well. "Stranger than fiction, they [Bill and Annie] died in London in 1985 a few hours apart—he of cancer, she of a heart attack," wrote the acclaimed art critic Clement Greenburg in *The Harold Letters, 1928–1965: The Making of an American Intellectual.*

Bill and Annie had sold La Consula in 1975, moving their belongings to their apartment in Madrid, and a mystery surrounded the estate that they left to Teo and his sister. The Jackson Pollock and Rothko paintings, as well as the rest of the art collection, were gone, and, a few biographers believed, most of the wealth as well. Teo and Nena inherited countless first-edition books, many of them signed, along with photographs and such valuables as the typewriter on which Hemingway worked at La Consula—apparently the same typewriter Teo had shown off at the MGM and Paramount studios when he worked there. Among those signed Hemingway books was *Death in the Afternoon*, which he inscribed "To Bill, Remembering May First-October 27, 1959 and all the roads and places, Ernest, La Consula." Inside the book, when it was sold at auction at Sotheby's, was a receipt from the Scribner Book Store in New York, dated June 1, 1959, for this first-edition copy, priced at $30.83 for delivery charged to "Ernest Hemingway, Author's Account." The other farewell gift Hemingway signed that day was a copy of *Across the River and Into the*

Trees, which he gave to Annie Davis. Understandably, Teo and his sister have been circumspect in talking about their inheritance, though friends believe it included a couple of million dollars apiece as well.

Hollywood, however, had been the wrong place at the wrong time in Teo's life. He had long before begun experimenting with drugs, and that culture was rampant on the West Coast. It was also the golden age of excess in Hollywood, memorialized by enthralling, lurid accounts of the drug- and sex-fueled decadence of the time. This became a decade when a new generation of maverick filmmakers took over the studios, exceeding their creative brilliance possibly only with their after-hours wild feats of self-indulgent hedonism.

For Teo, according to acquaintances from that time, for a while the drugs heightened his ability to talk about almost anything knowingly, even when he had no inkling of what he was saying. In Hollywood, that can be a door opener, which it was for him, but in those circumstances you have to be able to deliver on developing the idea into an outline or a treatment, at the very least, and certainly show up for work, appointments, or meetings, which is the essence of how the industry works at its root.

Teo, though, had little self-control when it came to hookers and heroin. He bragged to me that he spent tens of thousands of dollars a year on prostitutes from the notorious Hollywood madam Heidi Fleiss, and the heroin use that exhausted the rest of his inheritance eventually landed him in criminal trouble and in jail. To his credit, perhaps, Teo was no ordinary run-of-the-mill junky. His heroin pals were some of the top names in Hollywood, including Golden Globe–winning actor Ray Sharkey; character actor Richard Bright, known for playing Michael Corleone's bodyguard Al Neri in *The Godfather* films; and a movie darling considered by some as one of the greatest actors of all time.

"There were times when Teo was on the brink of dying from all the drugs he was doing—he worked at his self-destruction, he wanted to kill himself," said screenwriter Rod Hewitt, who befriended Teo and for years tried unsuccessfully to get him off drugs, even taking him into his own home before realizing his aid was only enabling Teo further into his downward spiral. Hewitt, who was one of Hollywood's hottest writers for a while in the late 1980s and 1990s, sensed that Teo had been deeply trau-matized by his relationship with his father but couldn't make the break-through to help him. "Pat Conroy [the best-selling author] says that the secret for success is to have had a fucked up childhood," said Hewitt, "and Teo had a fucking doctorate in that."

It was also an incredibly privileged and entitled doctorate, I would learn. One evening, we drove around Laurel Canyon for a couple of hours—lost, it seemed—while Teo tried remembering where a friend lived and insisting he had to find her. I was hoping he wasn't using me to make a drug buy and was planning to just leave him at whatever resi-dence we reached. All the while, he carried on talking eloquently about the tragic culture of wealthy, decadent youth in Los Angeles, the irony of him philosophizing on the subject never registering with him. When we finally located the house, Teo asked me inside and there disarmed my concern by quite matter-of-factly introducing me to its owner, heiress Aileen Getty, his longtime friend who was helping him get legal repre-sentation after his latest drug arrest.

"Teo, you have to get past this, you know that, don't you?" Getty asked him, gently begging him because confronting him was no use, as his few close friends had come to understand.

"Yes, I know," he said, drawing on that ever-present Camel of his. "I'm trying."

Over the years, this had become a costly routine that repeated itself often in Teo's life: drugs, arrests, and topflight lawyers. Usually his lawyers were able to get him sentenced to an alternative drug diversion program. There, as an inpatient and as he usually did with anyone on first meeting them, Teo would quickly impress the rehab center supervisors. At one center, they made him a resident counselor, even as he was a long way from ridding himself of his own addiction.

The rehab program that seemed to be little more than a revolving door for Teo was the Impact Drug and Alcohol Treatment Center in Pasadena, a 130-bed facility whose celebrity cachet of clients included actors Robert Downey Jr. and James Caan. Whenever I couldn't reach Teo on his cell phone, I knew I could leave a message at the Impact Center and usually get a reply in a day or two. California had become unique in dealing with drug offenders who, making up almost a third of the state's prison population, had prompted voters to overwhelmingly pass a ballot initiative that abolished jail or prison as a punishment for almost all nonviolent drug users, sending them instead to state-approved treatment centers. A major drawback for Teo, however, was that it only broadened his circle of drug acquaintances. Sometimes those new connections had found sobriety, though they unfortunately were unable to steer Teo onto the same path.

"My husband became friends with Teo back in 1989 when they were both at Impact treatment center," Kim Caldwell Park said in an e-mail she sent me after reading a newspaper column I had written about Teo in 2006, around the time when she and her husband Reggie were trying to track him down. "They shared a room and fastly became friends. Teo came to Orange County, where we lived several times and even stayed with us. I had to laugh because of your description of him and the chain smoking Camels. I remember that as though it was yesterday. He was a bit down on his luck then but I always had a soft spot for him. He was definitely always a smooth talker without a doubt. I never heard him speak much of his days in Spain but on occasion, he would mention his father and I guess he still kept in touch with his sister, I believe she lived in Arizona, if I'm not mistaken. He told us stories though of his time when he wrote and stories about the Gettys. I guess he was very close to Gail Getty."

At the time that the Parks were looking for him, Teo was back in rehab, though you would never suspect that if you were to have spoken to him on the telephone, as his up-tempo voice with his distinctive accent rarely intimated that he was down-and-out. Teo maintained his rare ability to engage writers, directors, and producers who were always willing to take meetings with him because he could spin a pitch on his feet, the first step toward a deal. Invariably, however, he usually failed to deliver on any promise to develop the story for subsequent meetings. Those who didn't know about Teo's drug problems wrote off his mood swings of going from thoughtful brilliance to utter forgetfulness to something else, possibly symptomatic bipolar disorder. And he was often forgiven. That Teo even got so far as to pitch projects to established producers and directors spoke for what some friends thought was nothing less than sheer genius. Rod Hewitt, for one, had read Teo's screenplay *West Coast Slide*, a modern L.A. crime story, and hailed it as "the best gangster screenplay ever written—and I've read them all." One of Teo's first acquaintances in Hollywood had been longtime agent Michael Hamilburg of the Mitchell Hamilburg literary agency, who knew about the Davis family connection to Hemingway but found it difficult to believe Teo had a serious drug problem. Convinced the idea had merit, Hamilburg tried on and off for more than two decades to get Teo to write an account of Hemingway's stay at La Consula.

"I'm afraid it's a book that Teo will wind up carrying to his grave," Hamilburg finally conceded as he wound down his business in 2015.

When he died on New Year's Day 2016, Hamilburg had given up thinking Teo would write the book. On top of his addiction issues, Teo also envisioned that book as being not about Hemingway but about his own life of decadence in Hollywood, tentatively calling the idea "Hollywood, Heroin, and Hookers." The problem, I came to understand, was Hemingway. Outsiders saw Hemingway as a high point in Teo's life, an experience most people wished had been their own. Teo saw Hemingway as a symbol of how small and inconsequential his own life had been in the eyes of his parents.

"Did I ever make peace with my father? No, I don't think that would have ever been possible," he told me once while we were talking about fathers and sons. "My father wasn't someone who would have ever acknowledged that there was something not perfect in his life. So, no, making peace with him wasn't something that would have happened."

In Los Angeles, Teo was also too busy having a good time and helping his acquaintances and friends out of addiction or out of an impasse in their screenplays. Numerous writers privately credited Teo for breakthroughs in their scripts or in their careers, some offering him payments of thousands of dollars, which he always refused to accept. If they insisted, Teo invariably ended up using it for drugs.

"He blew one windfall after another," said Hewitt. "His inheritance from his family? He blew it. Another inheritance? He blew that, too. An insurance settlement? He blew that as well. A million dollars inheritance, two million, whatever it was, or a hundred and sixty thousand dollar settlement. He blew all of it. There was just something inside him that drove him to fail on some level."

Friendship, though, was another matter. Anyone with smarts who met Teo was in for an intellectual roller-coaster ride that could easily swerve into a real-life long-distance sports car trip, as writer Rex Weiner would later recall. "It was at Teo's suggestion, one day in 1981, that I rented a brand new Camaro in Beverly Hills, and we drove 1,000 miles down Baja to the town of Todos Santos, trailing fumes from Camel filterless cigarettes—an epic journey that continues, in a way, for me and everyone whose lives have crossed at Casa Dracula. *Que le vaya bien, Teo!*"

Then there were times when it seemed that Teo's demise would be premature and have nothing to do with drugs. In 2002, after a book-signing party in Hollywood, he drove back to where he was staying in Pasadena and suffered the misfortune of being a Good Samaritan in the wrong place at the wrong time. Having stopped to help a motorist stranded on the old Pasadena Freeway, Teo stepped between his car and the stalled automobile just as another vehicle rammed his car's rear end, crushing him between the two vehicles. He almost lost a leg, spent months in the hospital recovering, and almost half a year in a wheelchair. At the time, Teo was broke and jobless, living where he housed the valuable books he had inherited and which he would sell from time to time. The accident, though, had a silver lining: Teo received a sizable insurance settlement that gave him new life. He rented an apartment, bought a Mercedes Benz two-seater sports car, and reconnected with a writing partner with renewed confidence about his future.

Teo also used some of his insurance windfall to revisit Spain, trying to reconnect with the beloved land of his childhood. La Consula was still standing, but it had been turned into a high-end cooking school. Ernest Hemingway and his momentous 1959 stay there had taken on legendary status, with the story retold by Spaniards to tourists in the local bars. However, Teo found that few of the old residents in neighboring Churriana were still alive or living in the area. Like much of Spain, the southern part of the country had changed dramatically, and Teo spent his time meeting new acquaintances and traveling the countryside looking for a past no longer there.

"I felt like Hemingway must have when he returned to Spain after being away so many years," he told a friend. "Maybe Spain hadn't changed as much as we had."

When he returned to Los Angeles, it was with a renewed commitment. As he had numerous times in his three decades in Hollywood, Teo Davis vowed to beat his addictions and fulfill the promise many saw in him. And those pulling for Teo seemed legion in numbers: writers whose scripts he had read and critiqued; directors who had bounced ideas off his mind; young actors; the children of his parents' friends whom he had met and known in Europe; ex-girlfriends who had fond memories of him; and even, in a couple of instances, husbands obligated to him for having introduced them to their brides. However, the person perhaps pulling most for Teo's full recovery had to have been his sister, Nena. She also lived in Southern California, and it was she on whom the duty most often fell of salvaging Teo from skirmishes with the law, from his repeated returns to detox recovery centers, from drug dealers trying to collect money owed to them and threatening harm if they were not paid. Married and divorced with no children, Nena had dedicated herself to championing nonprofit organizations working to improve the lives of low-income Latinos in East Los Angeles. She also carried on the work of representing her parents' legacy at La Consula with the Hemingway Foundation and Society.

Sometimes it fell upon Nena to field calls from Teo's friends and acquaintances who had tracked her down when they worried that her brother was missing. Their calls to Teo's cell phone usually went unanswered, and it was impossible to leave word for him on a message box that was almost always full. Often Teo's disappearances were not so mysterious. He was off with his drug pals doing heroin or cocaine, or he was back in rehab. However, around 2010, Teo got word back to friends that he was living in Connecticut in a turn of events that had surprised even him. He had been in contact with his first love, Lady Diana, and the old romantic sparks reignited. Teo relocated to the East Coast, where he tried to make a go of it a second time with Diana—along with Diana's teenage daughters from her second marriage.

"There was a lot of promise there," Teo said, looking back on it later. "There was always a lot of promise. But we learned that there needs to be more."

By 2013, Teo was back in Southern California, but unfortunately in the same old circles that had always gotten him in trouble. The only bad habit he had moved on from was heroin. He was now doing crystal meth. I didn't know that when I received a call from Teo, whom I hadn't talked to in months and had not seen in over a year. We met for lunch a few days later, getting together at our favorite spot, the Musso & Frank Grill, Hollywood's oldest restaurant, which had once been the hangout of Raymond Chandler, William Faulkner, and F. Scott Fitzgerald, not to mention Greta Garbo, Humphrey Bogart, and Marilyn Monroe. Teo said he wanted to meet there because he thought he was ready to work on a project we had long talked about and that Musso & Frank would be the appropriate place to start over again. Teo, though, was in no condition to work. That much was obvious when he showed up with a guy he introduced as a new writing partner who knew little about writing, looked as strung out as Teo, and was likely just another drug connection. They ordered enough food for what seemed like a small party of people, left with boxes of leftovers, and stuck me with a much bigger tab than I'd anticipated.

"I'm a junky," Teo later told me. "I think it's harder for you to acknowledge than for me to admit."

Of course it was, just as it was difficult to think of Teo as a convict, a number in the California penal system. His once dream life had descended into a drama of destruction in dire need of redemption but with little promise of any. Instead, the little boy who had been bounced on Hemingway's lap in Spain had now reached what appeared to be a sad finality to his life that Bill and Annie Davis could never have imagined. Could it have been mere coincidence that the tragedy that would befall the Davises was not unlike the misfortune that struck Gerald and Sara Murphy, the Bill and Annie Davis of the 1920s' Lost Generation? The Murphys's charmed life had been abruptly extinguished in 1929 when their youngest son, Patrick, was diagnosed with tuberculosis. Mortified by the health scare, the Murphys closed their salon and changed their lavish lifestyle, dedicating themselves to their children. But in 1935, while Patrick was hospitalized in a Swiss sanitarium, the Murphys's elder son, Baoth, was stricken with meningitis and died. A year later, they lost their younger son as well. Their sorrow and mourning devastated them.

"Life itself has stepped in now and blundered, scarred and destroyed," Gerald Murphy wrote to F. Scott Fitzgerald. "In my heart I dreaded the moment when our youth and invention would be attacked in our only vulnerable spot—the children." Touched, Fitzgerald replied, "The golden bowl is broken indeed, but it was golden." Hemingway, who in *A Moveable Feast* called the Murphys rich "bastards," had been even less kind in an unpublished portion of the memoir, especially considering their generosity to him years earlier: "They were bad luck to people, but they were worse luck to themselves and they lived to have all that bad luck finally."

Who would have imagined that tragedy would strike the Davises' golden son as it had the Murphys' two boys? Or was this just life and how tough it can be for anyone and everyone?

Still, Teo was right. It was difficult to think of him as a junky not to be trusted. As I had done in the past, I left numerous phone messages for him at several locations over several months. Almost a year passed before I heard from him in March of 2014. I almost didn't recognize his voice, which was week and hoarse, as if he was at death's door. Almost immediately, he told me that he feared he was dying and hoped I would come to see him at a hospital near the Fairfax District of Los Angeles. I rushed over, though completely unprepared for how I would find him. Teo's arms and legs were covered with needle marks, and there were large wounds, three inches long and an inch wide, on each inner forearm that were uncovered so that they could drain. His distinctive friendly smile was also gone. I couldn't fully understand why at first. Then I saw why: the effects of crystal meth had rotted most of his teeth, leaving him looking like a gaunt, homeless man of eighty. He had been diagnosed with a bad heart condition, he said, and needed a pacemaker. But doctors had insisted they couldn't perform any surgical procedure while he remained addicted to crystal meth as well as to narcotic pain medications.

"As Hemingway once said, I'm afraid tales of my demise are exaggerated and premature," Teo said, attempting to alleviate my concern, which must have been obvious. With doctors unable to do any more for him at the time, Teo was moved the next day to a nursing facility in Pasadena where every patient seemed be to waiting to die. I cried after my first visit there, returning home so distraught that my wife insisted on going back with me the next day. From then on, she and I took turns visiting Teo, bringing him healthy blended juices, protein smoothies, and liquid supplements because he was having difficulty eating with his damaged teeth. A month later, the wounds on his arms almost fully healed and having regained some weight, Teo was able to celebrate his sixty-third birthday with a big chocolate cake he wasn't supposed to have and a bottle of wine.

"Of course, you realize," I said as we sipped the California Chablis, "that you've now outlived Hemingway."

"Some consolation," he said.

Teo didn't want to live that way, he said. He had little going for him, however. His only income was a small monthly stipend, and he was in no condition to sell the books he had stored in his small apartment. Teo also had little realistic understanding of his medical condition and of the effect of the addictions on his mental health as well. It was only then that I realized that his circle of loved ones who would visit him was limited to his sister, his old friend from his childhood Tracy Tynan, and myself—and there were limitations to what we could and would do for him. No one was willing to open their home to him for his recovery, and Teo was the first to understand the risk and gamble involved. Could anyone truly trust Teo alone in their home, his dark junky side, and whomever he might invite over? Who could blame them? At that moment, it was academic anyway, as Teo was in no condition to leave the nursing facility. At one point, I asked Nena about getting her brother some new professional mental health counseling, aside from what the nursing care facility provided, only to get an eye-opening response from the person who knew Teo and his medical history best of all.

"As regards a psychologist—you should know that many psychologists have tried to get Teo to change his ways, ALL have failed," she said in one of several e-mails. "Many, many things have been tried with Teo, none have worked. Up to you if you want to try again. Personally, I think it's just company Teo wants at this point. A friend visiting, someone to talk to. (Most of his friends have died, he doesn't have many left)."

In another e-mail, she wrote:

"As regards his treatment. Nursing home facilities are the only place left to him, and I agree with you, this one is better than most. . . . I tend not to take anything he says very seriously, so when he tells me he has deteriorated—well, he may or may not have, but there's not much anyone can do, really. Everything that can be done is being done for him."

When I told Nena that Teo was complaining daily about the food, she wrote:

"I expect he is having difficulty eating because he doesn't like the food they serve him. But it is the right food, the type of food he should be eating. It is part of the problem that when he is not in the hospital or the nursing home, he eats the wrong things (i.e., real coke, desserts, fatty meats, fried foods) and makes himself worse. On top of that, he refuses to take his diabetes medicine, and still continues to smoke unfiltered cigarettes. For someone with a heart condition, bad lungs, and diabetes, you can imagine, that kind of diet is not helpful. So this is part of the reason why Teo has ended up in a nursing facility in such bad shape. Not to mention the drugs, of course. That has the effect it has, as we all know. Nevertheless, I will talk to them about a liquid diet."

And finally, Nena felt she had to concede that she was at her wit's end in taking care of Teo:

"Also, truth to tell, I am not the best caretaker," she wrote.

I chose not to have children, I was married only briefly—my world and my life is about my work, not taking care of sick relatives, who on top of everything else, pretty much made choices that resulted in these current circumstances. I have had 40 years of cleaning up after Teo. I am just not too interested, beyond the basics of making sure he has shelter, food, and medicated care.

Sorry, Tony, but that's the truth. Feel free to do whatever you want, can, or are willing to do for Teo. We've all tried. I'm only still here because I am the final relative still alive and I have my own code of ethics—I won't abandon him, but I long ago ran out of love, interest, or care.

I am grateful for your efforts, though, and I thank you sincerely. I wish it wasn't this way for Teo. But what I know is that there's very little that can be done. Nevertheless, your visits, your time with him, that is a true gift you are giving him. Thank you.

Perhaps Nena can be excused her hard line with her brother, for it was not just the hardships of a brother's misfortune she had been struggling with throughout most of their adult lives but the life of a hopelessly addicted junky. What a wonderful little boy he may have been when they were growing up together at La Consula, and how hopeless it must have felt to see that after years of heroin addiction, jail, detox, and recovery houses, he likely would soon be back out on the streets. And now, finally and sadly, she had come to terms with the fact that she could not help him, that the only one who could help him was himself.

How could she be blamed when Nena also wasn't alone in her conclusion that Teo had not just reached the crossroads of where life ends but had gone past it. Their longtime friend Tracy Tynan had reconnected with Teo since his early days in Hollywood, having been responsible for him meeting screenwriter-director Walter Hill, whose encouragement had led him to study at the American Film Institute. Tynan was a costume designer married to the film director Jim McBride, and they would have seemed a perfect networking opportunity in an industry where success so often hinges on who you know. Teo, though, had been seduced by the polar opposite side of Tinseltown. As he immersed himself in the drug culture, he stopped calling her and never returned any of her countless phone calls, despite her pleas in the messages she left. It was not until 2014, while at the Pasadena Meadows nursing facility, that he asked a friend to call her.

"I don't know how long I have," said Teo, "and I would love to see her, or at least hear her voice. But don't tell her that I'm dying. I think she'll see that for herself."

"Saw Teo last week and yes he is in very bad shape," Tynan wrote me in a Facebook message soon afterward. "Very down and self-pitying. I think he wants someone to get him out of that place but I pointed out that in his current shape he could not live on his own. I suggested some kind [of] half-way/sober house but he seems unwilling to take any of the necessary steps. I will visit him again this week, and try and bring him something to read. All he seems to do is lie on his bed over-medicated and unmotivated. Sadly, and I know it's such a cliché but he is the only one that can help himself and maybe, after all these years this really is his rock bottom. Nonetheless I know he really appreciates your visits. I think he has pretty much alienated the rest of his friends and family."

In another message, Tynan added:

So many attempts have been made [to help Teo], so many stays in rehab, a lot of therapy and yet nothing seems to stick. I don't want to say that the situation is hopeless but it is pretty close. This time I think it really is up to him to pull himself out of this hole that he has put himself in. I think the spectre of death, and he certainly will die if he continues abusing his body the way he has, may be some sort [of] wake-up call but I honestly don't know. Sorry to be so negative but I don't want you to have expectations of Teo that he can't meet.

Rehabilitation and redemption, though they are the journey and recovery up from personal abyss, are often mistaken for one and the same. But they are not. Accomplishing the first doesn't necessarily bring the latter, for redemption is usually accompanied by atonement brought on by an epiphany, an illuminating realization of what is most important in life. For Teo Davis, who had failed miserably at almost every turn of rehabilitation, that discovery, late as it came, appeared to have been of life itself. It may have happened the summer of 2014, after months at the Pasadena Meadows Nursing Center, where his body had recovered from the infected wounds of drug use even if his addictions continued. It was July 2, fifty-three years to the date of Hemingway's suicide by a gunshot wound to the head in his home in Ketchum, Idaho. Hemingway would have been sixty-two years old July 21.

Teo appeared more introspective than usual as we talked about Hemingway and the Davis family while secretly indulging in a sausage and pepperoni pizza with a bottle of Pinot Noir that a nurse helped me sneak in. I had also brought Teo a photograph taken during the summer of 1959 of him and his sister with the Hemingways and the La Consula staff. He remembered the moment immediately, describing the part of the grounds where the photo had been taken and recalling the names of some of the servants.

"Has it occurred to me that I have outlived Hemingway?" Teo repeated a question I had posed. He had to sip more of the wine to savor that. "I am older than Hemingway was when he died. I supposed he had a lot of mileage, more than most men his age, and I suppose I do, too. But I don't believe that I, or many people, for that matter, have outlived Hemingway, though I guess I have tried. And in my own way, I've looked up the barrel of my own [imaginary] double-barreled, 12-gauge shotgun, and what was it Nietzsche said about gazing long into the abyss?"

"That the abyss will gaze back into you."

Teo didn't say much more about death that day, but I sensed a moment of discovery, a personal feeling of elation or awe over one small wonder.

In 2015, as even his loved ones had given up on him, Teo surprised many who knew him by making it out of the nursing care facility and attempting one more time to put his life together. His friend Tracy Tynan helped him get an automobile, since his Mercedes sports car had disappeared along with many of his rare books and the so-called pal who was looking after them. Teo found a place of his own, got together with a new writing partner who replaced his late friend Bess, who had died, and went back one more time to his small business of buying and selling rare books.

I had faith in him, misplaced perhaps, but I believed he had it in him to make something of his life. What exactly, I had no idea. We talked about this book, and that seemed to inspire him to think he could finally write that book he wanted to write—not about Hemingway so much but about how presumably Hemingway had led to the hookers and the heroin. The Lost Generation? I was looking at its child.

"I'm a junky," he told me.

"I know," I said, regretting that I had to admit that. "There are worse things."

"I don't know what they'd be," he said.

"Being a murderer," I said. "A child abuser. A woman beater. A politician."

Teo had tears in his eyes. So did I.

Then 2016 rolled around. It was another year and another birthday more than Hemingway ever celebrated at La Consula amid the fiestas, the bulls, the wine, the pretty young girls, or anywhere, for that matter.

We commiserated about the death of our agent friend Mike Hamilburg and planned to attend his memorial at Santa Monica Beach. A heavy rainstorm, however, stranded us on the Pasadena and Santa Monica freeways for hours that Saturday, and there was an even worse thunderstorm downpour when we finally reached the site of the memorial long after it had ended.

Teo had begun the New Year with a lung infection that wouldn't respond to medication, though the fact he continued to chain-smoke cigarettes didn't help. He was finally hospitalized briefly before returning to his makeshift apartment in the back of a restaurant in Pasadena, which he turned into something that resembled a small bookstore lined with thousands of books on shelves along the walls.

Meanwhile, I had come up with a game plan to help get Teo working at what he did best. A producer I had known at Universal years earlier called me to see if I could spitball a baseball murder mystery for a cable network movie. He knew I had written a biography of Mickey Mantle and another book about Mantle and Joe DiMaggio and wondered if I had a story to pitch. Did I ever. Except it involved vampires, I told him. I was making it up as I went along, but he loved it. Could I come in and pitch it formally? Of course, I said, telling him I'd come in with my partner—and that was what I proposed to Teo, who could pitch stories like a revival-tent preacher selling religion. The old Teo could anyway. The down-and-out Teo, though, thought it was a stretch. For crying out loud, *Phantom of the Opera* meets *Field of Dreams*, I insisted. Some 112-mile-an-hour fastball flamethrower from Budapest thrills the major leagues—and on nights when he pitches, a fan leaving the stadium is routinely brutally murdered, with all the blood sucked out of the body. *Vampires in the Ballpark.* Ah! It clicked in Teo's mind, and he went off on inventing a possible vampire teammate of the Budapest southpaw—a toothy Mexican shortstop who had been raised by *brujeros* at Casa Dracula, an ancient two-story, adobe-brick landmark in Todos Santos, a Baja California Sur town so strange that it was officially designated as a *Pueblo Mágico* by the Mexican government. Teo was finally into it, and we planned to get together to work on it.

"It's blood lust," he said, "and it's beneath us."

"I know," I said. "But so's bullfighting."

Then Teo told me the good news he said he had been holding back. He had met someone, he said, and he had fallen madly in love again.

It sounded promising until he went into the details.

"She's this beautiful Uber driver who drove me home from the doctor," he began. "She's the ex-girlfriend of the son of . . ."

He began dropping names of movie stars, carrying on with a far-fetched notion that smacked of the drugs talking.

"Teo," I interrupted, "an Uber driver can be the first baseball vampire victim."

That got him into the story pitch, as I guessed it would, and he spun a story that was especially brilliant given that he still knew little about baseball, or vampires, for that matter.

Of course, as was his habit, Teo disappeared. Over the coming days, he didn't answer his phone, and his message box was full. And, not surprisingly, he missed our March 1 meeting, at which I succeeded in getting us to second base and another pitch at which Teo could swing from his heels, as they say about the sluggers in baseball. I figured I'd hear from him sooner or later. I was wrong.

Two days later, I got the news via a text message.

Teo had died sometime on March 1.

"His heart gave out," Tracy Tynan later posted on her Facebook page. "He was a funny, smart, infuriating, unique guy. He will be greatly missed. As his friend, Walter Hill, put it, 'I am a better person for having known him.'"

Teo's death still hit his friends hard. I didn't sleep for a couple of nights, thinking back on his life and all that wasted talent.

"Your brother had a brilliant mind," I told his sister in a text message a few days later. "Somewhere something happened."

"What happened to Teo was Bill Davis and his cruelty," Nena replied. "From day one, our father ridiculed him and humiliated him."

I told her of the time Teo broke into tears upon hearing my wife and me tell our toddler son that we loved him as he left our presence to return to his bedroom and of Teo revealing to us that he couldn't remember his parents ever once letting him know that they loved him.

"They never did," she wrote back. "Not to me either. They weren't parents, more like rival older siblings. That's what made Teo and I bond so closely. We had each other, and that was it. We never told stories or ratted each other out. We had each other's backs, always. But Teo bore the brunt of the cruelty, being the oldest and the boy."

It left an unexpected sadness the rest of the night, reassessing my late friend's childhood from the one of privilege and comfort I had always assumed he had had. Was that a symptom we didn't know about the rich? Was that one of the ways in which they were different? Was the road to riches and social status paved differently in how we love our children? Were they like incredible homes, expensive cars, beautiful clothes, lavish tastes, and famous friends? Little more than tokens of what extravagant wealth can buy?

"I've been looking for Hemingway for so long," Teo once said, though at the time it didn't seem like the mantra of his life. "For a sense of who he really was, that at times, I feel as if I've almost become Hemingway. Does that make sense?"

To the generations who have come after Hemingway, of course it does. Teo, though, feared he might never find him, and he was haunted by the elusive, self-created image of someone who had taken his place in his parents' hearts. With his self-destructive, wild life, Teo had seemingly abandoned his own dreams for an ill-conceived pursuit of that illusion, as if it were any more real than the great love symbolized by the green light on the dock that Jay Gatsby had stared at nightly. Sadly, like Gatsby Teo also didn't realize that what he was chasing was long behind him, buried in the past.

"Every man's life ends the same way," Ernest Hemingway once said, "and it is only the details of how he lived and how he died that distinguish one man from another."

Author's Note and Acknowledgments

"As you get older it is harder to have heroes, but it is sort of necessary."
—Ernest Hemingway

As a child of the 1950s who read *The Old Man and the Sea* thinking I was the boy Manolin, I suppose I have been looking for Hemingway all my life, and perhaps it is fitting that I think I have found him at an age when I now see myself in the old man Santiago.

Looking for Hemingway: Spain, the Bullfights, and a Final Rite of Passage is about Hemingway long past that time of the youth and romance of Paris in the 1920s and his first visits to Spain, when he discovered the bulls and wrote the novel that made him Hemingway, as author Lesley M. M. Blume put it in her recent book *Everybody Behaves Badly: The True Story Behind Hemingway's Masterpiece* The Sun Also Rises. It is also about Hemingway at an age that is not an easy time for most people to face, apparently publishers especially. More than a few just flat out said they didn't think any readers, especially Hemingway fans, wanted to read about him as an old man, pathetic at times, feeble, and paranoid.

Being a lifelong Hemingway lover, I found that hard to believe, unless it's simply old age some of us don't want to face, whether Hemingway's or our own. For those who fear this life stage, I can only say that I found it inspiring in the research to learn that Pablo Picasso in his sixties was having affairs with gorgeous, youthful women more than forty years younger—young enough to be his granddaughters. A dirty old man? Maybe not so dirty if you're Picasso.

Today, the aging, dying Hemingway is one I have come to love and appreciate as much as the young, romantic Hemingway, for in his mortality lie the same fears, regrets, and self-recriminations that all of us face in our own way as we reach that stage in our lives.

My lifelong fascination with Ernest Hemingway had its genesis in my youth when an English teacher who had taken a special interest in my insatiable appetite for reading introduced me to *The Old Man and the Sea*. I quickly found myself devouring that book, and in rapid succession dispatched every Hemingway short story and novel that I could find, along with almost every book at my hometown public library in Waco, Texas. The obsession with Hemingway eventually led to an unauthorized visit to Cuba in the 1960s along with a group of Chicano movement activists and members of the Students for a Democratic Society. The revolutionary romance of Fidel Castro's Cuba had made it a popular destination for the New Left, but I was hardly the political sort. I was an undergraduate at Baylor University, a conservative Baptist college in the heart of the South's Bible Belt, and through a Latin American studies professor at the University of Texas made the connection of a lifetime. The professor had known Fidel Castro in Mexico in the 1950s, and he arranged for me a special tour of La Finca Vigía, the Hemingway home in San Francisco de Paula, Cuba.

I was a romantic with a destiny of which I wasn't even aware. A few years after college, I moved into a writer friend's house in Houston, which had an unexpected connection to Hemingway. Was it simply an incredible coincidence that my friend's previous housemate had been Teo Davis, the son of the wealthy American expatriates who had hosted Hemingway in his last two visits to Spain before his suicide?

A couple of years later, while on a Nieman Fellowship at Harvard, I shared this story with the two professors with whom I was studying literature—the Mexican writer and future Nobel laureate Octavio Paz and Homeric scholar Robert Fitzgerald. Both urged me to also spend time during my fellowship studying the newly opened collection of Hemingway papers at the John F. Kennedy Presidential Library. Both Paz and Fitzgerald joined me the first time I visited the collection. Fitzgerald bailed on us afterward, but Paz and I closed down the Faculty Club at Harvard that night, toasting Hemingway with shots of tequila.

A decade or so later, in yet one more twist of coincidence, I finally met Teo Davis in Los Angeles, where we began a friendship that spanned three decades. It was Teo who introduced me to Mike Hamilburg, a literary agent who represented me until his illness and death. Mike had known Teo for several years, and he tried for well over twenty years to convince Teo to write a book about his experience as a child with Ernest Hemingway when he had stayed at La Consula in 1959. Mike said he didn't think Teo had ever written a single word, and if he did I never read a word of it either. Teo didn't want to write that book or couldn't. Finally, after years of trying to coax the story out of him, I gave up. It was then that Teo, somewhat relieved that I was going to stop pestering him about his story, said that I should write the story and that he would help as best he could.

This book, though, isn't the book Mike had envisioned Teo writing, nor is it the book I tried to get him to write. That book Teo took with him to the grave.

For me, there has always been in the story of Hemingway and Spain an allure so sharp and fresh that there was never any question of writing this book. There has been, from the start, the joy of rediscovering the world in which he walked and traveled, both in the 1920s and again in 1959. Here was a canvas as generous, colorful, and grand as any in Hemingway's life. As the story pushed forth, there was at every turn the excitement of history never told, of connections hidden for decades, of old mysteries answered. The story of Hemingway the icon was well known. The story of Hemingway the man and his friendship with Bill and Annie Davis at their magnificent home had been buried. Getting that story was slow work. After a good while, I felt I had become the crypt of *Hemingwayolé en La Consula*. As my patient wife used to say (but seldom aloud—for which I thank her) about this project, great effort went in but nothing came out until now.

I am thankful to my publishers for their extension of time, especially after Teo's death and then losing twenty-five hundred words of a revision in a computer glitch. For that generosity and for the chance to try my hand at this project, I have to thank first and foremost the late Mike Hamilburg, godfather to *Looking for Hemingway*, friend, and former agent, who helped in conceiving the book he suggested that I write—as different from the one he wanted Teo to write—and then having the patience and time to assist in its development. His passing on New Year's

Day 2016 weighs heavily and will be felt for years to come by those of us who loved him. My new agent and friend Leticia Gomez of Savvy Literary was instrumental in finding a home for the book at Lyons Press, and I am grateful to her for this and all her caring work on my behalf. I also wish to thank my diligent editor at Lyons Press, Keith Wallman, who fortunately understood the making of this book better than I did; and to everyone else at Lyons Press involved in the publication, especially Julia Loy for her dedicated copyediting and editing suggestions.

I was blessed to have the help on this book of four individuals, who were pivotal.

Renee LaSalle, my wife, has been supportive on all my books, though never to the degree she has assisted me in *Looking for Hemingway*. She knew Mike and Mike's wish that I undertake this project as a book with a broader scope than that of a young child's remembrance. Mike envisioned it as a biography of Ernest Hemingway from the perspective of his life near its end, and Renee convinced me that I could write the book no matter how long it took. Often we sat up long hours into the night and the following morning talking about Hemingway's life and work and breaking it down so as to fit it properly in a setting surrounding the summer of 1959 in Spain.

Our sons, Trey and Ryan, have always had their old man's back, and they were instrumental in helping shape the manuscript through a couple of revisions that involved the massive reshuffling of chapters to help in telling the story, perhaps in a less linear fashion but as a better narrative.

My black Labrador, Jeter, a muse every bit as inspiring as his Yankee namesake, was awakened too many times from his well-deserved naps by my reading aloud anecdotes and dialogue that needed some verbal laundering. His acute hearing sensibility continues to astonish.

Looking for Hemingway: Spain, the Bullfights, and a Final Rite of Passage would not have been possible without the assistance of many other individuals, but some bear special mention.

Teo Davis was an invaluable friend for almost half our lifetimes, and his unselfishness in sharing memories of his childhood in Spain, particularly of Ernest Hemingway's visit, vastly enriched this book's treatment of that time at La Consula. I am immensely grateful to Teo for trusting me with memories so close to him and for welcoming me into his history. Teo's sister, Nena, kindly shared her thoughts about her brother and their family. I appreciate her thoughtfulness and understand how painfully difficult those recollections may have been. She was both sister and parent to Teo, always at his side, and was his protector and primary health provider. Teo knew that and loved her dearly. "The one person I wish I'd not disappointed," he told me in one conversation, "is my sister."

I am eternally fortunate to have had friends and acquaintances in Houston in the 1970s who knew Teo while he worked at the *Houston Chronicle* and lived there in the broken-down old ranch-style house in Rivers Oaks with Peter Heyne, who kindly rented me Teo's former bedroom after he moved on. Peter also was gracious in talking to me so candidly about Teo, who had the talent of always making a memorably lasting impression on anyone who met him.

James Bacon, the longtime Hollywood insider and my former desk mate at the *Los Angeles Herald Examiner*, was an inspiring mentor with his friendship and countless stories about stars and celebrities from Frank Sinatra to Marilyn Monroe, not to mention his whiskey and his introduction to numerous contacts, among them Lauren Bacall and Orson Welles, who helped me in researching this book. Jim also introduced me, the new kid in town at the time, to the Polo Lounge and the since-gone Rangoon Racquet Club in Beverly Hills, where Orson and others who had known Ernest Hemingway added to my understanding of the man.

Lauren Bacall opened the doors of her New York apartment because of Jim and graciously shared her experiences with Ernest Hemingway and Luis Miguel Dominguín, as well as her remembrances of Spain in 1959.

As always, I am especially indebted to my late parents: my mother, Maria Emma, for always encouraging my interest in heroes in general and Mickey Mantle and Ernest Hemingway in particular; my father, Antonio Sr., for sparking my love of history as a youth and spending countless hours over the years talking about Spain and bullfighting.

Special thanks to these individuals for their support or assistance in tangible and intangible ways: Marty Appel, Jim Bacon, Allie Baker, Sallie Baker, Diana and Domingo Balderas, Simon Barzalay, Cameron

Bebehani, Jim Bellows, Keven Bellows, Eli Broad, Tony Brooklier, Jerry Brown, George W. Bush, Roger Butler, Frank and Lucy Casado, Patricia Casado, Ruben Castañeda, Laura Chester, Barbara Cigarroa, John B. Connally, Alfredo Corchado, Warren Cowan, Francis Dale, Tina Daunt, Nena Davis, Teo Davis, Arturo de la Riva, Mary Anne Dolan, James and Nancy Duarte, Mel Durslag, Robert Evans, Blanca and Armando Fajardo, Alexander Fiske-Harrison, Robert Fitzgerald, Don Forst, David Frost, Carlos Fuentes, Paul Gelb, Mikal Gilmore, Rudolph Giuliani, Carole Player Golden, Peter Golenbock, Caroline Cushing Graham, Johnny Grant, Kathy Griffin, Carlos Guerra, Mary Frances Gurton, Mike Hamilburg, Thomas Harris, Grant Hayes, Inez Balderas Hayes, Isabel Hayes, Carol Hemingway, Jack Hemingway, Margaux Hemingway, Jeffrey Herlihy-Mera, Walter Hill, Joe Holley, Ken Holley, Alex Jacinto, Christina Kahrl, Ron Kaye, Sally Kirkland, Liudmila Konovalova, Deborah Larcom, Ring Lardner Jr., Daniel Lastra, Tim Layana, Timothy Leary, Carole Lieberman, Ken Locker, Skip E. Lowe, Larry Lynch, Professor Ralph Lynn, Barbara McBride-Smith, Julie McCullough, David McHam, Maxine Messinger, Lidia Montemayor, Dave and Linda Montgomery, Jim Montgomery, Alice Montoya, Dennis Mukai, Marcus Musante, Edward James Olmos, Francisco Rivera Ordoñez, Bill Orozco, Reggie and Kim Caldwell Park, Teddy Jo Paulson Overley, Octavio Paz, Professor Thomas Pettigrew, John Robert Pharr, George Pla, George Plimpton, Thomas Ranco, Ignacio Redondo, Gregory Rodriguez, Emilio Sanchez, Dutch Schroeder, Vin Scully, Modesta Garcia Segovia, Gail Sheehy, Charlie Sheen, Jason Silva, Marty Singer, Ben Sonnenberg, Stephanie Sowa, Ben Stein, Oliver Stone, Sallie Taggart, Randy Taraborrelli, John Tuthill, Tracy Tynan, Chase Untermeyer, Keith Urban, Debby Veracruz, Antonio Villaraigosa, Sander Vanocur, John Vasek, Robert Vickrey, Judy Wammack Rice, Don Wanlass, Tommy West, and Tom Wolfe.

My appreciation to the entire staff of the Ernest Hemingway Collection at the John F. Kennedy Presidential Library and Museum in Boston, Massachusetts, for their cooperation on so many levels; to the Hemingway Museum at Finca Vigía in San Francisco de Paula, Cuba; to the Hemingway Collection at the University of Virginia; and to the Hemingway museums in Key West, Florida, and Oak Park, Illinois. I also wish to thank the Nieman and Guggenheim Foundations for their support, as well as the library staffs at Harvard and Princeton Universities.

I should also thank the staffs of the National Archives and Records Services; the Library of Congress; the Federal Bureau of Investigation records office in Washington, DC; and the Centro de Estudios Sobre America in Havana.

Gratitude, too, to the libraries of *Time*, the *New York Times*, the *Washington Post*, the *New Yorker*, the Associated Press, the *Los Angeles Times*, the *New York Post*, the *New York Daily News*, *Newsday*, the *Boston Globe*, the *Dallas Morning News*, the *Houston Chronicle*, the *Detroit Free Press*, the *Kansas City Star*, the *Oklahoman*, and the *Houston Chronicle*; CBS Archives; the reference departments at the New York Public Library, the Beverly Hills Public Library, the Santa Monica Public Library, the Dallas Public Library, the Library of Congress, the Hemingway Project, and the Hemingway Society.

Tony Castro

Appendix I: Hemingway's Nobel Prize Speech

As the laureate was unable to be present at the Nobel Banquet at the City Hall in Stockholm, December 10, 1954, the speech was read by John C. Cabot, U.S. ambassador to Sweden.

No writer who knows the great writers who did not receive the Prize can accept it other than with humility. There is no need to list these writers. Everyone here may make his own list according to his knowledge and his conscience.

It would be impossible for me to ask the Ambassador of my country to read a speech in which a writer said all of the things which are in his heart. Things may not be immediately discernible in what a man writes, and in this sometimes he is fortunate; but eventually they are quite clear and by these and the degree of alchemy that he possesses he will endure or be forgotten.

Writing, at its best, is a lonely life. Organizations for writers palliate the writer's loneliness but I doubt if they improve his writing. He grows in public stature as he sheds his loneliness and often his work deteriorates. For he does his work alone and if he is a good enough writer he must face eternity, or the lack of it, each day.

For a true writer each book should be a new beginning where he tries again for something that is beyond attainment. He should always try for something that has never been done or that others have tried and failed. Then sometimes, with great luck, he will succeed.

How simple the writing of literature would be if it were only necessary to write in another way what has been well written. It is because we have had such great writers in the past that a writer is driven far out past where he can go, out to where no one can help him.

I have spoken too long for a writer. A writer should write what he has to say and not speak it. Again I thank you.

Appendix II: Time Line of Hemingway in Spain

1921   At the end of the year, on his way to Paris to be a correspondent, he makes his first stop in Spain, at the port of Vigo, but for only four hours.

1923   His first visit to Pamplona for San Fermín; visits Ronda.

1924   Spends July in Spain watching bullfights; it was on this particular trip that he was inspired to write the novel *The Sun Also Rises*; he and his wife Hadley also visited the town Burguete in the Pyrenees.

1925   Spends July in Spain watching bullfights; he and Hadley visit Madrid, Valencia, and San Sebastian; following the trip, Hemingway starts writing *The Sun Also Rises*.

1926   Spends July in Spain watching bullfights.

1927   Spends the summer in Spain with his new wife Pauline; they visit Galicia and in particular Santiago de Compostela.

1929   Spends July in Spain watching bullfights.

1930   Spends the summer in Spain watching more bullfights, including Pamplona's *corrida*, while working on his book *Death in the Afternoon*.

1931   From May through August, he passes the summer in Spain, curious about the newly proclaimed Second Republic; arrives in Vigo; watches more bullfights in Pamplona; continues to write his book *Death in the Afternoon*; visits Ávila.

1933   In August, he travels to Spain with wife Pauline and two sons to see the bullfights in Extremadura.

1937–   Was a wartime news correspondent for Collier's, covering the
1938   civil war from March 1937 to May 1938 and stationed out of
        Madrid. He would also help with the production of the propa-
        ganda film *Tierra de España* (1937) and become involved with
        the International Brigade, fighting on behalf of the Republican
        forces. Hemingway also met future wife Martha Gellhorn dur-
        ing this period.

1953   Invited back to Spain to see Pamplona's San Fermín festivities
        in July.

1954   Watches the San Isidro bullfights in Madrid in May and June.

1956   Visited Spain in September and October: watched more bull-
        fights; visited El Escorial and went to friend Pío Baroja's funeral
        in San Sebastian.

1959   Went to Spain in July to document the *mano a mano* between
        Luis Miguel Dominguín and Antonio Ordoñez for *Life* maga-
        zine and stayed with his friends, Bill and Anne Davis, at their
        villa, La Consula, in Málaga.

1960   Vacationed in Spain: Pamplona's San Fermín Festival; and again
        Málaga.

Compiled by blogger *Not Hemingway's Spain*.

Appendix III:
Selected Letters from
Ernest Hemingway to Bill Davis

Finca Vigía, San Francisco de Paula, Cuba

March 31, 1942

Dear Emily and Bill:

We had a wonderful time with you guys. Marty [Martha Gellhorn] says she wrote you all the news. Our cat Pony is no better. Why couldn't Arty get sick instead of Pony? Also they let my quail die and the pigeons got badly flooded with that cloudburst we came in on. Hope it all takes the curse off something else.

We have never had any more fun than with you both nor ever liked anybody more.

Will try to get some pictures of the pictures to send you to make sure to have something to lure you down here. We look forward to you coming as big thing of this summer.

Love to Don Cayetano
Hemingstein

You might let our friends know from time to time that I am proceeding leisurely through the various Mexican states working on that book The Farewell to Arms Boys Take Telespalteper.

On board the French Line ship Liberté *en route to New York*

28 October 1959

Dear Negro,

It's very rough. Everything and the western ocean. Forceful and beautiful. Full gale. Never missed people so much—not ever—actually was always rather relieved to leave people—not any more—feel the way I've seen but couldn't really know about, when their twin brothers were killed. Miss you and Annie too much. But shit we are a too much outfit.

Thank you for all the things and for May, June, July, August, September and October through the 27th and for finally deciding to pass that truck . . .

Much love,
Ernest

From Ketchum, Idaho, 7 January 1960

Dear Negro:

Hope you and Annie had good holidays and Teo has a good school and likes it.

We were to leave here day after tomorrow but Mary's arm needs some more whirlpool bath and manipulation and leaving has been put off one week to 16th. I will go on to Cuba from Chicago but Mary wants to stop to see her cousin [Beatrice Guck] there 2 days. She will be at the Finca by or before the 25th.

Her arm is coming along OK. The piece about the size of a walnut (English) that was broken off the end of the humerus and was sewed back on seems solid now. She is getting better movement in the joint each day—lateral as well as up and down and under anaesthesia they bent it all the way up. There is one place that is not right and George has sent some special films off for consultation and opinion. But it is so much better than anyone expected it would be and with patience and fortitude she will have a useful arm with which she can both shoot and fish as well as write, use typewriter etc. But it has been very rough although any place else it would have been rougher. She could not have had better people to work on it, nor better facilities and I have been able to devote myself full time to her care, comfort etc. Will not molest you with details nor timetables. Shortly we'll be back in Cuba where there are servants trained to see these various duties and can get back to work.

Wanted to phone you at Christmas but we had a big storm with all wires out for 3 days. Since have had -20 degree -25 degree weather. But very beautiful. I try and walk enough to keep in shape and have held weight down to 202–203. Had some fair shooting for a while but the hours have been bad for it lately. Days very short and the mornings taken up with the hospital and errands. Been making up by really working with the hand trap—beautiful place to throw here with a grove of cottonwoods, the [Big Wood] river, and some fine willow thickets and have a shot at a few thousand targets and made some good runs several 50 straights—a 98, a 103–105 etc. George throws very well as do a couple of other friends here. Hotch shot well on targets but disastrously in the field on his last day and felt very badly. I felt worse as I thought he had really learned to shoot. But the hell of it was that he had learned to shoot targets that were falling and the damn ducks just towered. Haven't heard from him since he went to N.Y. from the coast for Christmas. May have been on acct. of the wires being down.

I wrote Val [Valerie Danby-Smith] the gen on getting to Cuba and our plans and when they were delayed day before yest cabled her we would be there absolutely by the 25th.

She needs a tourist visa for U.S. Needs a ticket to Havana and return Havana to Miami or Key West or N.Y. to be given Tourist card and Tourist Entry for and to Cuba.

Will get this off to you now on way to Hospital and find your other letters and send check for Pembroke coral. Please let me know other expenses.

Best love to you both.
Ernest

Finca Vigía, San Francisco de Paula, Cuba

May 9, 1960

Dear Negro, Thank you very much for doing such a wonderful job . . . Annamarie's letter finally came through & you were right that she does not know when she is well off. I cannot give her exact publication dates nor give her "some clarity as to her working program for the next few years" having just this morning before breakfast gone over 92,000 words on something that I hoped would not exceed 18,000 when I started it with still at least 15 days of steady work to go. I had to postpone the Paris Book from this fall. But you have to do one damned thing at a time. I see nothing to do about AMHH at the present time except to send her a letter which you . . . agree is fair. She certainly should not be allowed to weasel in on the TV deal. It was impossible for me to contract with Rowhowlt to write the book since over 60,000 words of it was written before he made the offer. It would be nice to have that money tax free not unless you can clearly show that you contracted to write it before you started it it would not hold up in court & I would have to pay it all back sooner or later. Another angle is that if Rowhowlt published it before Scribners did I could lose the American Copyright after the impression that you & I both have gained from seeing [him]. I would prefer not to have him advance me any money on anything where there are possible angles. For years I have never taken advances ever from people that I trusted. Then I took this advance from Life & it has been nothing but a headache. If I had not taken the advance I could have stopped the work at a certain date. Taken up the going over & rewrite on the Paris book, had it in shape for Scribners & then returned to the bullfight thing & finished it off. But my head was forced by having to produce that cash to pay out Rice's mistake. Now I have fought my way out of that into the clear & we have the Idaho place which is completely paid for & is worth at least 3 times what it cost. My cash position is OK & am building up a good tax reserve. So I think it would be a bad play to take an advance now which the Revenue Department at any time in the future might consider taxable & so hit you again with a heavy unexpected levy. If I

get short of cash at any time we can take an advance on the Paris book
. . . Going back to AMHH; what sort of contract does she have anyway?
Am I committed to translating future books? If not I should be in a
position to tell her she must accept an adjustment . . . From her letters
it seems as though they were reaching such a adjustment but that she is
being extremely difficult, is that the way you see it? . . . You worked so
damned hard on it & I am very grateful & hate for you to have had to
deal with people who were so unpleasant. Should have written all this
sooner but when Val told me that you were staying in London through
May I did not bite down on it since I was jamming every day until I was
too pooped when I finished work . . . to write a letter. AMHH's letter
showed that it was something that would drag on indefinitely between
her & R & she made me sore asking for definite dates before she would
lower her overblown percentages when she knew damned well I could
not furnish them. The only definite dates are with a paper & pen every
morning. Negro after all this work that you have done I hate to ask you
to do anything else but have some things written down that I have to
get to ask if you can help me out on them. Can you get me an account
of the Cuenca fight. All I remember is the terrible state of the piso and
how dangerous it was and that Pepe Casares would not deal with his
bulls and that Chicuelo II & Antonio could, due to greater experience,
etc. Any account of the fight brings the details back to me. But preoc-
cupation with the dangerous ring drives the rest of it out of my head. I
also need accounts in the local papers of the two fights in Muncia. I have
written them both, well I think, but I might be wrong in remembering
whether Antonio did the truco of kneeling in front of the bull & throwing away the minleta & the sword in the first or the second fight . . . do
you remember too what was done exactly about the picador's at Cuenca,
Villara . . . & Ronda? Juanito Quintana has looked up several of the
fights for me but I can't get a hold of him right now as he went down to
Andalucia. Have handled the picador business OK so far & have only
one more fight to write the Ronda one. It is a hell of a difficult book to
write, Negro because of the way [it] ended & the moral angle & what
transcends it is the only frame it goes on. But since I still have to keep on
writing about it better not tell about it. Sometimes it goes wonderfully

& the summer was well worth trying to make something permanent out of for Antonio & for us guys too. Have been having some trouble with my eyes the last two weeks. There is a good man here but he is away at the moment & I do not want to get mixed up with anybody else. It could very well be fatigue, or writing in a tricky light. Have had them bother at other times but never for quite as long as this. Otherwise everything fine here. Mary's arm much better steadily. Val has caught 2 good white marlin & is handling rod very well . . . Sorry this letter is all business & begging . . .

Ernest

BIBLIOGRAPHY

Arnold, Lloyd. *High on the Wild with Hemingway*. Caldwell, ID: Caxton Press, 1968.

Bacall, Lauren. *Lauren Bacall by Myself*. New York: Knopf, 1978.

Baker, Carlos. *Ernest Hemingway: A Life Story*. New York: Charles Scribner's Sons, 1969.

———, ed. *Ernest Hemingway: Selected Letters*. New York: Charles Scribner's Sons, 1982.

———. *Hemingway: The Writer as Artist*. Princeton, NJ: Princeton University Press, 1952.

———, ed. *Hemingway and His Critics*. New York: Hill and Wang, 1961.

Bald, Wambly. *On the Left Bank*. Edited by Benjamin Franklin V. Athens: Ohio University Press, 1987.

Beevor, Antony. *The Spanish Civil War*. New York: Peter Bedrick Books, 1983.

Benson, Jackson J., ed. *The Short Stories of Ernest Hemingway*. Durham, NC: Duke University Press, 1975.

Berg, A. Scott. *Max Perkins: Editor of Genius*. New York: Simon and Schuster, 1978.

Blume, Lesley M. M. *Everybody Behaves Badly: The True Story Behind Hemingway's Masterpiece* The Sun Also Rises. Boston and New York: Eamon Dolan Book/Houghton Mifflin Harcourt, 2016.

Botsford, Keith. *Dominguin: Spain's Greatest Bullfighter*. New York: Quadrangle Books, 1972.

Brenan, Gerald. *A Life of One's Own: Childhood and Youth*. London: CUP Archive, 1979.

———. *The Spanish Labyrinth*. Cambridge: Cambridge University Press, 1943.

Bruccoli, Matthew J. *Scott and Ernest*. Carbondale: Southern Illinois University Press, 1978.

Bruccoli, Matthew J., and C. E. Frazer Clark. *Fitzgerald/Hemingway Annual, 1973*. Washington, DC: Microcard Editions, 1974.

Buckley, Peter. *Ernest*. New York: Dial Press, 1978.

Castillo-Puche, Jose Luis. *Hemingway in Spain*. New York: Doubleday, 1974.

Conrad, Barnaby. *The Death of Manolete*. Essex, VT: Phoenix Books, 2007.

Cowley, Malcolm. *Exile's Return*. New York: Viking Press, 1969.

Donaldson, Scott. *By Force of Will: The Life and Art of Ernest Hemingway*. New York: Penguin Books, 1978.

Donnelly, Honoria Murphy, with Richard N. Billings. *Sara & Gerald*. New York: Times Books, 1982.

Dundy, Elaine. *Life Itself!* New York: Little, Brown Book Group, 2012.

Fiske-Harrison, Alexander. *Into the Arena: The World of the Spanish Bullfight*. London: Profile Books, 2011.

Fitch, Noel Riley. *Sylvia Beach and the Lost Generation*. London: Souvenir Press, 1983.

Fitzgerald, F. Scott. *Correspondence of F. Scott Fitzgerald*. Edited by Matthew J. Bruccoli and Margaret N. Duggan. New York: Random House, 1980.

Fuentes, Norberto. *Hemingway in Cuba*. Secaucus, NJ: Lyle Stuart, 1984.

Gardner, Ava. *Ava: My Story*. New York: Bantam, 1992.

Gardner, Ava, and Peter Evans. *Ava Gardner: The Secret Conversations*. London: Simon and Schuster, 2013.

Gathorne-Hardy, Jonathan. *Half an Arch: A Memoir*. London: Timewell Press, 2004.

———. *Gerald Brenan: The Interior Castle: A Biography*. London: Faber and Faber, 2014.

Greenberg, Clement. *The Harold Letters 1928–1943: The Making of an American Intellectual*. Berkeley, CA: Counterpoint Press, 2000.

Haynes, John Earl, and Alexander Vassiliev. *Spies: The Rise and Fall of the KGB in America*. Ann Arbor: Sheridan Books, 2009.

Hawkins. Ruth. *Unbelievable Happiness and Final Sorrow: The Hemingway-Pfeiffer Marriage*. Fayetteville: University of Arkansas Press, 2012.

Hemingway, Ernest. *Across the River and Into the Trees*. New York: Charles Scribner's Sons, 1950.

———. *By-Line: Ernest Hemingway*. New York: Charles Scribner's Sons, 1967.

———. *The Complete Short Stories of Ernest Hemingway*. New York: Charles Scribner's Sons, 1987.

———. *Conversations with Ernest Hemingway*. Edited by Matthew J. Bruccoli. Jackson: University of Mississippi Press, 1986.

———. *The Dangerous Summer*. New York: Charles Scribner's Sons, 1985.

———. *Death in the Afternoon*. New York: Charles Scribner's Sons, 1932.

———. *Ernest Hemingway on Writing*. New York: Charles Scribner's Sons, 1984.

———. *A Farewell to Arms*. New York: Charles Scribner's Sons, 1929.

———. *The Garden of Eden*. New York: Charles Scribner's Sons, 1986.

———. *Green Hills of Africa*. New York: Charles Scribner's Sons, 1935.

———. *Islands in the Stream*. New York: Charles Scribner's Sons, 1970.

———. *A Moveable Feast*. New York: Charles Scribner's Sons, 1964.

———. *The Nick Adams Stories*. New York: Charles Scribner's Sons, 1972.

———. *The Old Man and the Sea*. New York: Charles Scribner's Sons, 1952.

———. *The Short Stories of Ernest Hemingway*. New York: Modern Library, 1938.

———. *The Sun Also Rises*. New York: Charles Scribner's Sons, 1926.

———. *To Have and Have Not*. New York: P. F. Collier and Son, 1937.

———. *The Torrents of Spring*. New York: Charles Scribner's Sons, 1972.

Hemingway, Gregory H. *Papa: A Personal Memoir*. Boston: Houghton Mifflin, 1976.

Hemingway, Jack. *Misadventures of a Fly Fisherman*. Dallas: Taylor Publishing, 1986.

Hemingway, Leicester. *My Brother, Ernest Hemingway*. Cleveland, OH: World, 1962.

Hemingway, Mary Welsh. *How It Was*. New York: Knopf, 1951.

Hemingway, Valerie. *Running with the Bulls: My Years with the Hemingways*. New York: Random House, 2007.

Hendrickson, Paul. *Hemingway's Boat: Everything He Loved in Life, and Lost*. New York: Vintage, 2012.

Hotchner, A. E. *Papa Hemingway*. New York: Random House, 1966.

Ivancich, Adriana. *Torre Bianca*. Milan, Italy: Il Saggiatore, 1980.

Joost, Nicholas. *Ernest Hemingway and the Little Magazines: The Paris Years*. Barre, MA: Barre Publishers, 1968.

Keith, Slim. *Slim: Memories of a Rich and Imperfect Life*. New York: Simon and Schuster, 1990.

Kennedy, J. Gerald, and Jackson R. Bryer. *French Connections: Hemingway and Fitzgerald Abroad*. London: Palgrave Macmillan, 1999.

Keough, Terence. *My Green Age*. Bloomington, IN: Trafford Publishing, 2009.

Kert, Bernice. *The Hemingway Women*. New York: W. W. Norton, 1983.

Klimo, Vernon (Jake), and Will Oursler. *Hemingway and Jake*. New York: Doubleday, 1972.

Laprade, Douglas Edward. *Hemingway & Franco*. Madrid: Universitat de València, 2011.

Lewine, Edward. *Death and the Sun: A Matador's Season in the Heart of Spain*. Orlando, FL: Mariner Books, 2007.

Lewis, Jeremy. *Cyril Connolly: A Life*. New York: Random House, 2012.

Lynn, Kenneth S. *Hemingway*. New York: Simon and Schuster, 1987.

Luard, Elizabeth. *My Life as a Wife: Love, Liquor and What to Do about Other Women*. London: Timewell Press 2008.

McCaffery, John K. M., ed. *Hemingway: The Man and His Work*. New York: Cooper Square Publishers, 1969.

McLendon, James. *Papa*. New York: Popular Books, 1972.

Mellow, James R. *Hemingway: A Life Without Consequences*. New York: Da Capo Press, 1993.

Meyers, Jeffrey. *Hemingway: A Biography*. New York: Harper and Row, 1985.

Miller, Madelaine Hemingway. *Ernie: Hemingway's Sister Sunny Remembers*. New York: Crown Publishers, 1975.

Moorehead, Caroline. *Martha Gellhorn: A Life*. New York: Random House, 2011.

Nagel, James. *Critical Essays on Ernest Hemingway's* The Sun Also Rises. New York: Twayne Publishers, 1995.

———, ed. *Ernest Hemingway: The Writer in Context*. Madison: University of Wisconsin Press, 1984.

Nagel, James, and Henry Serrano Villard. *Hemingway in Love and War: The Lost Diary of Agnes Von Kurowsky*. New York: Hyperion, 1996.

Picasso, Pablo, Georges Boudaille, and Luis Miguel Dominguín. *Toros y Toreros*. Ann Arbor: University of Michigan Press, 2011.

Raeburn, John. *Fame Became of Him: Hemingway as Public Writer*. Bloomington: Indiana University Press, 1984.

Regler, Gustav. *The Owl of Minerva: The Autobiography of Gustav Regler*. New York: Farrar, Straus and Cudahy, 1960.

Reynolds, Michael S. *Critical Essays on Ernest Hemingway's* In Our Time. Boston: G. K. Hall, 1983.

———. *Hemingway: The Paris Years*. Cambridge, MA: Basil Blackwell, 1989.

Samuelson, Arnold. *With Hemingway*. New York: Random House, 1984.

Sanford, Marcelline Hemingway. *At the Hemingways: A Family Portrait*. Boston: Atlantic-Little, Brown, 1962.

Sarason, Bertram D. *Hemingway and the Sun Set*. Washington, DC: Microcard Editions, 1972.

Sims, Norman. *Literary Journalism in the Twentieth Century*. Oxford: Oxford University Press, 1990.

Sindelar, Nancy W. *Influencing Hemingway: People and Places That Shaped His Life and Work*. Lanham, MD: Rowman and Littlefield, 2014.

Skelton, Barbara. *Tears Before Bedtime*. London: Harnish Hamilton, 1987.

Stanton, Edward F. *Hemingway and Spain*. Seattle: University of Washington Press, 1989.

Stein, Gertrude. *The Autobiography of Alice B. Toklas*. New York: Harcourt, Brace, 1933.

Svoboda, Frederic Joseph. *Hemingway & The Sun Also Rises*. Lawrence: University Press of Kansas, 1983.

Thomas, Hugh. *The Spanish Civil War*. New York: Harper and Brothers, 1961.

Thomson, David. *Showman: The Life of David O. Selznick*. London: Trafalgar Square, 1991.

Tynan, Kathleen. *Tynan Letters*. New York: Random House, 2012.

Tynan, Kenneth. *The Diaries of Kenneth Tynan*. New York: A&C Black, 1982.

Tynan, Tracy. *Wear and Tear: The Threads of My Life*. New York, Scribner, 2016.

Vaill, Amanda. *Everybody Was So Young: Gerald and Sara Murphy: A Lost Generation Love Story*. New York: Broadway Books, 1999.

———. *Hotel Florida: Truth, Love, and Death in the Spanish Civil War*. New York: Picador, 2015.

Villard, Henry Serrano, and James Nagel. *Hemingway in Love and War: The Lost Diary of Agnes von Kurowsky*. Boston: Northeastern University Press, 1989.

Villareal, René, and Raul Villareal. *Hemingway's Cuban Son*. Kent, OH: Kent State University Press, 2009.

Vinolo, Juan Soto. *Manolete*. Madrid: Perfect Paperback, 1999.

Wertenbaker, Lael. *The World of Picasso*. New York: Time-Life Books, 1967.

Williams, Wirt. *The Tragic Art of Ernest Hemingway*. Baton Rouge: Louisiana University Press, 1981.

Woolsey, Gamel. *Death's Other Kingdom*. London: Eland Publishing, 2004.

INDEX

Esquire magazine: *Answered Prayers* in, 58; *Death in the Afternoon* in, 35; Mailer on Hemingway, E., in, 162
Eton, ix, xiii, 180, 183
Exile's Return (Cowley), 133
expatriates, 29, 47, 132, 158, 179; in Paris, 85; in Spain, xii, 26

Faces of Spain (Brenan), 24
A Farewell to Arms (film), 154
A Farewell to Arms (Hemingway, E.), 71, 73, 154
Faulkner, William, 59, 192
Federal Bureau of Investigation (FBI), 64
Fiesta de San Fermin, 3, 5, 41, 102, 210–11
Finca Vigia Estate, xxiv, 20, 47, 61, 96, 119
Fitzgerald, F. Scott: *Great Gatsby* by, xiv, 10; Hemingway, E., and, 53–54, 68–70; Hemingway, E., letters to, 19, 31, 47, 59, 137; letter from Murphy, G., 193; Lost Generation and, 132; "The Rich Boy" by, 69
Fleiss, Heidi, 186
Fonda, Afdera, 77
Fonda, Henry, 77
For Whom the Bell Tolls (Hemingway, E.), 4
Franco, Francisco, 6–7, 36, 37, 82; Manolete and, 129; as protector of bullfighting, 104
Fuentes, Carlos, 129–30

Gable, Clark, 58
gambling, 153
Garden of Eden (Hemingway, E.), 20, 174
Gardner, Ava: Dominguín and, 46, 48–49, 131, 151; as expatriate, 47; at Finca Vigia, 47; Hemingway, E., friendship with, 47
Gaythorne-Hardy, Jonathan, xvii

Gellhorn, Martha: *Collier's* magazine China assignment for, 86; Hemingway, E., marriage to, xvi, 4, 53, 79, 86; *Hotel Florida* by, 36
Getty, Aileen, 187
Getty, Gail, 188
Getty, J. Paul, 65
Gigi All-Stars, xxiv–xxv; Blas on, xxv; Villarreal on, xxv
Goya, Francisco, xvi, 67, 103, 135
Great Gatsby (Fitzgerald), xiv, 10
Greenberg, Clement: affair with Davis, Anne Bakewell, xx; *The Harold Letters* by, 185; letters of, xx
The Green Hills of Africa (Hemingway, E.), 177
Guernica (Picasso), 134
Guernica, Spain, 134
Guggenheim, Peggy, 83

Halda: Davis, N., on, 68; as Hemingway, E., typewriter, 68, 99, 183
Hamilburg, Michael: death of, 199; with literary agency, 189
Hard Times, xi
Harold Letters, 1928-1965 (Greenberg), 185
Harrison, Mervyn, 154–55
Hawkins, Ruth, *63*
Hawks, Howard: *To Have and Have Not* directed by, 57, 146; Hayward marriage to, 57
Hayward, Slim, 56–59
health, 74, 79–80, 96, 121, 143, 176, 217
Hemingway (Reynolds), 128
Hemingway, Clarence (father), 162
Hemingway, Ernest: *Across the River and Into the Trees* by, 75–76, 185; as Agent Argo, 86–87; anti-Semitism and, xvi; Bacall and, 53, 54, 146–50; Baker

About the Author

Tony Castro is the author of the critically acclaimed and best-selling *Mickey Mantle: America's Prodigal Son*, hailed by the *New York Times* as the best biography ever written about the Hall of Fame legend, and of the dual biography of Mantle and Joe DiMaggio, *DiMag & Mick: Sibling Rivals, Yankee Blood Brothers*. He is also the author of the rite of passage memoir *The Prince of South Waco: American Dreams and Great Expectations* and the landmark civil rights history *Chicano Power: The Emergence of Mexican America*, which *Publishers Weekly* called "brilliant . . . a valuable contribution to the understanding of our time."

A former staff writer at *Sports Illustrated* and political columnist, Castro's journalism has appeared in the *Washington Post*, the *Los Angeles Times*, the *Dallas Morning News*, and the *Texas Observer*. He is a graduate of Baylor University and formerly a Nieman Fellow at Harvard University. With his wife and two sons and black Labrador, Jeter, he lives in Los Angeles, California.